14.75

Behavioral Archeology

STUDIES IN ARCHEOLOGY

Consulting Editor: Stuart Struever

Department of Anthropology
Northwestern University
Evanston, Illinois

Charles R. McGimsey III. **Public Archeology**

Lewis R. Binford. **An Archaeological Perspective**

Muriel Porter Weaver. **The Aztecs, Maya, and Their Predecessors: Archaeology of Mesoamerica**

Joseph W. Michels. **Dating Methods in Archaeology**

C. Garth Sampson. **The Stone Age Archaeology of Southern Africa**

Fred T. Plog. **The Study of Prehistoric Change**

Patty Jo Watson (Ed.). **Archeology of the Mammoth Cave Area**

George C. Frison (Ed.). **The Casper Site: A Hell Gap Bison Kill on the High Plains**

W. Raymond Wood and R. Bruce McMillan (Eds.). **Prehistoric Man and His Environments: A Case Study in the Ozark Highland**

Michael B. Schiffer. **Behavioral Archeology**

in preparation

Charles E. Cleland (Ed.). **Cultural Change and Continuity: Essays in Honor of James Bennett Griffin**

Fred Wendorf and Romuald Schild. **Prehistory of the Nile Valley**

Kent V. Flannery (Ed.). **The Early Mesoamerican Village: Archeological Research Strategy for an Endangered Species**

Michael A. Jochim. **Hunter-Gatherer Subsistence and Settlement: A Predictive Model**

Stanley South. **Method and Theory in Historical Archeology**

Behavioral Archeology

Michael B. Schiffer
Department of Anthropology
University of Arizona
Tucson, Arizona

ACADEMIC PRESS New York San Francisco London

A Subsidiary of Harcourt Brace Jovanovich, Publishers

ACADEMIC PRESS, INC.
111 Fifth Avenue, New York, New York 10003

United Kingdom Edition published by
ACADEMIC PRESS, INC. (LONDON) LTD.
24/28 Oval Road, London NW1

Library of Congress Cataloging in Publication Data

Schiffer, Michael B
    Behavioral archeology.

    (Studies in archeology)
    Bibliography: p.
    Includes index.
    1.   Archaeology–Methodology.   2.   Joint site,
Ariz.   3.   Pueblo Indians–Implements.   4.   Indians
of North America–Arizona–Implements.   I.   Title.
CC80.S33   930'.1'028   75-32035
ISBN 0–12–624150–3

Contents

Preface

This is a work in archeological methodology. If it is consulted in search of ready-made explanations for the more popular issues in archeology—e.g., the adoption of agriculture, development of civilization, and Mousterian variability— the reader will surely be disappointed. If, on the other hand, the reader is concerned to ask these important questions in new ways and to devise more appropriate strategies for answering them, then this book may be of some interest.

My aims are several. First, I attempt to show that the bewildering variety of things archeologists do—e.g., experimental studies, culture history, ethnoarcheology—really fit together into a larger, coherent enterprise. This is accomplished by a consideration of the interdependent relationship between law-using and law-producing strategies of a behavioral archeology. Archeology is redefined as the study of human behavior and material culture, regardless of time or place.

Second, I wish to show that achievement of a genuine scientific study of the past depends on the establishment and rigorous use of laws. Laws can be acquired in many ways, and several of these, including literature searches, simulation, and ethnoarcheology, are illustrated.

And third, I argue that some of the principles of the new archeology form an inadequate basis for archeological research. In particular I raise doubts about the oft-repeated assumption that there is a direct relationship between a past behavioral system and its archeological remains. I substitute a more general principle, which states that because of intervening processes these relationships are seldom direct. Much of the present work is devoted to examining some of these processes, primarily cultural formation processes, which complicate the task of inferring past behavior and organization from the archeological record. I show that these processes must be considered in most phases of archeological research, from interpreting absolute dates to designating proveniences. My approach is not to underscore the difficulty in reconstructing the past, but to emphasize that this difficulty will decrease as we begin to confront head-on the numerous problems which inhere in the study of the past. The many models and principles presented illustrate ways that these processes can be taken into account in order to allow for more rigorous uses of archeological data.

The material in this book falls naturally into two parts: principles (and heuristic devices) and applications of them to the data from the Joint Site. It is tempting to group the chapters into principles and applications, but my own sense of order dictates that some of the general discussions, such as classification and interpretation of absolute dates, take place in close proximity to the Joint Site examples.

The Joint Site, a Pueblo III ruin in the Hay Hollow Valley of eastern Arizona, excavated by the Field Museum of Natural History, provides the data base I employ to illustrate the use of the general principles of behavioral archeology. The major class of artifacts treated is the chipped stone. Although problems in the data and the all-too-preliminary models preclude achievement of novel or startling results, I am confident that the many examples will convince the reader of the merits of the behavioral approach to archeology and stimulate development of better models for answering other, perhaps more significant, questions.

Acknowledgments

A study of this sort draws heavily upon the labors of many individuals, though it is scarcely possible to thank them all adequately.

I owe a special debt of gratitude to the many people—staff and students—of the Southwestern Archaeological Expedition of the Field Museum of Natural History who participated in the Joint Site project: (1970) David Burkenroad, Michael Ester, Gene Goode, Jan Goode, Frederick Gorman, David Gregory, Eric Gritzmacher, John Hanson, Martha Hanson, Richard Hevly, John Johnson, Colleen Maley, Sharon Ott, Paul Parker, Margaret Powers, John Rick, Wilbert Sampson, Stephen Saraydar, Jerome Schaefer, Annette Schiffer, and Susan Tracz; (1971) Susan Anderson, Daniel Andrews, Russell Barber, Scott Cox, Alan Engstrom, John Hanson, Martha Hanson, Mark Henderson, Elsa Hirvela, Stan James, John Justeson, Barbara Lehner, James Moore, Annette Schiffer, Paul Smith, Deborah Thompson (now Wilde), Susan Tracz, Carole Wiley, and Hanson Wong. I hope that in some small way this book does justice to their labors.

In particular I am grateful to the late Paul S. Martin, Director of the Southwestern Expedition, for his encouragement, criticism, and especially for support through the Field Museum of Natural History and the National Science Foundation. Without his support, encouragement, and friendship, this study would not have been possible. He provided the kind of intellectual climate, found in few other places, where even the smallest seed of an idea could develop, blossom, and eventually bear fruit. I deeply regret that he did not live long enough to see this study.

I also thank the James Carter family, formerly of Snowflake, Arizona, for allowing the Southwestern Expedition to undertake investigations in their pleasant portion of the Hay Hollow Valley.

The Department of Anthropology at the University of Arizona granted me the space to store and analyze the Joint Site collections, gave me ample time on the CDC 6400 computer, and provided me with financial support in the form of a National Science Foundation Traineeship and a Teaching Associateship.

The programming skills of Patricia Beirne and Timothy Klinger often rescued me from the insensate clutches of the indispensible computers.

I am grateful to the many creative, spirited, and hardworking students with whom I have had contact over the past several years at the University of Arizona and the University of Arkansas. I especially appreciate the effort that went into examining the implications of the inference model. My classes in archeological interpretation and behavioral archeology have been subjected to most of the ideas presented here, and the value of my students' ideas, comments, and occasional but good-natured complaints is acknowledged.

The illustrations are a product of the graphic skills of Thomas Levy, Charles Sternberg, and Sharon Urban. The map of the Joint Site was drawn at the Field Museum. Susan Luebbermann took the photographs of the chipped stone.

I acknowledge with considerable appreciation the individuals who criticized, often in depth, many of the ponderous chapters and their precursors or who otherwise provided useful comments on the ideas in this book. These people include Keith Basso, Cheryl Claassen, Jeffrey S. Dean, Jeffrey Eighmy, Albert C. Goodyear III, Donald Graybill, Paul Grebinger, John Hanson, John House, Mark Harlan, Arthur Jelinek, Edward Jelks, Timothy C. Klinger, Michael Levin, Charles Morgan, Merrilee Salmon, Sandra Scholtz, Stanley South, Alan Sullivan, W. Raymond Wood, and especially J. Jefferson Reid, John Fritz, Fred Plog, Raymond Thompson, H. A. Luebbermann, Jr., David Wilcox, James Rock, Annetta Cheek, Charles Cheek, Charles Baker, William Rathje, and William Longacre.

The Arkansas Archeological Survey, under the leadership of Charles R. McGimsey III and Hester Davis, deserves credit for supporting me while I completed this work. Few other area-based archeological institutions are as sensitive to the need to encourage theoretical and methodological research.

I thank *Plains Anthropologist, American Antiquity,* and *American Anthropologist* for permission to reproduce portions of previously published articles. David R. Wilcox and John H. House granted permission to use illustrations from their work. And J. Jefferson Reid and William L. Rathje graciously allowed me to include large sections of our joint paper, "Behavioral archaeology: Four strategies."

I thank Lewis R. Binford and James N. Hill for instilling within me during my undergraduate years many important principles, a feel for what are the appropriate questions to ask, and a large measure of skepticism for received ideas. I thank John M. Fritz for a timely six-page critique of the five-page typescript that eventually became "Archaeological context and systemic context."

Many of the important methodological insights in the present volume are a product of the intense and exciting interaction that J. Jefferson Reid and I have enjoyed over the last few years. Our collaborative efforts are continuing and will soon yield other major statements and applications of behavioral archeology.

In the field and in the laboratory, my wife Annette cheerfully contributed her own effort, while setting high standards of careful data retrieval and analysis for others to follow. For this unrecompensed toil, as well as her loving patience and constant encouragement throughout the several stages of this project, I cannot begin to express my gratitude.

List of Figures

List of Tables

1

Introduction

From the perspective of the mid-1970s, the "new" or "processual" archeology finally has reached maturity. As symbols of this new status, it now boasts textbooks (Watson, LeBlanc, and Redman 1971; Woodall 1972; Thomas 1974), collections of classic principles and applications (Leone 1972; Binford 1972a), lengthy case studies (e.g., Plog 1974; Zubrow 1975; Hill 1970a; Longacre 1970a), and even a long-established introductory work that is beginning to make the heresies of the 1960s seem eminently respectable (Hole and Heizer 1973). At the present time, when the paradigm of the new archeology is becoming consolidated and even entrenched, I sense in the discipline both ferment and complacency. Ferment, manifest in publications and recent symposia, focuses on major avenues of promising research including computer applications, settlement location studies, simulations, the design of classificatory systems, and model building (e.g., Clarke 1972a; Redman 1973; Renfrew 1973). The observable ferment may be interpreted to mean that archeology is in a healthy state. However, such an interpretation may be deceiving. Complacency, too, is evident in many quarters, and it is symptomatic of a profound neglect of many unresolved epistemological, theoretical, and methodological issues of the past decade. Complacency represents premature closure of discussion and debate on a number of important topics (see also Reid 1973).

A period of normal science (Kuhn 1970) has emerged in archeology. As in many normal science periods, basic concepts and principles are beginning to submerge into the murky inaccessible depths of the discipline, where they no longer can be easily questioned or challenged—until, of course, the next major paradigm clash (Kuhn 1970). It is time to step back from the calm of the current archeological scene and ask if the paradigm under which we now labor, ushered in by the new archeology of the 1960s, is fully adequate for genuine scientific studies of the past.

PROCESSUAL ARCHEOLOGY

The developments of the 1960s, although bringing about substantial improvements in theory and method (Martin 1971), did not succeed in fully liberating archeologists from their persistent practices of "interpreting" rather than explaining their data. To be sure, the principles that facilitate the new interpretations are different, but they are often crude, undeveloped, and misapplied. We simply have substituted one set of all-purpose causes—population pressure, environmental change and stress, various forms of intercultural contact, and assorted cybernetic processes—for an equally inadequate set of predecessor causes, such as innovation, diffusion, and migration. At the level of explaining behavioral and organizational variability and change, much of the new has not surpassed the old. In far too many instances, we simply have grafted a borrowed, precise-sounding terminology into a set of poorly developed principles and overlain the entire frail structure with the appealing magic of mathematics and the computer.

The borrowing of principles for the purpose of explaining the events of the past is sometimes necessary; archeologists certainly should exploit the inventiveness of scientists in other disciplines, such as cultural anthropology, ecology, and systems engineering. But by borrowing sophisticated explanatory principles and techniques, we cannot escape the need for securely documenting *archeologically* the events we attempt to explain. To date, processualists have not always seen to it that there is a close fit between their principles and the archeological data. It is in this respect, especially, that the new archeology does not differ measurably from what preceded it.

It is the main thesis of this work that archeologists must be concerned first and foremost with devising principles and methods for reliably reconstructing past behavioral variables from archeological remains (Binford and Binford 1968; Binford 1968a, b; Schiffer 1972a; Fritz 1972). This is not to say that efforts at *explaining* the past should cease, but only that such efforts be coupled to the design of appropriate instruments for measuring the variables of interest (Fritz 1972). To be successful at all, then, explanation in archeology must occur on two levels. First, the documentation of a specific behavioral or organizational property of a past cultural system functions to explain archeological observations.

And, second, such documented properties become the object of further explanation. It should be clear that explanation of systemic phenomenon (for example, adoption of agriculture, the Pueblo IV population aggregation) is contingent upon the prior or concomitant explanation of the facts of the archeological record (Binford 1968a). Many new archeologists, in their understandable haste to be relevant to both modern society and anthropology, have short-circuited the process of archeological explanation by failing to confront and resolve the complex problems of using archeological data.

The paradigm shifts precipitated by the new archeology occurred at many levels. In areas such as artifact classification, sampling, use of ethnographic analogy, and research design, major reorientations in approach have taken place. But beneath the surface of an apparently coherent set of paradigms for archeological research lie serious inconsistencies, ambiguities, and lacunae. These deficiencies in the overall program of the new archeology cannot be remedied fully without modest alterations to lower levels of the paradigm hierarchy. This study is aimed at providing the epistemological and methodological bases for effecting such changes (see also Reid 1973).

That the developments of the 1960s did not go far enough in important respects is demonstrated easily. The fact is evident that much of what stood for archeology in decades preceding the 1960s has yet to be reintegrated into the discipline; such reintegration is an expectable consequence of major paradigm change in a science (Kuhn 1970). For example, the new archeology, in properly stressing intersubjective verifiability, provides no stated role for expertise or the subjective element; yet no one who has practiced archeology can deny the contribution that covert knowledge makes to any research project. Although most of us share the desire to report as fully as possible all aspects of our research procedures, it remains to determine the nature of the subjective element and to ask how it can be of explicit use to archeologists. As another example of incomplete synthesis, one can point to the familiar tension existing between archeologists who are oriented toward the collection and analysis of data and others concerned primarily with model building and the conceptual basis of archeology. Although disciplines such as physics and biology long ago have resolved these incipient splits, the framework has yet to be offered for appreciating how the disparate activities of modern archeologists fit together into a larger, coherent enterprise. As a final index to the superficial and transitory nature of the current era of good feelings, I note that two of the most respected theorists of the new archeology have assessed the present state of paradigm mix in very different ways. While Binford (1971, 1972b) still finds it necessary to joust with "traditionalists," Clarke (1972b) is unable to reconcile what he believes are four competing paradigms in the contemporary conceptual repertoire of archeology (morphological, anthropological, ecological, and geographical). Although archeology is no longer divided into warring camps, the impression remains that we are in a state of fatigue-induced cease-fire rather than one of peace. The reintegration of archeology as a discipline must receive top priority, and with it must come the resolution of the problems left unsolved by the processualists.

BEHAVIORAL ARCHEOLOGY

Behavioral archeology is the particular configuration of principles, activities, and interests that we offer to reintegrate the discipline (Reid, Schiffer, and Rathje n.d.). The formulation and realization of a behavioral archeology depends on making explicit the multiple roles of laws in archeological research, and on showing how the strategies of a behavioral archeology, whether they emphasize the *use* or *discovery* of laws, are interrelated. In this work, the term "law" is used frequently, and a working definition is therefore needed.

Philosophers of science employ "law" as a technical term to denote certain relational statements having empirical content. Nagel (1961) refers to these principles as "experimental laws," while Hempel (1966) uses the designation "covering law." In applications of these terms, no connotations of immutability or compulsion inhere. Laws are simply one kind of relational statement, which function (in conjunction with other information) to explain or predict empirical phenomena. Statistical and probabilistic laws are, of course, encompassed by this formulation (see Salmon 1971). In this work, the philosophical perspective on laws is maintained. A law is an atemporal, aspatial statement relating two or more operationally defined variables. Because many relational statements in archeology possess these properties and also function to explain and predict empirical phenomena, the appropriate designation for these principles is *laws*. This usage naturally leaves ample room to subject all such relational statements to discussion, retesting, or, in many cases, extraction from the archeological literature and initial testing.

Reid, Rathje, and I (Reid 1973; Reid, Rathje, and Schiffer 1974; Reid, Schiffer, and Rathje n.d.) propose that the subject matter of archeology is the relationships between human behavior and material culture in all times and places. The kinds of questions that can be asked about these relationships form

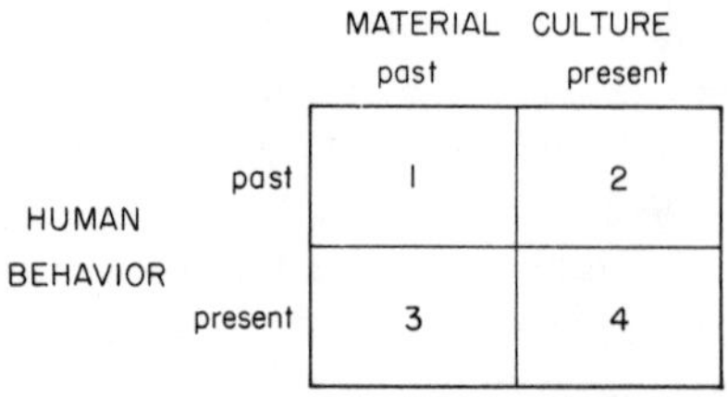

Figure 1.1   The strategies of a behavioral archeology. (Based on Reid 1973.)

the framework of a behavioral archeology consisting of four strategies. These strategies, defined on the basis of question type, are displayed in Figure 1.1.

Strategy 1

This strategy is concerned with using material culture that was made in the past, to answer specific descriptive and explanatory questions about the behavioral and organizational properties of past cultural systems. For example, one might ask: What was the average population of Grasshopper Pueblo between A.D. 1275 and 1400? When was the Eva Site occupied? What plant and animal resources were exploited by the Upper Pleistocene inhabitants of Tabun? Why was there a decrease in dependence on agriculture in the Hay Hollow Valley from A.D. 1200 to A.D. 1300? Such questions, bound to specific time–space loci, form the basis of archeology as it has been practiced traditionally, whether it is prehistoric, classical, or historical.

It should be emphasized that, although particular questions deal with both description and explanation of past events and system properties (Binford 1962a), explanatory goals have come, properly, to dominate studies of the past (Willey and Sabloff 1974). As archeologists grappled with the nature of explanation, they found it necessary to draw on a wide variety of behavioral laws to facilitate documenting and explaining past events. Regardless of whether or not one subscribes to the Hempel–Oppenheim model of explanation, the emerging importance of laws in archeology is apparent.

Archeologists working within Strategy 1 are law users (Binford 1968a; Spaulding 1968; Trigger 1970; Stickel and Chartkoff 1973; Fritz and Plog 1970; Watson, LeBlanc, and Redman 1971; Schiffer 1972a, n.d.a). Some fail to recognize this fact, yet proceed, nonetheless, to make ad hoc generalizations that function as laws. It usually is argued that the laws used in Strategy 1 derive from ethnology or other social sciences (Trigger 1970), and it is now quite fashionable to discuss the interrelationship of archeology and ethnology (Chang 1967), even though this relationship is said to involve a one-way flow of laws into archeology. While it is certainly true that some archeologists use laws that originated in other disciplines, especially ethnology, it is not true that all archeological laws are borrowed (Schiffer n.d.a). Many archeologists have recognized that a science is likely to generate only the laws for which it has a use. Consequently, there is no reason to expect that ethnology, or any other discipline, has produced, or can produce, all the laws required to describe and explain the events of the past. The thrust of this realization has been the development of Strategy 2.

Strategy 2

Research within Strategy 2 pursues general questions in present material culture in order to acquire laws useful for the study of the past. Some general questions that typify this strategy are: What are the traces of various techniques of manufacture on a given type of material? What is the relationship between the population size of a community and its habitation area? How long does it take various materials to decay under given conditions of deposition? Why are whole, usable items sometimes discarded? These are *general* questions because they are not bound to specific time–space referents. The answers to these questions take the form of experimental laws. "Experimental archeology" (Ascher 1961), "action archeology" (Kleindienst and Watson 1956), "ethnoarcheology" (Oswalt and VanStone 1967), and "living archeology" (Gould 1968) are labels for variants of Strategy 2.

One can distinguish two major types of research design within Strategy 2. The first, probably the one more aptly called "experimental archeology," consists of carefully contriving a situation in which to observe the interaction of selected variables. In this activity, the archeologist can control relevant variables and boundary conditions by direct intervention and manipulation. The second type of research design requires the observation of interacting variables in an ongoing system that is selected on the basis of certain boundary conditions. This latter approach has been termed "living archeology" (Gould 1968). As the work of White and Thomas (1972) has shown, however, the distinction between experimental archeology and living archeology is not hard and fast. Nor should it be.

Several major shortcomings characterize much of the research undertaken to date within Strategy 2. Although many of these studies have produced interesting and useful results, in general, they have been restricted in the scope of variables examined. Most investigations deal with manufacturing behavior, the traces of use wear on specific artifacts, or the processes of decay and noncultural deposition (Heizer and Graham 1967; Coles 1973; Clark 1957; Hole and Heizer 1973). But I emphasize that this strategy subsumes the entire range of behavioral and organizational variables in relation to material, spatial, and even environmental variables. Fortunately efforts guiding the necessary expansion of Strategy 2 are underway along a broad front (e.g., White and Thomas 1972; Donnan and Clewlow 1974; Salwen 1973; Leone 1973; Saraydar and Shimada 1973; Shimada n.d.; Binford 1973; Longacre 1974).

Not only are these studies, taken as a body, narrow in scope, but they also are scattered widely in the literature and are unsystematized (see also Coles 1973). Many are purely descriptive, and others fail to express results in lawlike form (Schiffer 1974). A bibliography of experimental archeology (Hester and Heizer 1973) is a needed first step, but to salvage useful principles, one must extract the laws and assemble related ones. By this process, we can increase the set of accessible laws for understanding the past, and discover what is undiscovered.

As archeologists investigated a variety of questions on present material culture, they found, like cultural anthropologists before them, that ethnographic data are not very useful for testing laws about long-term processes of cultural change.

There have been two solutions to this problem. The first was to turn to nonanthropological disciplines in search of potentially useful laws. Thus, a major trend now evident in archeology is interdisciplinary borrowing. Principles, methods, and techniques from fields as diverse as systems theory, biological ecology, information theory, and geography now frequently punctuate the archeological literature (Clarke 1968 being the classic example). Although the ultimate utility of many of these ideas remains to be demonstrated, such borrowings are inevitable and necessary.

The second solution was to explore the possibility that the archeological record itself might be an ideal laboratory for deriving laws of cultural change processes (Binford 1962a; Wauchope 1966; Leone 1968; Schuyler 1970; Zubrow 1971, 1975; Woodall 1972; Plog 1973a,b, 1974). Once available, these laws also could be applied to explain and predict contemporary behavioral change. The realization that archeologists could use their data base from the past to answer questions about long-term change processes has led to the conscious emergence of Strategy 3.

Strategy 3

Strategy 3 is the pursuit of general questions in the study of past material remains to derive behavioral laws of wide applicability that illuminate past as well as present human behavior. The questions that typify this strategy, like those in Strategy 2, do not have specific time–space referents. Examples include: What are the determinants of variability in organizational complexity? What factors explain variability in storage capacity? How do cultural systems adapt to changes in population? As in Strategy 2, these types of question are answered in terms of laws. An implication of this strategy is that such laws are potentially relevant to modern social problems and issues.

Strategy 3, with its prominent theme of social relevance, is rooted deeply in the writings of the late Paul S. Martin (1954, 1971; Martin, Quimby, and Collier 1947; Martin and Plog 1973; also Fritz and Plog 1970). This theme of relevance has been stifled in the past for lack of an appropriate methodological vehicle, and remained only a muted plea until the emergence of explicit concern with formulating laws. Since laws are atemporal and aspatial, they should be applicable to any situation in which the initial and boundary conditions are met (Hempel 1966; Reynolds 1971). Although concern with laws provides the long-awaited methodological breakthrough, relevance and the search for laws are not bound inseparably. Laws can be formulated and tested without being applied in a socially relevant context. This is an investigator's prerogative. However, the converse does not hold. If statements derived from the past are to be applied in a socially relevant context, they must conform to the format of a law.

Strategy 3 gives substance to the claim that, within anthropology, only archeology possesses the requisite time depth necessary for studying long-term cultural change (cf. Plog 1973a, 1974). It is difficult to imagine insisting on the importance of time depth without also insisting on the need for generating and testing laws. Archeology's contributions to predictive anthropological theory are contingent on these statements (Titiev 1961:183).

Time depth is not archeology's only potential contribution to anthropology. By virtue of years of research within Strategies 1 and 2, archeologists now possess an expanding body of theory, method, and behavioral laws for the study of material objects and human behavior regardless of time and space. As archeologists in urban environments have sought to teach and test archeological principles, they have turned to modern material culture as a largely untapped, renewable data base. In exploring the relationships between archeological principles and material culture, they have discovered that archeology can make contributions to the understanding of present human behavior and have, thereby, opened the way to Strategy 4 (Salwen 1973; Reid, Rathje, and Schiffer 1974; Rathje 1974).

Strategy 4

Strategy 4 is the study of present material objects in ongoing cultural systems to describe and explain present human behavior. This strategy, then, includes the study of contemporary industrial as well as nonindustrial societies. However, its potential contribution to social science derives from the research possibilities of studying material culture in industrial societies.

The questions asked within Strategy 4 are usually specific questions about ongoing societies. For example: What patterns of meat and liquor consumption characterize different ethnic groups in Tucson, Arizona? Do members of higher socioeconomic groups waste nonrenewable resources in Fayetteville, Arkansas? How many times is a television set owned before it is discarded in Los Angeles? The Garbage Project at the University of Arizona is now exploring solutions to many interesting questions in Strategy 4 (Rathje 1974; Harrison, Rathje, and Hughes 1975). It is anticipated that Strategy 4 holds much promise for those concerned with archeological relevance and for those wishing to contribute to the analysis and explanation of human behavior.

The expansion of research into Strategies 2, 3, and 4 more accurately reflects the development of archeology as a discipline, and should permit a meaningful processual history of this subject to be written in the near future. The importance of this expansion to present discussions is that it reflects the essential interrelatedness of all four strategies. The pursuit of Strategy 1 always has required information gained through Strategy 2, and these requirements need not be met exclusively by ethnologists. In like manner, Strategy 3 embodies procedures that seek to contribute to anthropological theory and, thereby, to an understanding of contemporary behavior. Recognition of Strategy 4 merely closes a logical set of research options to embrace the attainment of goals common to most archeologists. I emphasize that a behavioral archeology is a synthesis of what archeologists have done and aspire to do, and that the essential interrelatedness among the strategies has roots deep in the progressive development of the discipline.

INFORMATION FLOW IN A BEHAVIORAL ARCHEOLOGY

Viewed as a conjunction of four strategies, archeology is more than a loose aggregation of subfields. Instead, the strategies are integrated into a coherent behavioral science by the flow of general questions and general laws. A behavioral archeology exceeds the sum of its parts, since it depends upon interaction among the four strategies. This interaction further distinguishes the uniqueness of individual research and highlights the unity of combined research activity.

Strategies 1 and 4 are the idiographic component of archeology, whereas Strategies 2 and 3 are the nomothetic component. Within this framework, the tiresome debate about archeology as history or science (e.g., Trigger 1970) is seen to reflect overemphasis on one or the other component. A viable behavioral archeology must have both.

Strategies 1 and 4, concerned with answering particular questions about the past and present, cannot exist without Strategies 2 and 3 to provide needed laws. On the other hand, specific questions raised within Strategies 1 and 4 can lead to the discovery that no appropriate laws are available. This impasse is resolved when a general question, formulated and fed into Strategy 2 or 3, serves as a basis for law construction and testing.

I cannot emphasize too strongly that these research strategies are interdependent and together contribute to a more substantial body of theory and method and a more powerful behavioral discipline. This is not to say that any individual must be competent in the execution of all four strategies. That would be inefficient. It is also apparent that a single investigator may operate simultaneously in more than one strategy. If questions raised within Strategies 1 and 4 are to be answered successfully, it is necessary that the discipline as a whole support studies in Strategies 2 and 3. Furthermore, if Strategies 2 and 3 are to succeed in producing useful laws, appropriate questions must be obtained from Strategies 1 and 4.

The development of Strategies 2, 3, and 4 has led to a redefinition of archeology based on a broad conception of its subject matter and the kinds of questions that are asked. It no longer seems possible to view archeology as only the study of the past. To be sure, questions in Strategy 1 properly will continue to occupy the research efforts of most archeologists, but a more productive view of the field as an integrated whole recognizes the essential contribution of other archeologists. In the framework of a behavioral archeology, the study of urbanization at Teotihuacan, stone chipping in the Outback, human adjustments to environmental stress, and meat consumption in Tucson, Arizona, all are legitimate and productive archeological research activities.

2

A Synthetic Model
of Archeological Inference

The early years of the new archeology witnessed the frequent and unquestioning repetition of major methodological principles. One such principle was enunciated by Binford (1964:425) in perhaps its most explicit form:

> The loss, breakage, and abandonment of implements and facilities at different locations, where groups of variable structure performed different tasks, leaves a "fossil" record of the actual operation of an extinct society.

Closely paraphrased variants of this statement have continued to appear in the literature, frequently as part of an introductory section to empirical studies. Under the aegis of this principle, new archeologists have approached the remains of the past in bold and exciting ways, seeking with sophisticated techniques assorted patterns in artifact distributions and interpreting them directly in terms of past behavior and social organization. As often happens in times of normal science, few investigators have noticed that the principle is false.

It is false because archeological remains are not in any sense a fossilized cultural system. Between the time artifacts were manufactured and used in the past and the time these same objects are unearthed by the archeologist, they have been subjected to a series of cultural and noncultural processes which have transformed them spatially, quantitatively, formally, and relationally (see also Collins 1975). If we desire to reconstruct the past from archeological remains, then these processes must be taken into account, and a more generally applicable methodological principle substituted for the one that asserts that there is an

11

equivalence between a past cultural system and its archeological record. The principle I offer is that archeological remains are a distorted reflection of a past behavioral system. However, because the cultural and noncultural processes responsible for these distortions are regular, there are systematic (but seldom direct) relationships between archeological remains and past cultural systems.

With this principle in mind, it becomes possible to frame the basic problem of archeological inference: How can we take into account the intervening processes when using archeological remains to inform on the past? These intervening processes and the multifaceted relationships between behavior and material objects form the basis of the synthetic model of archeological inference. Before that model is presented, some preliminary definitions are in order. *Archeological knowledge* is defined as consisting of the laws that are employed implicitly or explicitly to retrieve knowledge of the past from archeological data. In confining the meaning of archeological knowledge to sets of laws, I do not imply that other kinds of knowledge are unimportant.

An inference is a descriptive statement of high probability about past cultural behavior or organization. By this definition, a positively tested hypothesis within Strategy 1 becomes an inference. *Inference justification* is the archeological knowledge and data—and their structure—that give an inference its credibility.

THE SYNTHETIC MODEL

The basic problem in constructing this synthetic model is to determine the general nature of archeological knowledge. The model presented here is based on what I suggest is the knowledge required to solve the problems that confront every archeologist as a result of the three basic properties of archeological data:

1. They consist of materials in static spatial relationships.
2. They have been output in one way or another from a cultural system.
3. They have been subjected to the operation of noncultural processes.

Because a solution to each of these problems must be reached in the justification of any inference, three sets of laws, or at least assumptions within each problem domain, are employed. I now present the basic problems in greater detail and discuss the corresponding law sets.

Correlates

Let us begin by visualizing an ongoing cultural system. Such a system consists of material objects, human actors, foods, and fuels, and is manifest in the repetitive occurrence of activities. What one pictures is a system of action—of energy transformations and material flows occurring in space. If the human participants and all other energy sources completely halt their actions, the activities cease, as does the operation of the behavioral system. What remains (assuming no modification by other processes) is the closest conceivable approximation to a "fossil" of a cultural system—its material elements in a system-relevant spatial matrix. Even though most archeologists would accept gratefully a site produced under those conditions, when confronted by one, there still would be left a major problem to solve by the application of laws before inferences could be made.

Because the data themselves are totally silent and do not apprise the investigator of the ways artifacts once participated in a behavioral system or how they reflect the organization of that system, a set of laws must be acquired and applied to the materials. These statements relate behavioral variables to variables of material objects or spatial relations. They also may involve organizational and environmental variables. Such statements have the important property of being operationally definable and therefore testable in an ongoing cultural system. Principles of this sort—without which no archeologist possibly could know anything about the operation of a cultural system, past or present, by observing its material objects and their spatial relations—are termed "correlates" (after Hill 1970a:63). I have referred elsewhere to these laws as "arguments of relevance" (Schiffer 1972a,b), but that usage is misleading. In a strict sense, all principles that link an inference to specific archeological observations are arguments of relevance (Binford 1968a:23, 1968b:273).

One important kind of correlate relates variables of behavior to variables of material objects. Such correlates are used often (but not exclusively) to infer the manufacturing operations that produced an artifact, or the use(s) to which it was put. Statements that relate the fracturing properties of a lithic material and the particular applied forces to attributes of the resultant products and by-products are examples (Schiffer 1974). Crabtree's (1968) experiments on the removal of blades from polyhedral cores have produced many correlates of this type:

> Assuming that obsidian has been properly preformed into a core with ridges, the platform is ground until it has the appearance of frosted glass. . . . The pressure crutch has been made, and the specimen is now ready for removal of the first blade [Crabtree 1968:463].

> Blade types are governed by the manner in which the pressure tool is placed on the edge of the core. The triangular blade is made by directly following one ridge, and the trapezoidal type is made by positioning the tip of the pressure tool in line with but between, two ridges [Crabtree 1968:465].

Armed with this correlate (and several others not made explicit), an investigator examining materials in the hypothetical stalled cultural system could recognize the attributes of certain artifacts and waste products as indicative of a particular kind of manufacturing behavior. Or viewed in another way, if he were seeking to identify this kind of behavior, the application of the correlates would readily produce test implications.

Correlates are often exceedingly complex and may involve multiple variables of behavior, system organization, spatial relations, and material objects (see Rathje 1973 for an example of a correlate relating social mobility to status symbols). The terms "behavioral–material" or "behavioral–spatial–material" or any other meaningful combination may be applied to these laws (Schiffer n.d.a). Despite the potential complexity in both laws and terminology, all correlates function in inference justification by allowing the derivation or identification of some aspects of an operating cultural system from knowledge of those aspects, spatial and material, which would be or are present in the archeological record.

C-Transforms

The formulation and use of correlates is the procedure that archeologists employ to solve the problem posed by the nonbehavioral nature of archeological data. The second problem, solutions to which also lie embedded in the justification of any inference, requires the construction and use of laws that relate variables of an ongoing cultural system to variables describing the cultural deposition or nondeposition of its elements.

It is possible to define more precisely the nature and function of these laws by returning to the hypothetical cultural system. If the operation of the energy sources resumes, one notes that continuous activity results in periodic outputs of exhausted tools, waste products of food and fuel consumption, obsolete items, and others. Items discarded during the normal operation of a cultural system constitute a major source of the archeological record. Another source of materials that begins a path to the archeological record is de facto refuse, produced when the inhabitants abandon a site and leave usable materials behind (Schiffer 1972b).

The general problem of *cultural formation processes* typified by normal outputs, de facto refuse, and other sources is taken into account by laws of the cultural formation processes of the archeological record (Schiffer 1972b). These principles permit an investigator to specify the ways in which a cultural system outputs the materials that eventually may be observed archeologically. Application of these laws is necessary to relate the past qualitative, quantitative, spatial, and associational attributes of materials in systemic context to materials deposited by the cultural system. Such laws are termed "c-transforms" (Schiffer 1973a; Schiffer and Rathje 1973).

Unfortunately, c-transforms are the most seriously embedded principles of archeological knowledge; the necessity of their use is generally unacknowledged and only a very few are explicit (Schiffer 1972b, 1973a). One hypothesis that functions within the c-transform domain is that

> *with increasing site population (or perhaps site size) and increasing intensity of occupation, there will be a decreasing correspondence between the use and discard locations for all elements used in activities and discarded at a site* [Schiffer 1972b:162; emphasis in original].

Employing this principle (untested though it is) one can justify the use of data from limited activity sites (Wilmsen 1970) to postulate locations of past activity performance, since most elements of such a site are discarded at their locations of use (assuming no modification of spatial relationships by subsequent processes). Many inferences that rest on similar c-transforms are found in Binford *et al.* (1970) and Brose (1970); in both of these monographs, the assumption is made of a correspondence between use and discard locations for many classes of debris.

Other c-transforms relate quantitative variables of a cultural system to quantitative variables of cultural deposition. For example, Howells (1960) developed several c-transforms that allow the reconstruction of site population size through the use of data from the retrieved burial population.

Superficially, c-transforms resemble correlates. At one level, they both apply to the dynamics of ongoing cultural systems. But only c-transforms contain information about system outputs, such as discard rates, discard locations, loss probabilities, burial practices, and others. *Only c-transforms can be used to predict the materials that will or will not be deposited by a system.*

For purposes of presenting the synthetic model, this discussion of c-transforms and cultural formation processes will suffice; in the next chapter, a more developed discussion unfolds.

N-Transforms

The last major problem presented by the nature of archeological data concerns the postdepositional changes in site and artifact morphology caused by noncultural processes, such as wind, water, rodent activity, and chemical action. *Noncultural formation processes* are taken into account in inference justification by the use of principles called "n-transforms" (Schiffer 1973a; Schiffer and Rathje 1973). N-transforms comprise the most highly developed area of archeological knowledge, and many are explicit. As two simple examples of n-transforms, I note that pollen is preserved in acidic soil, but bone is destroyed in acidic soil (all other variables constant). Additional examples of n-transforms may be found in works by Clark (1957), Coles (1973), Hole and Heizer (1973), and others. N-transforms allow the archeologist to predict the interaction between variables of culturally deposited materials and variables of the noncultural environment in which the former materials are found.

Stipulations

It has been argued thus far that archeological knowledge consists of corre-lates, c-transforms, and n-transforms. To complete the synthetic model of inference, several elements must be added. In the first place, one often must make assumptions within the domains of the three law sets. These additional but necessary bits of information are termed "stipulations." I have refrained deliberately from calling them "assumptions." The point to be emphasized is that they are assumed or stipulated only in a specific inference justification; in

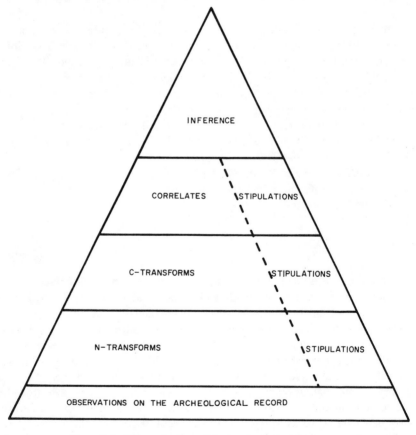

Figure 2.1 The synthetic model of archeological inference.

principle, stipulations are subject to independent testing. Assumptions, on the other hand, seem never to be tested.

Stipulations convey information about other conditions that were present in the past. These may pertain to the cultural system under study, to its natural and cultural environment, or even to subsequent cultural systems. As an example, in applying Howell's c-transforms, discussed earlier, it is necessary to stipulate that population remained constant during site occupation.

In addition to archeological knowledge, stipulations, and the inference itself, the completed synthetic model requires that inference justification include statements about observations made on the archeological record. Figure 2.1 illustrates this structural model of archeological inference and inference justification.

Archeological Explanation

The synthetic model specifies that the explanation of archeological observations is achieved when they are shown to be the expectable consequence of the initial conditions, given the relevant laws (see also Fritz and Plog 1970; Watson, LeBlanc, and Redman 1971). The inference itself and the stipulations are seen as the initial and boundary conditions, while correlates, c-transforms, and n-transforms constitute the laws. Together, these statements function to explain aspects of the archeological record. In other words, a given behavioral or organizational property, other features of a past cultural system and its environment, post-depositional variables, and the relevant laws provide the conditions to account for (or allow the prediction of) aspects of material items and their interrelationships in the present. When coupled to stipulations and laws, an inference is justified to the extent that it makes certain archeological observations expectable. Of course, alternative inferences and explanations are never precluded.

ACQUISITION OF ARCHEOLOGICAL KNOWLEDGE

The basic structure of archeological inference, simple though it is, has eluded previous archeological epistemologists for the understandable reason that very few inferences are completely justified in the literature. The general lack of explicit laws not only has misled archeological epistemologists, but it has important implications concerning the means by which correlates, c-transforms, and n-transforms are acquired. In advanced scientific disciplines, most laws are explicit and can be learned by the diligent study of textbooks (Kuhn 1970). This is not yet the case in archeology. Even if one internalized every law contained in archeological textbooks, he would be incapable of generating from the data all the knowledge of the past that we claim is accessible. Conspicuously absent in all introductory textbooks (e.g., Hole and Heizer 1973; Fagan 1972; Rouse 1972) or in any texts, for that matter, is a section or sections describing the archeological knowledge required to infer some aspect of a past cultural system.

Clearly, the laws composing archeological knowledge must be acquired by prospective archeologists, but the question is: How? I believe that the process of law acquisition is not unlike the way a child learns the grammar of a language. After ploughing through a large sample of site reports and syntheses, a student unconsciously proposes and internalizes trial relational statements to account for the linkage between the data an investigator presents and his inferences about the past. These relational statements correspond to what I have termed "correlates," "c-transforms," and "n-transforms."

Because archeological knowledge rarely reaches the printed page, residing primarily in the conceptual framework of individual investigators, there is no shortcut method of learning these principles beyond the laborious and wasteful task of reinventing them while reading and comprehending the literature. The nonpresentation of laws is perhaps the most efficient way to write site reports, syntheses, and interpretive papers, but, in the absence of good textbooks, we are left without an efficient means of enculturating aspiring archeologists. More importantly, we cannot take stock of the conceptual progress of the discipline or easily determine the undeveloped areas of archeological knowledge. I suggest that writers of future textbooks will have to devote much more space to listing and illustrating the use of relational statements of archeological knowledge. I envision, for example, several introductory texts covering separately many complex subjects in reconstruction, such as social organization, lithic technology, and subsistence. Such texts would be nothing less than catalogs of law statements with examples of their applications to specific archeological situations and with discussion about the extent to which they had been tested.

TESTING THE MODEL

The domain of the synthetic model consists of all statements about past cultural behavior and organization derived from or applied to archeological data. This domain is manifest in the archeological literature of site reports, regional syntheses, topical books, and combinations of these.

Implications

The following implications of the synthetic model may be examined in light of data from this vast domain.

1. Inferences about the past may be presented with or without the explicit justification of archeological data and knowledge.
2. Although most inferences will not be accompanied by rigorous justifications, a sample of the literature should reveal the occasional explicit use of instances of each type of law.
3. If archeological knowledge is internalized in the manner I have suggested, a large sample of inferences, especially those concerning the same subject matter of reconstruction, will reveal repeated uses of a single, independently invented principle.

Data Collection

In order to examine these implications of the synthetic model, undergraduate students enrolled in a course entitled "World Prehistory" during the fall of 1972, at the University of Arizona, were assigned a term paper that required, in part, the gathering of a sample of the archeological literature and its perusal for explicit laws of archeological knowledge. Specifically, students were given this set of instructions.

A. The student will choose an area of the world that he or she finds interesting. By use of the card catalog, or in conversation with faculty who know this area, the student will select two archeological books or monographs. Normally one of these should be a site report. The other may be an areal synthesis or topical book. This selection process is critical—take time to ensure that the site reports contain interpretive sections as well as data. . . .

B. Read your books through once to get a general idea of what they contain.

C. After you become familiar with the author's presentation, you are ready to reread the work carefully and begin the analysis. The basic task is to identify and record the correlates, c-transforms, and n-transforms, that serve as the basis for the author's interpretations and predictions. . . .

D. Copy down word-for-word each correlate, c-transform, and n-transform, giving the page number next to the quotation. This is your basic data and should be complete. . . .

E. Make notes in the above sections as to which inferences and predictions are made by an author for which he *does not* present the appropriate principles.

The sample of archeological literature obtained by the students is not, of course, statistically adequate nor totally representative; but, after examining these data (which were derived from a surprising variety of sources), I believe it unlikely that a more rigorous search of the literature would uncover any new or unusual inference justification patterns. Sites used by the students included early man, petroglyph, cave, Neolithic villages of the Old and New World, sites of complex cultural systems of both hemispheres, and numerous others. In short, the 56 pieces of literature examined span 40 years of archeological reporting, all levels of cultural complexity, most major data classes, including representational art, and all continents except Australia.

Results

IMPLICATION 1

There is a range of variability in the extent to which inference justifications are explicit. The data provide strong support for this implication, so much so that several important varieties of inference justification can be noted. The oversimplified examples discussed here are contrived to illustrate the points as clearly as possible.

Example 1: "A brush was used for decorating this pottery." This is the least explicit kind of justification, consisting of an assertion about an event or behavioral property of a past cultural system with no relevant data or explicit laws.

Example 2: "Because of the striations on the painted surface of these sherds, a brush was used to apply the decoration." This type of justification is an archeological approximation to the classic "elliptical explanation" (Hempel 1966:52) and includes reference to some of the relevant data but contains no explicit laws. This type of inference justification is by far the one encountered most often and gives support to the emic value of Thompson's (1958) inference model as an accurate description of the way most archeologists describe their processes of deriving archeological inferences. In other words, this inference appears to follow directly from the observations of archeological phenomena (striations). It does so only because of the conceptual link provided by unstated but implicitly held laws.

Example 3: "Only the application of paint by a brush to pottery of this sort will leave striations of this form; because this pottery possesses the requisite striations, we can infer that a brush was used in the last stages of pottery decoration." This third form of justification is nearly complete (though lacking specific content in its terms) and includes the law and relevant archeological observations. This type of justification was exceedingly rare.

In addition to the three basic kinds of justification just noted, we also found evidence for what Hempel (1965) has termed the "explanatory sketch." This kind of justification occurs when the principle relates two or more *categories* of variables rather than specific variables. These justifications give only a general indication of the variables that might be involved in a correlate or transform if it were made explicit. For example, the following statement was found: "As evident from the location and nature of the finds, the shallow and not very roomy grotto of Kiik-koba served as the dwelling place of a small, primitive community [Movius 1953:6]." Implicit within this statement is the correlate that an amount of living space is related to a specific group size. This type of justification and its implicit correlate can lead one to formulate useful questions about how exactly group size and settlement area are related (e.g., Naroll 1962; LeBlanc 1971). In the context of a specific monograph, however, such an inference justification must be considered weak because the variables it contains are so general and because the reader has no evidence available as to the outcome of tests, if any, on more specific versions of the correlate (or other law) employed.

IMPLICATION 2

Although most justifications will contain implicit laws, occasional explicit principles of each type should be encountered in the literature. By far, the type of law made explicit most frequently is correlates followed distantly by c-transforms and n-transforms. C-transforms unfortunately conform quite closely to my characterization of them as "an underdeveloped branch of archaeological theory" (Schiffer 1972b:156), at least in terms of explicitness. Although n-transforms are not often explicit, they are easy to reconstruct and seem on the whole to be relatively reliable principles. C-transforms, rarely explicit, are exceedingly difficult to reconstruct. At best, they sometimes are indicated vaguely within explanatory sketches.

IMPLICATION 3

As evidence of independent invention of laws through inefficient enculturative processes in the culture of archeology, some laws should recur. Although only 86 correlates, 29 c-transforms, and 15 n-transforms were uncovered, there was some duplication. One of the most common c-transforms is the "Schlepp Effect" (Daly 1969). This law states that, with more butchering of an animal at a kill site, fewer bones will be carried back and discarded at the base camp or village. Variants of this c-transform were encountered three times (I also have found it in four other sources during previous searches of the literature for explicit laws). A correlate that appeared twice takes the general form that features of a large site required a sizable manpower pool and directed organization. Strictly speaking, this principle is an explanatory sketch, but the idea that every architectural feature implies a certain prerequisite labor force seems widespread. Another correlate was discovered three times and relates to procurement systems, to wit: When exotic materials are found at a site, some kind of procurement system, perhaps a trading network, existed in the past.

As further evidence for the independent invention of laws, we observed that in no case was an explicit law ever attributed to another author by citation. This is really a remarkable finding, which demonstrates conclusively the noncumulative character of archeological principles.

With respect to the three implications examined, the synthetic model has held up under testing. However, it should be noted that, in the context of confirming epistemological models, the term "test" is used somewhat loosely. At best, it is possible to state that the synthetic model accords with presently known patterns of inference justification. (Additional findings of the inference model test are presented in Schiffer 1973:50–52.)

USING THE SYNTHETIC MODEL

The synthetic model is intended to be more than a contribution to archeological epistemology; it is also a practical research tool. The primary use of the synthetic model is in eliciting the structure of specific inferences. With the insight provided by the synthetic model, that inferences are justified in terms of principles or stipulations in the three domains, one can raise questions about an inference and reveal weaknesses in its justification. I will illustrate this use of the model with a familiar example from processual archeology.

The inference to be examined is the identification of uxorilocal residence (units) at the sites of Carter Ranch (Martin *et al.* 1964; Longacre 1968, 1970a) and Broken K Pueblo (Martin, Longacre, and Hill 1967; Hill 1970a). These inferences stand particularly vulnerable to close examination because many of the underlying principles and stipulations have been published previously by Longacre and Hill. In this discussion, I treat only that part of the justification that concerns the spatial distribution of ceramic design elements. In addition, problems of the contemporary occupation of residence areas and the statistical interpretation of nonrandom patterning are not discussed. And, finally, no alternative inferences and justifications are presented that could account for the same archeological phenomena.

Longacre (1970a:28) states the major hypothesis (a correlate) as follows:

> Social demography and social organization are reflected in the material system. In a society practicing postmarital rules stressing matrilocality, social demography may be mirrored in the ceramic art of female potters; the smaller and more closely tied the social aggregate, the more details of design would be shared.

The next statement, that "differential relative frequencies of designs may suggest the delimitation of various social aggregates [Longacre 1970a:28]," does not follow as directly as Longacre implies. In this example, he attempts to spell out the nature of some of the correlates that underlie his analysis. What he does not present, nor does Hill, are the important remaining correlates and transforms that are embedded in the justification of this inference.

The incomplete presentation of the uxorilocality inference justification by Longacre and Hill has had an impact on research undertaken after, and stimulated by, their early published statements (Longacre 1964; Hill 1966). Stanislawski (1969a:30), for example, has set out among the modern Hopi to examine "the method of Hopi pottery training, and the association of family unit and pottery style or type." This research, although important in its own right, is completely irrelevant with respect to testing the laws justifying the uxorilocality inference (see also Longacre 1970b). Had Stanislawski attempted the analysis undertaken here with benefit of the synthetic model, he would have discovered an essential implicit stipulation (which also can be represented as a correlate). This stipulation is that the social unit of pottery manufacture is the same as, or a subset of, the social unit of pottery use. This is certainly not the case among the modern Hopi. Most of their pottery has been made for export since the ceramic art was revived there before the turn of the last century; only a very few pots actually are used by Hopi households. And, although Stanislawski (1969b:12) is aware of these conditions, the implications seem to escape his notice. Only under the above conditions of the relationship between use and manufacture social units would one expect designs to be transmitted intergenerationally within a localized social unit.

In addition to the stipulated relationship between the social units of pottery manufacture and use, an implicit c-transform (or stipulation) underlies this inference. The tables presented by Hill (1970a:63, 1970b:39) and Deetz (1965: 93) purport to represent relationships between postmarital residence patterns and the intrasite spatial distribution of female- and male-associated style elements. Such relationships totally omit factors of cultural formation processes. Hill (1970b) has termed these relationships "correlates," and they do meet the definition for correlates presented in the present volume. Such statements relate a behavioral aspect of a cultural system (marital residence pattern) to material variables (ceramic design elements) and spatial variables (design element distributions). As such, they contain no terms that deal with aspects of the archeological record.

Using such principles, it might be possible to infer residence pattern by examining design element distributions in a modern community (making the appropriate stipulations), but only by inclusion of c-transforms and n-transforms (or stipulations within those domains) can one make a complete linkage to archeological observations. Thus, unless it is assumed that at least some pottery was discarded or abandoned at the location of pottery use, there is no reason to expect the occurrence of a nonrandom distribution of design elements in the rooms where the pottery was used. This aspect of the inference justification has, to date, been overlooked but is as essential to the rigorous explanation of the

Table 2.1 The Uxorilocality Inference and Its Justification

Inference: Localized uxorilocal residence units

Correlates

1. If there is uxorilocality, and the social unit of pottery manufacture is the same as, or a subset of, the social unit of pottery use, and there is matrilineal transmission of style, then uxorilocal units will be equivalent to design units, and there will be more sharing of designs within units than between units.

2. If the social unit of pottery manufacture is the same as, or a subset of, the unit of use, and women make the pottery, then there will be matrilineal transmission of style.

3. If uxorilocal residence units are localized, then by (1) and (2) above, there will be differential relative frequencies of design elements in the community, corresponding to the various uxorilocal residence units.

1. The social unit of pottery manufacture is the same as, or a subset of, the social unit of use.

2. Women make the pottery.

C-Transforms

Stipulations

1. Some pottery is discarded or abandoned at its location of use and the design elements on this pottery are a representative sample of the design elements made by the manufacture unit.

N-Transforms

1. Pottery paste and fired-on design elements are preserved under most soil conditions.

2. Items will remain at their locations of discard unless there is postoccupational disturbance of the site.

Stipulations

1. There is no postoccupational disturbance of the site.

Archeological observations

1. At the site in question, there will be differential distributions of pottery design elements across residential areas.

---

data and the justification of the inference as is any other aspect. Limitations of space prevent a detailed presentation of the complete justification for the uxorilocality inference. But the entire justification as I have reconstructed it is presented in Table 2.1.

Examination of Table 2.1 illustrates that the entries in any of the law domains can be presented as either a stipulation or a relational statement. A stipulation can be changed readily into the respective relational statement; that is, it becomes a law that specifies the former stipulated information in one term and one or more additional variables of the past system under examination in its other term. This leads through another logical path to the archeological data. For example, the stipulation that the use and manufacture social units are related could be transformed into a general statement: In villages where pottery is made without wheels or molds and where there is no intervillage exchange of the pottery, the social unit of pottery manufacture is the same as, or a subset of, the social unit of pottery use. One can then either stipulate that the conditions for the applicability of this law are met (such as handmade pottery with no external exchange) or produce other correlates and transforms that specify which sets of data at that site would tend to confirm the presence of these prior conditions. Of course, all inference justifications must contain at least one correlate.

This discussion is not intended to be the last word on the uxorilocality inference—other reconstructions are both possible and desirable (see Binford 1968c:270; Watson, LeBlanc, and Redman 1971:34–37; Allen and Richardson 1971). And relevant tests of the actual principles that justify it still must be produced, as Longacre (1974) is now attempting. The examination of the inference with benefit of the synthetic model has indicated what some of these additional principles might be.

SUMMARY

In this chapter, I have attempted to lay bare the general structure of inference justification and the nature of archeological knowledge. Despite the many ways archeologists have devised to gain knowledge of the past, the basic structure of inference justification seems to be the same.

Some of the important implications of the synthetic model are:

1. All descriptive statements about the past—inferences and tested hypotheses—are part of a complex explanatory framework that accounts for aspects of the archeological record.
2. Some of the laws in these explanations—correlates and c-transforms—are laws of cultural dynamics.

3. All knowledge of the past is inference in the sense that there is no epistemically tenable or otherwise useful distinction between direct and indirect knowledge of the past. All knowledge of the past acquired through archeological means is made accessible by the use of laws.

The brief examination of the inference model in light of archeological inferences has indicated the vulnerability and weaknesses of implicit approaches to both the explanation of archeological observations and the derivation of knowledge of the past. Although many laws of archeological knowledge are shared widely, others are contradictory, and still others appear hopelessly embedded and inadequate. The case made earlier for extricating, systematizing, and testing of extant laws still seems to be an appropriate strategy for expanding the small set of explicit, reliable laws of archeological knowledge. Some investigators may feel such an activity is relatively unproductive because of the great amount of effort required to find the extant laws. Individuals who hold this view may desire to expend their energies in Strategy 2 of behavioral archeology. The remainder of this study demonstrates the viability of both approaches for deriving laws.

The examination of a body of archeological inferences and the uxorilocality inference in particular has given substance to my previous claim (Schiffer 1972b) that the cultural formation processes of the archeological record are poorly known at present. In order to increase the set of useful c-transforms, a general framework for understanding the operation of cultural formation processes is required. It is to the construction of such a framework that the next chapter is devoted.

3

Cultural Formation Processes

It is established in the previous chapter that knowledge of the past is accessible only when formation processes are considered. In order to build models that explicitly take these processes into account, it is necessary to understand in more detail the varied cultural processes responsible for forming evidence of the past. The primary purpose of this chapter is to identify and describe in one encompassing framework *cultural formation processes* (Schiffer 1972b, 1973a). The record or evidence of the cultural past exists in two forms. The first, used principally by historians, consists of materials—documents and other items—present within an ongoing cultural system. The second form is made up of materials in the archeological record, and these are studied primarily by archeologists. I designate the two types of evidence as the *historical record* and the *archeological record.* Let the reader note that my use of these terms differs from customary usage: In the present framework, a clay tablet at Babylon is part of the archeological record, whereas a nineteenth-century loom in a museum is a historical record.

ARCHEOLOGICAL CONTEXT AND SYSTEMIC CONTEXT

Before one can understand the formation of the archeological record, it is necessary to emphasize its principal characteristic. The archeological record differs from other cultural phenomena because the materials that comprise it—artifacts, features, residues—are no longer participating in a behavioral system. The nonbehavioral state of cultural materials is known as the *archeological context* (Schiffer 1972b). On the other hand, materials within an ongoing behavioral system—they are handled or observed—are in *systemic context* (Schiffer 1972b).

Under some circumstances, it is tempting to use archeological context and systemic context in other ways. With respect to the archeological record, for example, the systemic context is both inferentially derived and distant in time, but the archeological context can be observed directly in the present. Thus, some would use "systemic context" to mean past or inferred, and "archeological context" to mean present and observable. These usages are perfectly acceptable if one keeps in mind their limitations. For instance, in Strategy 2 of behavioral archeology, the systemic context is both presently existing and observable. In the remainder of this discussion, I will adhere to the original, strict definition of the two contexts based on behavioral criteria (Schiffer 1972b). Less rigorous usages have their place, but, for proper understanding of the formation of the archeological record, the behavioral—nonbehavioral dichotomy is crucial.

To summarize, the *archeological record* consists of materials in archeological context (prior to excavation by the archeologist). The *historical record* is simply defined as those items in systemic context which can provide information about prior system states. The meanings of these latter terms are clarified in a following section.

TYPES OF CULTURAL FORMATION PROCESSES

It is very difficult to construct a definition of cultural formation processes that is narrow enough to exclude cultural activities not of interest and broad enough to encompass all the phenomena that directly affect the formation of the archeological and historical records. Instead of attempting such a definition, I will define the four types of cultural formation processes.

The first type of process corresponds roughly to what many archeologists recognize as "cultural deposition" (Willey and McGimsey 1954). In any ongoing system, many of the activities performed will result in tangible contributions to the archeological record of that system. These activities exemplify the major type of cultural formation process, *whereby materials are transformed from systemic context to archeological context.* I name them *S–A processes.* My previous writings and definitions have emphasized, perhaps overemphasized, S–A processes (Schiffer 1972b, 1973a; Schiffer and Rathje 1973).

Quite clearly, S–A processes constitute the dominant factor shaping the archeological record. However, if attention is focused on the archeological record itself, it can be seen that still other processes of a cultural nature must be considered when providing explanations for its structure. Activities such as scavenging, collecting, pot hunting, and even archeological excavation remove and modify materials in archeological context. These activities, which comprise the second, or *A–S*, type of cultural formation process, *transform materials back from archeological context to systemic context.*

A lesser number of processes, which nevertheless are markedly affecting archeological deposits in many parts of the world, *transform materials from state to state within archeological context.* Examples include plowing, land leveling, channelization, and other land-modification activities that disturb culturally deposited items. Although *A–A processes* cause materials briefly to enter systemic context, they really do not participate in a behavioral system in the same way as do other materials.

Together, S–A, A–A, and A–S processes account for most properties of the archeological record; yet they do not exhaust the domain. To interpret correctly some aspects of the archeological record, it is necessary to understand processes entirely internal to the past sociocultural system, those which do not result in cultural deposition or in modification of extant deposits. This type of process is also primarily responsible for formation of the historical record. That is, because some items do not leave systemic context, they can inform on prior states even though they still may be in use. As the reader may have guessed already, the processes by which *materials are transformed through successive system states* are termed *S–S processes.* Chipped-stone bifaces, trade pottery, ornaments, documents, and an assortment of other items persist through numerous system states by changes in form, use, and transfers from individual to indivdual, and by deposit in entities such as shrines, museums, libraries, and archives.

Clearly, it is difficult to delimit S–S processes precisely; it all depends on the minimal change an investigator deems necessary to constitute a new systemic state. Fortunately, a somewhat arbitrary, object-centered definition can resolve this problem quite productively. For any object, an S–S process has occurred if, after some period of use, there is a change in the social unit of use (user) or the activity of use. For example, when Aunt Marti gives away her darling old lamp, when a lawnmower is bought at the thrift shop, when that lawnmower is stolen 2 weeks later, and when a house is sold to permit a family to move into a crime-free neighborhood, S–S processes (known as "lateral cycling") have occurred. Other types of re-use (for example, recycling), more widely appreciated, are also S–S processes.

Of the four types of cultural formation process, S–A processes are perhaps the best-known—although by no means are they very well-known; A–S, A–A, and S–S processes have received scant attention. As a consequence, their effects on the formation of the archeological and historical records are scarcely perceived.

In the remainder of this chapter, I shall discuss generally what is known about each kind of process, delineate subvarieties, and, especially, indicate gaps in present knowledge. Although this survey is not comprehensive, it should provide the foundation needed to generate models in the next chapter by which these processes can be taken into account.

S–A PROCESSES

S–A processes are broadly divisible into two types: *normal* and *abandonment* processes. Normal processes are those which characterize an activity area throughout its duration of use. The three major kinds of normal S–A processes are *discard, disposal of the dead,* and *loss.* Abandonment processes begin operation only when activity areas are being abandoned.

Discard

When objects break or wear out and are not recycled and when useless waste products are produced, the materials will be discarded, perhaps in one or more specialized activity areas known as "dumps." If trash is discarded at its location of use, it forms *primary refuse,* and if away from its location of use, *secondary refuse* (Schiffer 1972b). Thus, an *olla,* used and broken inside a dwelling, is discarded as secondary refuse in the dump at the edge of the village, whereas flakes used for skinning a rabbit in the plaza may be discarded there casually as primary refuse when they become dull. Additional varieties of refuse could be defined, based on other dimensions of variation in discard processes.

There is an increasing body of descriptive material concerning discard processes, most of which is widely scattered in the literature and borders on the inaccessible. In many ethnographic monographs, one sometimes finds passing reference to the customary way this or that object or waste product is discarded. Because information of this sort is so dispersed and unsystematized (not even Murdock has tried to deal with it), it cannot readily play a role in generating and testing c-transforms. Although some useful knowledge might result from a concerted effort to comb the ethnographic literature for these archeologically relevant morsels, I suspect that the returns probably would not repay the investment in time. Archeologists have resolved this dilemma in two principal ways: by invention and by ethnoarcheology.

The term "invention" applies to the numerous attempts made by archeologists to generate c-transforms, in the absence of relevant ethnographic test data, to account for their archeological observations. Invention has yielded a not insignificant quantity of c-transforms. For example, many of the reconstructions of dietary and population variables from shell midden data (Ascher 1959; Heizer and Cook 1956; Cook 1972) are based on assumed quantitative c-transforms. In Chapter 5, several of these laws are made explicit and formalized. Potentially quantifiable c-transforms pertaining to the discard of faunal remains also are found in the archeological literature (e.g., Thomas 1971; Daly 1969; Read 1971; Ziegler 1973; Medlock 1975; Chaplin 1971).

Other c-transforms have been invented to account for differential discard activities. For example, I have hypothesized that the larger the population of an activity area, and the greater the intensity of occupation, the larger the ratio of secondary to primary refuse produced (adapted from Schiffer 1972b). Although this c-transform still awaits testing (but see Yellen 1974), like others that have been invented, it does make intelligible a realm of archeological variability not understood previously. Many similar c-transforms lie embedded in the literature and require only extraction and testing.

Ethnoarcheology, wherein an archeologist studies an ongoing sociocultural system, has become a respectable research activity (see Donnan and Clewlow 1974). More and more investigators are realizing that the best place to test c-transforms (and some other archeological laws) is in living communities. McKellar (1973), who observed discard behavior on the campus of the University of Arizona, noted that object size has an effect on whether materials become primary or secondary refuse. Several other ethnoarcheological studies have paid cursory attention to discard activities, although the absence of relevant questions and hypotheses somewhat diminishes the usefulness of these investigations (e.g., Robbins 1973). Richard Gould and Lewis R. Binford (personal communications) are conducting promising ethnoarcheological studies of discard processes.

Disposal of the Dead

Activities involved with disposal of the dead comprise another major type of normal process. Even though burial practices have been a serious area of archeological study for centuries, it is remarkable how few explicit and formalized c-transforms are presently available. Burial practices sometimes are well-described ethnographically, and a systematic review of that literature would reward the investigator with a wealth of material useful for generating and testing c-transforms. Invention has been applied fruitfully to burial practices. Howells (1960), a physical anthropologist, devised a quantitative c-transform that relates the variables concerning the population of a community and duration of activity to the size of the burial population (see also Collins and Fenwick n.d.; Longacre n.d.). Although most archeologists recognize that basic elements of social organization determine patterns of grave good accompaniment, only since the early 1960s have any appropriate c-transforms been framed explicitly (see Rathje 1973; Binford 1962a; Ucko 1969; the papers in Brown 1971). One of the earliest c-transforms in this domain, long used for a variety of purposes, is Worsaae's Law (Rowe 1962). This law states that objects placed together in the same grave were in contemporary use. I anticipate that the domain of c-transforms related to burial practices soon will develop into a body of genuinely predictive principles.

Loss

A third major type of normal S–A process consists of loss activities. It would be the height of understatement to suggest that no one has ever looked at "loss" as a regular process. To propose, as I do, that there are laws of loss is tantamount to contradicting oneself—or is it? Even though individual instances of artifact loss are certainly random and probably unpredictable, when such activities are viewed in the aggregate, regularities should be readily discernible. I now offer a few thoughts on how one might begin to acquire these laws.

Some c-transforms of loss processes, applicable to object types having similar (but presently unspecifiable) behavioral and morphological properties, might be expressed as loss probabilities. The loss probability for any such object is simply the ratio of the number of items lost to the number transformed by all normal S–A processes. By studying the loss probabilities for object types within and between systems, an investigator may uncover significant regularities. For example, I suggest that (all other variables constant) loss probability varies inversely with an object's mass. Another hypothesis might be (again, all other variables constant) that loss probability varies directly with portability or transportability. Given these two hypothetical c-transforms, one could predict that, although ships are large, they will have higher loss probabilities than otherwise might be expected because they are seldom stationary. Shipwrecks, an important source of archeological data, then would come under the purview of general processes of archeological record formation.

Regularities of loss processes will be found not only in loss probabilities, but also in the kinds of loci where loss occurs. For example, if an object of a certain size is dropped to the ground, what is the probability that it can be picked up again? This probability will vary among the set of activity areas in which an object type is used. Thus, coins dropped on a linoleum floor, sidewalk, lawn, sand, sewer grating, and privy will be retrieved differentially with decreasing frequency. When loci are compared within and between systems, certain artifact "traps" will be discovered. These traps, containing a disproportionate amount of materials acquired by loss processes, will be identifiable by common variables related to physical properties and conditions of use. Privies and wells, for example, are notorious artifact traps. Fehon and Scholtz (n.d.) have expressed these hypothetical c-transforms in their most general form as statements of conditional probability and defined important varieties of loss behavior.

As our appreciation for the nature of loss processes increases, we will be able to make better use of our archeological data. For example, if one excavates the remains of a log cabin, it makes a considerable difference whether the material found resting on the original ground surface arrived there through the loss processes of the cabin's inhabitants or the discard processes of the previous use of the area. The same holds true for the materials recovered from a privy; some will have resulted from loss, and others from discard. For many kinds of research problems, it is absolutely essential to identify which process(es) is responsible for deposition of the material under study, although this point certainly is not appreciated as widely as it should be.

Discard, disposal of the dead, and loss constitute the three major types of normal S–A process. These processes most certainly do not exhaust the variety of activities that transform materials to archeological context during the use of an activity area. For example, "caches" of various sorts are produced by normal S–A processes and also deserve attention (cf. Baker n.d.). However, I leave the identification of additional processes for future occasions.

Abandonment

When activity areas are abandoned, another set of S–A processes is set in motion. The most important of these is *de facto refuse* production. De facto refuse consists of the tools, facilities, and other cultural materials that, although still usable, are abandoned with an activity area. The nature of de facto refuse deposited in an activity area should relate not only to what was used there, but also to the conditions under which abandonment took place, to available means of transport, to distance to the next occupied activity area, and to whether or not return is anticipated (see Schiffer 1972b). One would expect that, where transport is limited to what people can carry on land, heavy objects, stationary facilities, and easily replaced light objects will be deposited as de facto refuse when distance to the next site is appreciable (adapted from Lange and Rydberg 1972:430). Knowledge of c-transforms pertaining to de facto refuse production is limited at present. Again, the ethnographic literature contains scattered observations; such information remains to be synthesized, systematized, and tested. Some ethnoarcheological observations, however, are becoming available (Binford 1973; Longacre and Ayres 1968; Bonnichsen 1973).

Abandonment of an activity area results not only in de facto refuse production but sometimes in the modification of other S–A processes. For example, if abandonment is anticipated by a group, its members may begin to accumulate refuse in areas like house interiors, which usually would have been kept relatively free of debris. Such materials might be considered primary refuse but they really are formed by an abandonment, not normal, process. Naturally, serious errors could creep into one's interpretations if the correct process is not identified.

A–S PROCESSES

The second major type of cultural formation process (A–S)—responsible for transforming materials from archeological context to systemic context—is even more poorly understood than S–A processes. We have not progressed even to the point at which major varieties are definable. We can, however, find examples of potentially recurrent activities which eventually may be classed as distinct types of process.

Ascher (1968), in carrying out an ethnoarcheological study of the Seri, observed that, in unoccupied areas of a community, previously abandoned items were removed (or *scavenged*) for use by the remaining inhabitants. Scavenging behavior probably occurs to some extent in every community that is differentially abandoned. It is necessary to note, however, that this type of scavenging behavior involves an A–S transformation of de facto refuse. When materials produced by various normal A–S processes, such as primary refuse or burials, undergo A–S transformations, different types of scavenging behavior have occurred. I shall restrain myself and not give names to these important varieties of scavenging behavior, although names eventually will be required so that cumbersome constructions like "A–S transformation of secondary refuse" can be avoided.

To this point, attention has been directed to A–S transformations of *materials;* some A–S processes act on the *deposits* themselves as a unit. For example, in Mesoamerica, deposits of primary and secondary refuse were scooped up and used as a fill material in construction of monumental architecture (see Heider 1967 for an additional example of deposit modification in New Guinea). Clearly, when an A–S process operates on a deposit as opposed to an artifact, a qualitatively different type of activity has taken place. Again, I defer to others in the task of describing and defining varieties of this A–S process. Let us simply keep in mind their existence and the fact that their operation has important effects on the nature of the archeological record.

Archeological excavation itself comprises a major kind of A–S process. And, although that fact is sufficiently obvious, its implications may not be. In the first place, the investigator must be aware of possible effects of previous archeological work at a site. J. Jefferson Reid informed me (personal communication 1973) that, during recent investigations at the Grasshopper Ruin (Reid 1974; Thompson and Longacre 1966), Longacre attempted to test the hypothesis that certain surface modifications resulted from the previous excavation of rooms by Hough in the earlier part of this century. Although the hypothesis tested negatively, the example suggests how knowledge of such formation processes can lead to better interpretations of the archeological record and to the design of more appropriate data-gathering strategies (see Reid, Schiffer, and Neff 1975). In the second place, when one attempts to assess the archeologist's uses of the data, it is necessary to view his activities as cultural formation processes. For example, the extent to which counts of artifact types in a report correspond to artifact type counts in the original deposits depends on the nature of recovery and processing activities. It is gratifying to see archeological procedures now being considered as a process having tangible and predictable effects on the archeological record as described by the archeologist (e.g., Wilcox n.d.; Collins 1975).

If the archeologist's activities are A–S processes, then so, too, must be pot hunting and other kinds of collecting behavior. Pot hunting has been an ongoing A–S process for many years in most areas, although seldom does the archeologist consider the extent to which such behavior—sometimes difficult to detect after a long period of time has passed—can influence the structure of the site being studied. James Ford's work at the Menard Site in Arkansas provides a rare example. In comparing the quantity of burial goods per burial in his excavation sample with that obtained from the same site in 1908 by C. B. Moore, Ford found a significant increase in the number of burials without accompanying artifacts. He explained this discrepancy in terms of the recent occurrence of pot hunting (Ford 1961:156). Pot hunting, like all cultural formation processes, exhibits certain regularities. In the Southwest, for example, the first areas dug in "pristine" pueblo sites are extramural secondary refuse deposits where graves, and thus grave goods, frequently occur. In sites with severely disturbed secondary refuse deposits or no obvious extramural deposits, rooms will be dug in search of de facto refuse. I have observed these processes in operation over a 4-year period in the Hay Hollow Valley of east central Arizona.

Not only does pot hunting materially affect the archeological record at a site but so does surface collecting. Some information on the nature of collecting behavior is beginning to accumulate, although it is not yet in the form of fully general c-transforms. It is certain, however, that collecting activity is characterized by some regularities; for example, the items usually collected are finished tools in which a great deal of effort was invested during manufacture. These artifacts often are collected for the purpose of selling them, especially in parts of the Mississippi Valley (House and Schiffer 1975; Morse 1973, 1975).

In the face of widespread damage to, and destruction of, archeological sites all over the world, it may seem peculiar for an archeologist to suggest that we begin to study the nature and effects of pot hunting and collecting processes. Nevertheless, there are compelling reasons for doing so. In some areas of the United

States, almost any site an archeologist wishes to investigate has been subjected already to a variety of A–S processes. In future years, unless collecting and pot hunting decrease—an unlikely prospect—most sites to be scientifically investigated will have been modified already by collecting and pot hunting. Even if that gloomy future fails to arrive, many modified sites will be excavated. It thus becomes a practical necessity, when using data from such sites, to consider the nature and effects of collecting and pot hunting. To do this effectively requires one to use information on the regularities of these processes.

A–A PROCESSES

Other destructive activities of modern society (and prehistoric ones as well) are viewed as A–A processes. Land-modification activities, such as dam construction, channelization, suburban sprawl, farming, oil exploration, and myriad others, either directly modify the archeological record or bring into operation various noncultural processes that do. In all A–A processes, one must consider both cultural and noncultural factors. For example, plowing and discing not only damage and disperse archeological materials and deposits but also subject once-buried items to a wider range of noncultural processes, such as alternate freezing and thawing, oxidation, and erosion, which further affect the structure of the archeological record. As another example, dam construction will affect sites in areas where construction activities are conducted. But, once the dam is in operation, the noncultural processes operative in reservoirs, such as currents, fluctuating levels, and siltation, have other effects on archeological remains (Garrison n.d.).

Only in recent years have archeologists, under the impetus of federal and state legislation, begun to study the regularities in these processes. When called upon to assess the direct and indirect impacts of a proposed project on sites, archeologists must utilize these all-too-scarce c-transforms (and n-transforms) to make predictions. Studies have been conducted to determine effects of various agricultural practices on archeological sites (Medford 1972; Ford and Rolingson 1972; Baker 1974; Schiffer and House 1975), and others now are planned or in progress to examine processes operative in reservoirs (e.g., Garrison n.d.). But this information is useful beyond the confines of conservation archeology or cultural resource management studies, for again, many archeologists will scientifically study sites subjected to the operation of one or more of these processes. Although some effects are obvious upon excavation, such as mixing of levels, deflation, and sedimentation, others, like chemical changes in soil and horizontal artifact displacements, are more subtle. If archeologists are to succeed in approximating aspects of the systemic context of such sites, much more refined knowledge concerning A–A processes must be forthcoming.

The varieties of A—A processes enumerated here serve only to illustrate the diversity of this domain. By and large, A—A processes are poorly studied—although this situation is beginning to change. I believe we have a clear practical mandate, as well as scientific need, to study in detail all of the cultural processes that act on a site following (and even during) its original deposition.

S—S PROCESSES

The last basic type of cultural formation process, termed "S—S" earlier, results in a material's transformation from state to state within systemic context. Before discussing several kinds of S—S process, I want to emphasize the dualistic perspective necessary to comprehend their operation and significance: the archeological record of a systemic state and subsequent systemic states. That is, in order to infer aspects of a sociocultural system at a point in time—the task of the archeologist, historian, and historical archeologist—it is necessary to utilize evidence that endures from that system into the present. This evidence may be in the form of materials placed into the archeological record through S—A processes of that system, or it may consist of materials transmitted through time within systemic context. An appreciation for S—S processes affects the interpretation of both kinds of evidence.

First, if one were interested in, let us say, jewelry designs of the early nineteenth century for a given city, it would be necessary to understand the nature of presently obtainable evidence of those manufacturing practices. Several lines of evidence come readily to mind: museums, where actual specimens and perhaps manufacturing equipment is stored; antique shops and jewelers, where specimens are available; libraries, where books in which jewelry designers or their contemporaries may have recorded their observations or designs in print, and where periodicals with advertising may be found; private individuals who may have heirloom jewelry from that time period; company records, where jewelry manufacture has been continuous; and others. How one *finds and uses* each line of evidence depends, of course, on the specific question being asked, *and* on a knowledge of the S—S processes that have resulted in the preservation of these materials in systemic context.

Second, an understanding of S—S processes leads to successful explanation of what is and what is not subject to the operation of S—A processes, and under what conditions. For example, an archeologist of the twenty-second century, working only in secondary refuse and cemeteries from a modern city, would erroneously conclude, were he ignorant of S—S processes, that jewelry made of precious gems was not in widespread use as indicated by its rare occurrence in his excavated samples. Of course, should this archeologist encounter a fashion magazine, a distinct anomaly would present itself. Naturally, to interpret properly this archeological record, it would be necessary to know or correctly infer that jewelry incorporating precious gems was endlessly circulated, spiraling through time in systemic context from individual to individual by gift, sale, theft, or inheritance.

It is now necessary to define and describe S–S processes in more detail. Once again, this listing is by no means exhaustive; its purpose is merely to focus inquiry on unanswered questions. Unanswered questions typify the domain of S–S processes to a large extent. It is fair to state that very few archeologists ever have considered them when making interpretations, and fewer still have offered generalizations approaching the status of a c-transform. Nevertheless, it is possible to delineate several varieties of S–S processes.

Recycling

A major type of S–S process is *recycling*. Recycling is

> an activity whereby a secondary material is introduced as a raw material into an industrial process in which it is transformed into a new product in such a manner that its original identity is lost [Darnay and Franklin 1972:2].

"Secondary materials" are those which

> (1) have fulfilled their useful function and cannot be used further in their present form or composition and (2) materials that occur as waste from the manufacturing or conversion of products [Darnay and Franklin 1972: 3].

Major varieties of recycling exist (see Darnay and Franklin 1972 for some definitions), but completely general types useful for archeological purposes remain to be defined. Recycling may or may not involve a change in the user. There are many archeological instances of recycling behavior in which the original user, remanufacturer, and final user are the same (for example, a dull bifacially chipped knife is rechipped into a spokeshave; a sherd is ground up for use as temper in other pottery).

Secondary Use

Often, there is no need for extensive modifications to make an object suitable for its new use. The latter type of process is termed *secondary use* (Darnay and Franklin 1972:3). Familiar examples include: A *metate* is used as a wall stone; an exhausted core becomes a hammerstone; and a storage pit serves as a repository for secondary refuse. As in recycling, secondary use may involve a change in the user. "Secondary use" is a term that is sufficiently general to warrant adoption by archeologists; in fact, I recall having already seen it somewhere in the literature.

There appear to be several significant dimensions within which recycling and secondary use processes vary; variables within these dimensions eventually should permit isolation of general types of recycling and secondary use processes relevant for archeological research. Quite clearly, a major aim of future studies should be the designation of significant varieties, and the explanation of their differential occurrence within and between sociocultural systems.

Lateral Cycling

Another major type of S–S process is known as *lateral cycling* (Schiffer 1972b, 1973a). Lateral cycling occurs when an object is transferred from one user to another. It includes the many processes by which used, but usable, objects circulate within a sociocultural system and persist in time. Lateral cycling differs from recycling and secondary use in that no change in the object or its use occurs, although some repair or maintenance may take place between episodes of use. In modern industrial sociocultural systems, used material culture circulates by two major kinds of lateral cycling mechanisms: *formal* and *informal.* Formal lateral cycling mechanisms include auctions, thrift shops, real estate brokers, and various retail and wholesale handlers of more limited ranges of material culture. Formal mechanisms are characterized by sustained activity and sanctioning, via taxation, by local, state, and federal governments.

Informal lateral cycling mechanisms are those which occur beyond the periphery of sanctioned economic activity; records of transactions are seldom kept, locations of transactions are transient; and, often, lateral cycling occurs simply by barter or gift. Examples of informal lateral cycling mechanisms include patio and garage sales (see Young and Young 1973), some rummage sales, some swap meets, theft, and gifts within and between various social units. Claassen (n.d.) has shown that some of these mechanisms (formal and informal), which simply facilitate transfers in the ownership of used objects, also involve items that are recycled or secondarily used. Perhaps "cycling" mechanisms would be a more appropriate general term.

There are very few explicit c-transforms of lateral cycling processes in existence. Since 1972, however, a number of my students have examined some types of lateral cycling mechanisms in order to begin generating c-transforms, and, especially, to begin formulating relevant general questions. Several of these studies are described in Chapter 13.

Conservatory Processes

It should be apparent that the continuous operation of S–A processes and various types of recycling will tend to bring about the dispersal, modification, and deposition of most cultural materials. Although lateral cycling processes can postpone the time when materials are transformed to archeological context, they cannot entirely prevent such occurrences; eventually, all objects will break, wear out, be damaged beyond usability, or be lost. In part, concern for the preservation of past remains has led to the development, especially in state-level systems, of processes that countervail the tendency of materials to enter the archeological record. For example, libraries and archives concentrate manuscripts and books; museums accumulate material culture of all kinds; and private individuals and institutions collect everything from beer cans to toy trains. A general definition of what I call *conservatory processes* can be provided. A conservatory process is one that brings about a change in the function (but not form) of an object such that (often permanent) preservation is intended. Usually, the change in function is accompanied by a change in the social unit of use.

In the long run, even conservatory processes must be viewed as stopgap measures which, although serving to make materials from the past temporarily accessible to scholars and antiquarians, ultimately do not prevent materials from reaching archeological context (as the librarian from first-century Alexandria readily could testify). The attraction of the archeological record is an inexorable force that few objects can resist indefinitely. Even Lenin someday will be buried.

No one yet has suggested that there are any marked regularities inherent in conservatory processes, even though there clearly must be. As with other cultural formation processes, conservatory processes have yet to be widely appreciated as an important domain of unified phenomena worthy of scientific study. To be sure, in order to carry out effective historical research, one must know the kinds of materials collected by various institutions (Winks 1969:xvii–xviii). But that level of knowledge, casually acquired during scholarly training and research, is based on descriptive information, not on the comparison of variables that underlie the processes operating. A comparative study of private and public conservatory processes among different sociocultural systems doubtless could uncover significant regularities.

The processes just discussed do not, of course, cover entirely the S–S domain. It would be pointless, however, to continue subdividing and naming these processes until additional empirical studies are carried out. I have developed the discussions only to the point of indicating some broad areas of needed research.

SUMMARY

The processes responsible for forming evidence of the cultural past are diverse and, at present, poorly understood. Four major kinds of cultural formation process have been defined. S–A processes, also known as "cultural deposition," transform materials from systemic context to archeological context. A–S processes, on the other hand, transform items in archeological context back to systemic context. The third type of cultural formation process is known as "A–A"; these transform objects from state to state in archeological context. S–S processes comprise the fourth and last type, and are often known as "re-use." They transform materials from state to state in systemic context. A small repertoire of explicit c-transforms is presently available for S–A processes; fewer are known for the other types.

Regardless of the impoverished state of knowledge concerning cultural formation processes, one general conclusion seems inescapable: The archeological record is a complexly formed phenomenon in which the constituent materials have been transformed in many ways since their participation in a past behavioral system.

Future work is needed both to synthesize extant information about cultural formation processes and to originate and test new principles (by means of simulation studies or ethnoarcheology). In Chapters 5 and 6, I attempt to apply both approaches for deriving c-transforms. Another area of needed investigation is the formulation of general models by means of which c-transforms and specific information about cultural formation processes can be put to use in reconstructions of the past. It is to that task that I now turn.

4

Transformation Models

The consideration of cultural formation processes in the previous chapters has led to an appreciation for the differentiated nature of archeological remains and also to a reevaluation of generally accepted assumptions about how the archeological record is produced. Statements to the effect that the patterning of remains in a site directly reflects the structuring of past activities and social groups there can be abandoned decisively now. The more realistic principle is that the structure of archeological remains is a distorted reflection of the structure of material objects in a past cultural system. Such distortions are caused by cultural and noncultural formation processes. These distortions are taken into account and corrected by constructing appropriate conceptual and methodological tools to act as lenses through which the structure of the past can be perceived by observing the structure of the present. Just as all information needed to produce a sharp print is encoded in even the most poorly focused negative, the information for reconstructing the past is encoded in the structure of the present—but, instead of applying holographic restoration techniques, we apply c-transforms, n-transforms, and justifiable stipulations to eliminate the distortions introduced by formation processes.

STRUCTURES OF THE PAST AND PRESENT

The structure of the archeological record at a site—as it is perceived by the archeologist—can be described more precisely. It consists of material objects, features, and residues in a static, three-dimensional spatial arrangement. A complete description of the present structure also includes materials that were deposited by the operation of noncultural formation processes, such as soil. Thus, besides artifacts and ecofacts (Binford 1964), purely environmental facts of interest are contained within the present structure of the archeological record. Such a structure is described in terms of quantitative, formal, spatial, and relational properties of the various constituent materials.

The past structure of material objects also can be described by spatial, quantitative, formal, and relational variables. But such a description is very different from the static structure of the present. Systemic structures are synchronic slices of a dynamic system. Variability and change in the past are caused by the operation of energy sources, such as humans or machines, which effect changes in the quantitative, spatial, relational, and formal variables. For example, the formal properties and spatial locations of an object vary according to the systemic process under consideration. Naturally, events of the systemic structure occur at different times and the temporal parameter often must be considered.

It must be emphasized that there is no single systemic structure; there are many, depending on the interests of an investigator. For example, Wilcox (1975) introduces the useful concept of "site structure," defined as the set of all occupation surfaces that were in contemporary use in the past. This concept can be applied flexibly at different scales. (The flooring-over of a pit may or may not signify a change in the site structure, depending on how one defines the units of activity space.) The site structure is only one of many concepts that pertain to the complex systemic structure.

TRANSFORMATIONS

Quite clearly, the structures of the past and present are not equivalent; and this fact poses the basic problem faced by all archeologists: How does one relate the archeological and systemic structures? Although one might be tempted to suggest that this is achieved by "transforming" the archeological structure into a systemic structure, this is true only in a metaphorical sense. The task is one of modeling the transformations wrought by formation processes on systemic materials to produce the archeological structure. When one successfully models or specifies the nature and effects of these processes, then, and only then, can the two structures be related. Throughout the remainder of this work, reference is made to "transformations." It should be understood that, in "transforming" the present into the past, one is accounting for the transformations of the past into the present by formation processes.

All archeologists make assumptions about the cultural and noncultural formation processes that have operated to produce the materials being studied. Usually, these assumptions are implicit, and only on rare occasions have they been subjected to scrutiny, discussion, and testing. Unfortunately, many of these transformations, upon which the success of one's reconstructions depends, are ill-founded, and their use—implicitly and explicitly—for explaining the archeological structure and deriving information about the past has led to erroneous questions, sometimes spurious inferences, and a seeming ignorance of the complexity of the transformation problem itself.

Equivalence Transformation

The single most common inappropriate transformation is known as an *equivalence* transformation (Schiffer 1973a:73). An equivalence transformation asserts an identity between variables of the archeological and systemic structures. Several examples will illustrate the nature and pitfalls of this type of transformation.

It is tempting to assume that artifacts spatially associated in archeological context were associated also in systemic context, especially during use. Discussions in the preceding chapters should have indicated why this will be so only in some situations (see also Jelks 1972). Another equivalence transformation states that archeological quantities are related directly to systemic quantities; for example, some have assumed that, because there are 20 bowls per jar archeologically, there were 20 bowls in use for every jar. Because many other variables intervene, however, this is clearly a risky, and usually erroneous, transformation. More complex quantitative variables, such as frequency distributions, also have been subjected to equivalence transformations. Another type of equivalence transformation involves the assumption that variability in the formal properties of archeological remains directly corresponds to systemic variability. For example, projectile point types, often defined on the basis of shape and characteristics of the haft area, are assumed to correspond to past social or temporal variables. In recent studies, formerly distinct projectile point types have been shown to represent simply different degrees of maintenance and recycling processes (e.g., Goodyear 1974).

What archeologists have failed to note previously is that equivalence transformations are a special, not a general, case. A consideration of formation processes and the need to keep the archeological and systemic contexts conceptually distinct forces us to recognize that, in most instances, variables in the archeological structure have been transformed considerably from their values in the systemic structure. Thus, all transformations are nonequivalent; however, in some few instances, the degree of nonequivalence may be trivially small.

Equivalence transformations usually reflect an implicit merging by an investigator of the archeological and systemic contexts. This habit of thought also is reflected in a welter of terminological confusion which has hindered efforts to construct reliable transformation procedures (see Reid 1973:21–24). Many of our terms, such as "room," "site," and a host of functional names for artifacts, are indiscriminately used to designate both archeological and systemic context phenomena. To relieve archeology of this conceptual messiness and to facilitate construction of reliable transformation models, it is necessary to use terms that apply unambiguously to one context or the other (see Schiffer 1973a:77–88 for examples of mixed-context terms). I begin this process by presenting several of the systemic terms used throughout this and the remaining chapters.

SOME BASIC TERMS

The principal unit of archeological observation is the artifact. An artifact, in systemic context, is an *element*. I define elements to include foods, fuels, tools, facilities, machines, and human beings. Provisionally, elements can be divided into the categories of *durables, consumables,* and *energy sources* (Schiffer 1972b). Durable elements are tools, machines, and facilities—in short, transformers and preservers of energy (Wagner 1960). Consumables are foods, fuels, and other similar elements whose consumption results in the liberation of energy. Elements of both kinds often are joined physically to form more complex elements; and, of course, *raw materials* of one sort or another are combined or separated to form elements. When broken, elements become *fragments.* An energy source, such as a human being, is capable of performing work, thus expending energy.

The basic unit of behavior is the *activity.* An activity is defined as the interaction between at least one energy source and one cultural element (Schiffer 1972b:157). An *activity structure* consists of all activities participated in by a designated social unit (this definition differs slightly from my earlier use of the term "activity structure," (Schiffer 1972b:157)). For example, one can discuss the activity structure of a community (which may or may not be isomorphic with the activities performed at a site) or the activity structure of a nuclear family.

A location of activity performance is termed a *locus* (Binford 1964). An *activity set* (Struever 1968:135) consists of all activities repetitively performed within a specified unit of space, which is called an *activity area* (Struever 1968:135) and is made up of the loci of individual activity performance. For some purposes, an entire site may be considered an activity area, whereas smaller units of space are more appropriate for other problems.

FLOW MODELS

Perhaps the simplest way to solve the transformation problem is to focus on the life history of elements in systemic context. The sequence of activities in the systemic context of any durable element can be grouped into a set of *basic processes* and represented by a flow model (Schiffer 1972b). These processes include *procurement, manufacture, use, maintenance,* and *discard.* A process consists of one or more *stages,* such as the stages in the manufacture of a clay vessel. A stage, in turn, consists of one or more activities. Activities are discussed further in Chapter 7.

The terms describing the processes within the systemic context of consumable elements are parallel to, and adapted from, the flow model of durable elements. They are *procurement, preparation, consumption,* and *discard* (Schiffer 1972b). For the sake of convenience, the discussions to follow make exclusive use of the processes of durable elements.

In addition to the five basic processes of systemic context, it is necessary for some problems to consider storage and transport, activities that provide, respectively, a temporal and spatial displacement of an element. Transport and storage may take place singly or in combination between any two processes, stages, or activities of a stage.

Some items undergo a more devious set of processes within their systemic context. Elements can be rerouted at strategic points to processes or stages through which they already have passed. This general condition is known as

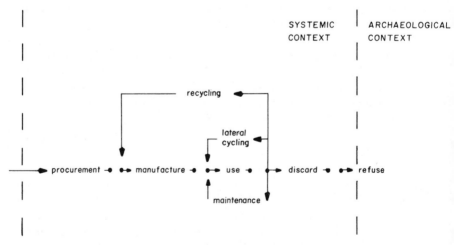

Figure 4.1 Flow model for durable elements. *Key:* − − − system under analysis; −● ●− opportunity for storage and/or transport. (From Schiffer 1972b.)

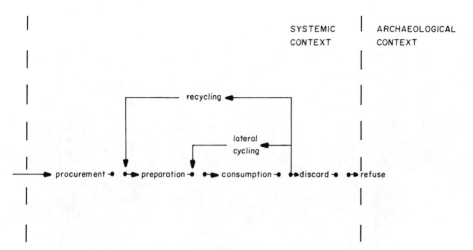

Figure 4.2 Flow model for consumable elements. *Key:* − − − system under analysis; −● ●− opportunity for storage and/or transport. (From Schiffer 1972b.)

re-use, and includes the various S–S processes discussed in the previous chapter.

Figures 4.1 and 4.2 illustrate the basic flow models for durables and consumables, respectively, by which the coarser aspects of any element's systemic context can be described. It is up to the individual investigator to modify the model as appropriate for specific materials and questions.

To date, flow models have been used principally to handle the transformation problem with respect to chipped-stone artifacts. Muto (1971) and Collins (1971, 1974) have pioneered these efforts, and other investigators now are following suit (e.g., Shafer 1973; Schiffer 1973a; Gregg 1974). Perhaps the most ambitious use of flow models in lithic research is House's (1975) treatment of the Cache Basin assemblages of northeast Arkansas (Figure 4.3). In all of these examples, a description of the technological processes was the problem at hand, and, thus, although cultural formation processes are considered to some extent, in no instance is the treatment exhaustive. In future applications of flow models, it should be possible to account for all relevant cultural formation processes.

Flow models are particularly well-suited for characterizing reductive technologies like chipped-stone industries. In addition, they can be coupled with experimental data produced by modern flintknappers for constructing quantitative models. These kinds of research are in their infancy, but major discoveries stand poised in the wings. Further research will reveal whether or not flow models can be used efficiently for solving the transformation problem on other cultural materials. Flow models also can be quantified directly, as will be shown in Chapter 5.

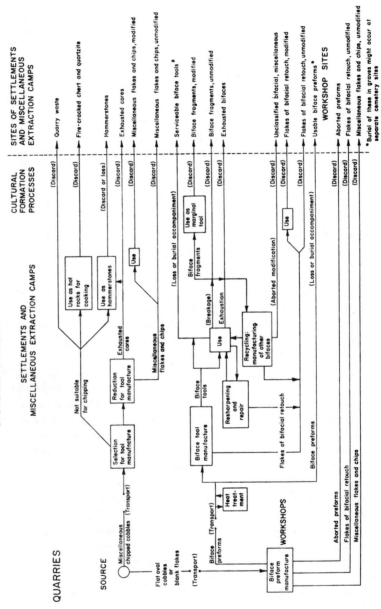

Figure 4.3 Flow model for prehistoric chipped stone of the Cache River Basin, Arkansas. (From House 1975.)

BEHAVIORAL CHAINS

A second type of transformation model is the *behavioral chain,* used to systematize activity hypotheses and generate their test implications. A similar but more specific model has been put forward by Krause and Thorne (1971; see also Fritz 1974). The perspective of Harris (1964) was utilized in the development of the behavioral chain model (Schiffer 1975a). I have substituted for his actor-activity orientation an artifact-activity orientation, which is more appropriate for archeological uses.

A behavioral chain is the sequence of all activities in which an element participates during its systemic context (Schiffer 1975a). Behavioral chains may be divided into designated portions called *segments,* of which the smallest is a single activity. Behavioral chain segments may be defined to correspond to gross system processes, as described in the previous section, but they need not be. Each activity is defined by seven *components:*

1. a specific behavioral description of the activity;
2. the nature of the constituent human and nonhuman energy sources;
3. element(s) conjoined or associated with the one under consideration;
4. time(s) and frequency of activity performance;
5. the locus of activity performance;
6. points at which other elements integrate with, or diverge from, the element under consideration;
7. the pathways created to the archeological record by the outputs of activity performance.

These essential components of any activity now are given more explicit definition. The examples in the following discussion refer to a behavioral chain segment for Hopi maize, derived from ethnographic sources (Figure 4.4). Where no authors are cited specifically for the information listed under an activity component, I simply have made a reasonable guess in the absence of the relevant data.

Activity Definition

The nature of the activity is one of the most important components. Activities should be described in terms of the dynamic relationships among the participating elements. For example, use of the term "grinding" is an attempt to be precise in designating a set of behaviors. Grinding implies that the object of the activity, such as maize, is being worn down by the application of a tool. Because the attributes of tools make them more or less suitable for behaving in a certain way, the precise specification of a behavior can lead to a listing of the attributes a conjoined element must have possessed (or acquired through use). These inferences are made possible by application of correlates that state relationships

ACTIVITY	ENERGY-SOURCES SOCIAL UNITS / NON-HUMAN	CONJOINED ELEMENTS	TIME AND FREQUENCY	LOCATION	OUTPUTS	INTERSECTIONS ADDITIONS / DELETIONS
HARVEST	ABLE VILLAGERS OF BOTH SEXES 3,4	BASKETS 4	SEVERAL DAYS IN SEPTEMBER 4	FIELDS OF H.H. 3,4	STALKS ; WASTED OR UNHARVESTED MAIZE	
TRANSPORT	ABLE VILLAGERS OF BOTH SEXES 3,4	BASKETS BLANKETS 3,4	ONCE IN SEPTEMBER	FROM FIELDS TO ROOF OF H.H. AREA	POLLEN	
HUSK	WOMEN OF H.H. AND OTHER FEMALES 3,4	WOODEN OR BONE PEG 6	ONE OR SEVERAL DAYS IN SEPTEMBER	ON ROOF OF H.H. AREA 3,4	POLLEN	HUSKS
DRY	4 / SUNLIGHT	ROOF OF H.H. AREA 4	SEVERAL DAYS IN SEPTEMBER	ON ROOF OF H.H. AREA 3,4	POLLEN	
TRANSPORT	WOMEN OF H.H.	BASKETS	ONCE IN SEPTEMBER	FROM H.H. AREA TO STOREROOM	OCCASIONAL KERNELS, POLLEN	
STORAGE		STOREROOM 3,4,6	1 TO 100 WEEKS · 6	STOREROOM 3,4,6	OCCASIONAL KERNELS, POLLEN	
TRANSPORT	WOMEN OF H.H.	BASKETS	SEVERAL MORNINGS WEEKLY	FROM STOREROOM TO HABITATION ROOM		
REMOVE KERNELS	WOMEN OF H.H. 3	SHORT STICK YUCCA BASKET 3	SEVERAL MORNINGS WEEKLY	HABITATION ROOM	OCCASIONAL KERNELS, POLLEN	COBS
COARSE GRIND	WOMEN OF H.H. 1	MEALING BIN, STICK, COARSE MANO AND METATE, YUCCA BASKET· 1,2	SEVERAL MORNINGS WEEKLY	HABITATION ROOM 1	WASTED KERNELS AND MEAL POLLEN	
REMOVE CHAFF	WOMEN OF H.H. / WIND	YUCCA BASKET 3	SEVERAL MORNINGS WEEKLY	OUTSIDE OF STRUCTURE	CHAFF	
MEDIUM GRIND	WOMEN OF H.H. 1	MEALING BIN, STICK, MEDIUM MANO AND METATE , BOWL 1,2	SEVERAL MORNINGS WEEKLY	HABITATION ROOM 1	WASTED MEAL	
FINE GRIND	WOMEN OF H.H. 1	MEALING BIN, FINE MANO AND METATE STICK , BOWL 1,2	SEVERAL MORNINGS WEEKLY	HABITATION ROOM 1	WASTED MEAL	
TRANSPORT	WOMEN OF H.H.	BOWLS 2	SEVERAL MORNINGS WEEKLY	HABITATION ROOM TO STOREROOM	WASTED MEAL	
STORAGE		BOWLS 2	SEVERALS DAYS TO A WEEK	STOREROOM	WASTED MEAL	
TRANSPORT	WOMEN OF H.H.	BOWLS 2	TWICE DAILY	STOREROOM TO HABITATION ROOM	WASTED MEAL	
MAKE DUMPLINGS	WOMEN OF H.H.	COOKING JAR, BOWL	TWICE DAILY	HABITATION ROOM	WASTED MEAL	WATER, OTHER INGRE- DIENTS
COOK	/ FIRE	JUNIPER TWIGS COOKING JAR FIRE PIT · 6	TWICE DAILY 3	HABITATION ROOM	SPILLAGE- WASTE	
SERVE	WOMEN OF H.H.	SERVING BOWLS COOKING JARS LADLES· 5	TWICE DAILY 3	HABITATION ROOM	SPILLAGE- WASTE	
EAT	ENTIRE H.H.	BOWLS 5	TWICE DAILY 3	HABITATION ROOM	WASTE	
DIGEST TRANSPORT	ENTIRE H.H.		ALMOST CONTINUOUSLY	LOCATIONS OF H.H. MEMBERS		OTHER FOODS
DEFECATE DISCARD	ENTIRE H.H.	A BROAD LEAF	ONCE DAILY	AWAY FROM OCCUPIED ROOMS	A BROAD LEAF, RESIDUES	

Figure 4.4 Behavioral chain segment for Hopi maize. *Key:* 1 = Bartlett (1933); 2 = Bartlett (1936); 3 = Beaglehole (1937); 4 = Stephen (1936); 5 = Turner and Lofgren (1966); 6 = Whiting (1939); H.H. = household. (From Schiffer 1975a.)

between morphological attributes of objects and behavior, and the results of behavior in terms of use-related attributes. Naturally, this kind of activity definition can lead to the construction of test implications for any hypothesized activity (when coupled to the relevant transforms or transform stipulations).

Energy Sources

The number and nature of human energy sources are a designation of the social unit of activity performance (Freeman 1968). This unit consists of any and all humans associated with the element during a specific activity. The concept of social unit of activity performance applies minimally on two levels: the individual and the societal level which is recurrent. For example, it might be pointed out that, among the Hopi, a postpubescent woman does the coarse-grinding of maize. At another level of analysis, it may be desirable to specify that the social unit of coarse-grinding maize is all postpubescent women of a society; in this case, a status is specified. It also should be possible to consider and describe patterned internal variability in a society for a social unit of activity performance.

Nonhuman energy sources include the sun, wind, fire, animals, and machines.

Conjoined Elements

The conjoined elements are those (excluding energy sources) associated with the one under consideration during the activity. They should be conceived of in terms of the attributes critical to their interaction. This implies that not all attributes of form are relevant for the description of an element or its identification.

Times and Frequency

Reference is made here to the class of usual performance times and frequencies (with the stipulation that variability can be encompassed in specific applications). As an example, among the Hopi, the activity of metate stone procurement took place yearly in the winter (Bartlett 1933).

Locus

The locus of activity performance ordinarily refers to a location or class of like locations within an activity area; they can be specified relative to each other or with respect to stationary objects.

Chain Intersections

In constructing the behavioral chain of an element, it is necessary for some problems to specify when another element has become attached to, or deleted from, the reference chain. For example, spices and other ingredients become part of the maize behavioral chain during "dumpling preparation" activities. In the case of divergence, one can cite the separation of kernels and cob (Figure 4.4).

Outputs or Pathways

At every point in the behavioral chain that is labeled "output," a path exists through which materials may become part of the archeological record. This includes waste products and elements that terminate their uselife during activity performance. In the case of some outputs, such as pollen grains and seeds lost during storage, the material may undergo no further cultural transport or discard. Other pathways are more complex. For example, waste produced from cooking or mixing activities constitutes an obvious inconvenient and unsanitary residue that most likely would be cleaned up, transported, and discarded as secondary refuse. In societies with highly developed refuse disposal systems, most elements make their way into the archeological record at locations other than those of their use, and it is necessary to specify in the appropriate component of the behavioral chain exactly how and where these discard activities take place. (Data are incomplete in the Hopi maize example.)

As the Hopi maize example illustrates, behavioral chain models are especially useful where ethnographic data are available. It should be noted, however, that no ethnographic observations were available for over half the entries in Figure 4.4. Further, the lack of archeologically relevant data in ethnographic reports is systematic. The likelihood of finding ethnographic observations on a component decreases in the following order: conjoined elements, energy sources, location, time and frequency, and outputs. Not surprisingly, a similar pattern of ethnographic reporting bias has been found repeatedly in other attempts to construct behavioral chains (Magers n.d.; George and Rose 1973; Claassen 1975). The archeologist relying on ethnographic data to build behavioral chains will have to make educated guesses at many components. Generalized behavioral chains, based on correlates, eventually may be constructed to obviate partially this difficulty. Elsewhere, I have presented several correlates that can be used to expand the corpus of activity hypotheses (Schiffer 1975a:142–144).

The use of behavioral chains, once constructed, is relatively informal. An attempt is made to match the output components of each activity with available archeological evidence. A close fit between expectations and observations results in the retention of an activity hypothesis, and a poor fit results in hypothesis rejection or modification (e.g., Stier n.d.; Magers n.d.). The matching process is not carried out in a rigidly prescribed manner but is flexibly applied to allow consideration of multiple lines of evidence.

Several investigators have added significant elements to the construction and use of behavioral chain models. Rock (n.d.) has formulated the concepts of *conjoined chain* and *alternative chain segment.* A conjoined chain covers what I have referred to as "chain intersections." It may be *divergent* (for instance, maize cobs after separation from kernels) or *convergent* (say, spices when added to dumplings). An alternative chain segment is a substitutable portion of a chain. For example, after maize is ground into meal, it can be prepared in several different ways. These additional sequences of cooking activities are alternative chain segments.

In the report on the El Sol–Vail Transmission Line Project, Phillips has adapted the behavioral chain model for intersite use. He attempts to describe the past interaction between sites on the basis of the flow of materials and the differentiation of activities. To operationalize this approach, he defines two types of behavioral chains:

> (1) ... a *site-continuous* behavioral chain, in which the life history of an element occurs entirely at one site, and
>
> (2) a *site discontinuous* chain, in which only part of the element's life history occurs at one site ... [McDonald *et al.* 1974:136; emphasis mine].

Use of these concepts for different elements allows precise behavioral characterizations to be made of components in a past settlement system as required for studies of cultural adaptation.

It seems that the behavioral chain model lends itself to a wide variety of applications, most of which have yet to be explored. As more applications are attempted, it will become easier to gauge its areas of usefulness and limitations.

THE PATHWAY MODEL

Behavioral chain models force one to consider individual activities as generators of archeological remains; that is, the performance of an activity can be viewed in terms of its potential contribution to the archeological record. Activities, then, create pathways to the archeological record. The pathway model is an outgrowth of behavioral chain analysis (Schiffer 1975a), and is simply a more formalized and quantified version of the output component of the behavioral chain model. Because it can be used separately from behavioral chains and because it too can be engaged in a variety of important uses, especially the production of simulated data, I treat the pathway model separately. In addition, it was my failure to differentiate the two models, in an earlier discussion, that resulted in cumbersome and unnecessary shifts in the frame of reference from activities to elements back to activities (Schiffer 1973a:117–123).

To begin, it is noted that many pathways do not lead directly to archeological context, because of the occurrence of lateral cycling, recycling, and other processes (Schiffer 1972b, 1973a, 1975a). Further, decay and other noncultural formation processes can effect additional transformations. Nevertheless, a general equation can be provided that describes the pathways initiated by activity performance, and other terms introduced to allow for the operation of some subsequent processes.

If each instance of activity performance is defined as one *use* for all constituent elements (except consumables and waste products), then the quantity of any element type terminating its uselife during an instance of activity performance may be expressed as follows:

$$C = 1/b \tag{1}$$

where

C = the quantity of an element type exhausted during one instance of activity performance. This variable is termed the *output fraction*.

b = the number of uses per uselife. The quantity b is statistical and designates an average number of uses.

As a result of this relationship, one instance of activity performance creates the following pathways to the archeological record:

$$Y = rdC_1 + rdC_2 \ldots + rdC_n \tag{2}$$

where

Y = the total number of exhausted elements of each type $(1 \ldots n)$;

$C_1 \ldots C_n$ = the respective output fractions of all elements $(1 \ldots n)$ of an activity;

r = coefficient of recycling;

d = coefficient of decay (or other noncultural loss).

Thus, the total pathways (Z) created by one instance of performance of an activity set is equal to

$$\Sigma\, Y. \tag{3}$$

Because the performance rates of the activities that comprise an activity set are likely to vary, a more useful expression takes into account both the duration and rate of activity performance. To construct this equation, several more items must be introduced. The activities of any activity set are $A_1 \ldots A_n$, and the performance rates of each are represented as $F_{A_1} \ldots F_{A_n}$. In addition, let t equal the interval of time over which an activity set is conducted. The total pathways formed by the operation of an activity set during time t can be expressed as

$$Z = t(YF_{A_1} + YF_{A_2} \ldots + YF_{A_n}). \tag{4}$$

A principal use of the pathway model is the generation of simulated data for evaluating analytic techniques and testing other transformation models (Schiffer

1975b). Other uses might include more formal applications of behavioral chain models. For example, as experimental and ethnoarcheological data accumulate on uselives and other systemic variables, it will be possible to offer a precise set of archeological predictions for any set of activities. One could change the value of various variables, such as duration of activity performance or relative performance frequencies, to provide even closer fits to the observed quantities of artifacts in archeological context. It seems safe to predict that the pathway model and as yet undeveloped analogs will become extremely important in future studies of archeological context variability (see also Schiffer 1975c).

THE REID TRANSFORMATION MODEL

From discussions in preceding chapters, it should be clear that the materials produced by differing formation processes may be appropriate for answering different kinds of questions. In the most obvious example, a study of textiles scarcely would be carried out on sites where conditions did not favor their preservation. In another example, it would not be desirable to compare primary and de facto refuse from one site with the secondary refuse from another if the problem consisted in discussing variations in abandonment behavior. Nor would it be wise to take secondary refuse locations as directly indicative of activity locations within a site. These examples relate to the important question of establishing comparability among units of analysis. The criteria for establishing comparability is the focus of the Reid model (Reid 1973; Reid, Schiffer, and Neff 1975; Schiffer 1973a; Reid and Schiffer n.d.). It is billed as a general transformation model, and, indeed, it very likely subsumes the others that have been presented. The basis of the model is that transformation procedures must explicitly identify and model the processes responsible for the archeological remains under study within specified analytic units.

The presentation of this model requires the introduction of additional technical terms (this discussion closely follows Reid and Schiffer n.d.). *Transformation procedures* are the application of the general conceptual toolkit (correlates, c-transforms, and n-transforms) to the pragmatic problems of archeological research. These applications are directed toward establishing relationships between the systemic context and archeological context relevant to the solution of research problems on a specific body of archeological data. Research problems are framed within the *systemic context of information,* which includes specific behavioral and cultural variables of the past that are the objects of archeological descriptions and explanations. These variables, not directly observable in the archeological record, are related through *systemic transformations* to specific *units of analysis,* which, in turn, are operationalized to *units of observation* in the archeological context by identification transformations. Systemic transformations relate systemic context information to units of analysis, and are facilitated by the use of correlates, c-transforms, and n-transforms. Units of analysis are the materials produced by specified formation processes that have been argued to be relevant—by systemic transformations—to the systemic context information. *Identification transformations* relate units of analysis to units of observation within the archeological context; it is through identification transformations that units of analysis are operationalized. Units of observation are the units of space and material remains recognizable in the archeological record from their formal, spatial, quantitative and relational attributes.

An Example: Curate Behavior

In studying the Nunamiut Eskimo throughout the seasonal round, Binford identified what he calls *curate behavior,* which consists of removing objects from one site and transporting them elsewhere in anticipation of future use (Binford 1973). It should be recognized that curate behavior occurs to a certain extent in all cultural systems; very few activity areas are abandoned with a complete inventory of cultural elements left as de facto refuse. Suppose, then, that an archeologist asked the following systemic context question of a site: What items did the occupants carry off elsewhere? In other words, what items were curated? If problems of recycling, preservation, occupation span, and systemic change are eliminated from this example, a fairly straightforward set of transformations yields the desired answer.

The basic systemic transformation (adapted from Reid 1973:27–28) is the following:

$$C = (P + S) - D$$

where

P = set of element types in primary refuse;
S = set of element types in secondary refuse;
D = set of element types in de facto refuse;
C = set of curated element types.

The set $(P + S)$ consists of an inventory of normal system outputs and thus provides an inventory of element types used at the site. De facto refuse consists of the residual element set after curated elements are removed from the total inventory. This transformation specifies that an inventory of cultural element types from each kind of refuse must be acquired.

The problem remaining is to predict the locations of, or to identify the deposits of, each type of refuse at the site under study. In other words, the analytical units—element sets within refuse types—must be related to actual observational units (proveniences). This involves construction of identification transformations. For example, one type of primary refuse produced is burial goods, which are identified readily in archeological context. Secondary refuse consists of worn-out and broken materials and usually occurs in deposits of high material density and diversity. De facto refuse is found in the last-occupied activity areas, which are identified through another set of transformations. Having located and inventoried the element types contained within each kind of refuse, the archeologist feeds these element sets into the above-mentioned systemic transformation and derives the set of curated elements.

In principle, the simplest transformations are those whose analytic units are operationalized to the observational unit "site." Many quantitative estimates of systemic properties, such as dependence on specific resources, utilize "community" or "settlement" as the analytic unit. These units generally are defined as all the refuse produced by a social unit at one location. Thus, single-component sites are the appropriate observational unit. Grahame Clark's (1954, 1972) studies at Star Carr provide one of the more successful examples of this kind of transformation. Although the identification transformation is quite simple, the six-stage systemic transformation used to relate aspects of prehistoric diet to animal bones is quite complex (see Shawcross 1972 for an outline of Clark's systemic transformation).

Other analytic units require complex identification transformations, and studies of these are now in their infancy. For example, a topic of increasing importance is the detection and explanation of horizontal artifact patterns on occupation surfaces. Most investigators have assumed tacitly that they are dealing with primary refuse in these situations (e.g., Goodyear 1974; Whallon 1973), but recent ethnoarcheology findings (Yellen 1974) suggest that occupation floor deposits are formed by more complex processes than merely primary refuse disposal. Research now should be undertaken to develop identification transformations for partitioning occupation floors into behaviorally meaningful analytic units which will allow the materials to be treated with appropriate statistics.

The Reid model is particularly well-adapted for use with computer-assisted analyses. This is so because the analytic units of the model are equated easily with the statistician's "case," and artifact type frequencies within the units readily become the variables. In Chapter 12, this model partially forms the basis of a reconstruction of chipped-stone artifacts related to activity sets, from secondary refuse deposits at the Joint Site.

5
Quantitative Transformations

In this chapter, I provide a set of explicit, quantitative transforms derived in part from the archeological literature. This exercise has several purposes. First, it attempts to demonstrate that there is already available a respectable number of quantitative archeological laws. Second, by systematizing some of these laws, it is possible to extend them and perceive interesting and useful implications. And, third, this discussion serves as a background to Chapter 12, in which several of the principles are used to reconstruct quantitative systemic variables of the chipped-stone assemblage from the Joint Site.

PRELIMINARY DEFINITIONS AND PRINCIPLES

Our starting point is the flow model for durable elements (see Chapter 4). The processes occurring during the systemic context of durable elements are represented by the following symbol set:

P—procurement D—discard
M—manufacture T—transport
U—use S—storage

All elements participate during their systemic context in one or more members of the set of processes. If p designates a process, then F_p stands for the frequency or rate of that process. For example, F_M represents manufacture rate, which is expressed as a quantity of objects per unit of time. The equations using these symbols apply to the normal outputs population (that is, *discarded* materials). In most applications, this would be limited to primary and secondary refuse; burial items would be treated separately. Another boundary condition is that no import or export is occurring.

A given process p occurring at a rate F and acting through time t involves a total number of elements T_p; in short:

$$T_p = F_p t. \tag{1}$$

T_P is an important variable since, in some cases, T_D equals the total number of elements recovered by the archeologist (T_e), or T_D can be estimated from the recovered sample. Thus, the most useful version of Equation (1) is obtained when $p = D$:

$$T_D = F_D t. \tag{2}$$

As an example of its use, if the discard rate of hammerstones is 5 per year, then, in a 4-year period, 20 will be discarded.

Equation (2), like most of those which follow, applies at the level of a community. Another useful expression can be obtained for treating subunits of a community, such as households. To construct that equation, we first set F_D equal to two new variables:

$$F_D = f_D c, \tag{3}$$

where f_D is the discard rate for a social unit, such as household, that is a subunit of the community, and c is the number of those social units present. The form of F_D thus produced can be inserted into Equation (2) to generate the important expression:

$$T_D = f_D t c. \tag{4}$$

Use of this formula would permit the calculation that, if 5 households were present in a community for 5 years, each discarding 3 manos per year, a total of 75 manos will be discarded. This transform is used in Chapter 12 to estimate household discard rates for various chipped-stone tool types at the Joint Site.

THE BASIC EQUATION

One can approach T_D from a different path; many quantitative studies in archeology have made implicit use of a general equation that is relevant to the determination of T_D. In fact, since 1960, a handful of archeologists have rediscovered independently the variables affecting T_D. The first such variable is the uselife of a cultural element (Binford 1973; David 1971, 1972; Foster 1960; Schiffer 1972b, among others). Uselife, symbolized by L, is the average length of time that elements of a type are in use. If all other variables are constant, T_D varies inversely with uselife, or $T_D = f(1/L)$.

Another variable that determines T_D is t, the time span over which the systemic process operates for an element type. In many cases, t equals the occupation span of the site under examination (see Willey and McGimsey 1954). If all other variables are constant, T_D varies directly with t. Symbolically, $T_D = f(t)$.

The last variable of interest is the average number of elements normally in the use process (Binford 1962b). This variable, represented by S, is termed the *systemic number*. Clearly, as S varies, T_D follows directly; in short, $T_D = f(S)$.

By combining the foregoing statements of functional relationship, one produces the law:

$$T_D = \frac{St}{L}.$$ (5)

For this equation to operate properly, the temporal units of t and L must be the same. Uselife (L) is expressed in units of time, such as weeks or years, but S is dimensionless (note that the units here differ from an earlier formulation in Schiffer 1973a:101). Performing a dimensional analysis on Equation (5) reveals that T_D is expressed as a quantity of elements. This law and its derivatives are based on the following assumptions:

1. During its period of use (t) by a community, the uselife (L) of an element type is constant.
2. During its period of use (t) by a community, the systemic number (S) of an element type is constant.
3. No S–S processes operate.
4. No instances of the element type are traded in or out.

It should be noted also that, because S and L are statistical quantities, the equations that employ them are necessarily statistical laws (Merrilee Salmon, personal communication, 1974). The implications of this fact have yet to be formulated.

This law can be illustrated easily. Let there be a community in which there are, on the average, 15 end scrapers in use ($S = 15$). If the uselife of end scrapers is taken to be 6 months and the period of use 4 years ($t = 4$), then 120 end scrapers (T_D) will have been discarded by the community.

Moving on, we note that Equation (2) holds a term in common (T_D) with Equation (5). Two quantities equal to a third quantity are equal to each other; therefore

$$F_D t = \frac{St}{L}.$$

Canceling the t on each side produces:

$$F_D = \frac{S}{L}. \tag{6}$$

With this equation, it is possible to observe that an object having an S of 4 and an L of 2 years will be discarded at the rate of 2 per year. This is a useful relationship because S often can be reliably estimated archeologically and L frequently can be obtained from experimental or ethnoarcheological studies.

T_D AS A FUNCTION OF USE VARIABLES

Perhaps the most common way the archeological record is discussed, or the items in it summarized and compared, is by frequency of occurrence or relative frequency. Archeologists then use intersite and intrasite diachronic and synchronic statements of variation as a basis for interpretation. "Increasing use" and "changing popularity" often are cited as explanations for observed changes in artifact frequencies through time, while the age–area hypothesis or variants of it are cited as explanations for synchronic variability. Unfortunately, all such explanations are inherently ambiguous because of the multiple, use-related factors that can cause variability in T_D.

There are at least two ways that differences in T_D can be explained by patterns of use: If S (systemic number) or F_U (use frequency) varies, then, by Equation (5), so too will F_D. Let us now construct an equation relating T_D to other variables of use. The basic question is: How can T_D be made a function of F_U? The answer is quite simple because L is a function of F_U and another variable, b, which represents the average number of uses per element. As b increases, L increases; but L varies inversely with F_U. This relationship is expressed as:

$$L = \frac{b}{F_U}. \tag{7}$$

Substituting b/F_U in Equation (5) for the quantity L, one arrives at

$$T_D = \frac{St}{b/F_U}.$$

Rearranging terms produces the law:

$$T_D = \frac{StF_U}{b}. \tag{8}$$

The operation of this equation is illustrated easily by bestowing concrete values on the variables. For example, let there be a community in which the use frequency (F_U) of adzes is 150 per year, and the number of uses per uselife (b) is 25. With 3 adzes in the community (S), on the average over a 5-year period (t), 90 adzes will be discarded.

In many cases, it is possible to express S as a function of population or the number of social units of a particular composition. This equation takes the following form:

$$S = kc, \tag{9}$$

where k refers to the average quantity of an element type in use per given type of social unit, while c is the number of such social units in the community (as in Equation (3)). This value of S can be inserted into Equation (5) to yield a value of T_D dependent on social unit quantity:

$$T_D = \frac{kct}{L}. \tag{10}$$

The operation of this law also can be shown by contrived example. If there are 5 households in a community (c), each of which uses 2 storage jars (k) having a uselife of 1 year (L), then, in 10 years (t), a total of 100 jars will be discarded. Various transpositions of this equation yield formulas useful for estimating the other variables.

For some purposes, a more useful expression would be one relating patterns of use to discard rate. Such a formula is constructed readily. Since $F_D t = T_D$ and $(SF_U t)/b = T_D$ (by Equations (2) and (8)), it follows that $F_D t = (SF_U t)/b$. Canceling the t, which appears on both sides of the equation, yields:

$$F_D = \frac{SF_U}{b}. \tag{11}$$

This is the basic equation for discard rate expressed as a function of patterns of use. We can transpose still further and arrive at discard rate as a function of social unit variables. Using the form of S provided by Equation (9), we arrive at:

$$F_D = \frac{kcF_U}{b}. \tag{12}$$

As an illustration of this equation, we note that, if there are 15 households in a community (c), each of which uses one razor blade ($k = 1$) having a life of about 15 uses (b), one use per day (F_U) will result in a discard rate of one razor blade per day. By substituting $1/L$ for F_U/b (by Equation (7)), we may present a simpler expression for discard rate as a function of social unit variables:

$$F_D = \frac{kc}{L}. \tag{13}$$

The equations in this section, which point out just the basic use-related variables that can affect F_D or T_D, should make it abundantly clear why most explanations for variability in artifact frequencies are inadequate. In Chapter 12, several of these equations are applied to explain changes in chalcedony usage at the Joint Site.

WASTE PRODUCTS

If there is a constant rate of waste production (and ultimately waste discard) with respect to the rate of manufacture of an element, then it is possible to learn about manufacture rates by observing the discarded waste products (Orton 1970). One can express the rate of waste production (F_{M_w}) as a function of the manufacture rate (F_{M_a}) times a waste production constant:

$$F_{M_w} = F_{M_a} k_1, \tag{14}$$

where k_1 is the ratio of waste materials to the number of elements manufactured. Substitution of T_w/t for F_{M_w} (by Equation (1)) in Equation (14) also results in the useful expression:

$$T_w = F_{M_a} k_1 t, \tag{15}$$

where T_w is the total occurrence of the waste products from the manufacture of an element. When T_a (total elements discarded) is substituted in Equation (15) for $F_{M_a} t$ (again by Equation (1)), one readily derives the important relationship:

$$T_w = T_a k_1. \tag{16}$$

By a similar process of derivation, one can employ conjoined elements to estimate F_M or T_D for an element type that is recycled (Schiffer 1973a: 107–109). One also can readily handle instances of import or export by means of analogous equations (see H. Wright 1972:99 for the implicit use of such a principle).

Equation (16) is especially appropriate for estimating manufactured quantities of elements that have been either recycled or discarded at other loci. For example, Flenniken (1975) has estimated the total number of dart points manufactured in an Ozark Bluff Shelter site from the number of bifacial thinning flakes present. In order to accomplish this, he substituted for k_1 a value obtained from his experimental manufacture of similar dart points.

PROCESS DURATION RELATIONSHIPS

To this point, it has been assumed that various processes within the life history of an element type occurred over the same span of time and at the same average rate. For many problems, this simplification is useful and justifiable; but other problems require one to establish more refined relationships between the duration of various processes. This point is illustrated by examining traditional monistic views of the concept "life span" and observing how the uncritical use of this concept may obscure important variability. Some solutions to these problems are indicated.

The life span of an element type, in years, is a complex variable, and its meanings must be specified precisely and kept distinct. One may be referring, for example, to the total number of years an element type was being manufactured, used, or discarded by a system. These quantities need not correspond in magnitude nor in absolute time. For many types of problems, especially the construction of archeological chronologies from tree-ring-associated ceramics (e.g., Breternitz 1966), it is crucial to distinguish the different spans and find ways of relating them to one another. Several variables must be defined first. The *use span* (S_U) is the period of time during which an element type was in the use process, while the *manufacture span* (S_M) and the *discard span* (S_D) designate the spans of manufacture and discard, respectively. The use of these terms expands upon a discussion by South (1972:76). These quantities are defined as the difference, in absolute years, between the beginning of the process M, U, D and its termination. For example, if the manufacture of St. Johns Polychrome began at A.D. 1200 and terminated at A.D. 1300 (Breternitz 1966), then S_M = 100 years. Each of these quantities can be symbolized by the following notation: pt_1 and pt_2, where pt_1 equals the initiation of process p and pt_2 is the absolute date at which that process terminates.

By definition, the following relationships are obtained:

$$S_U = Ut_2 - Ut_1 \tag{17}$$

$$S_M = Mt_2 - Mt_1 \tag{18}$$

$$S_D = Dt_2 - Dt_1. \tag{19}$$

Because no use or discard of an element can occur before manufacture, the smallest quantity among those just listed is Mt_1. It should be possible to express the other variables in terms of Mt_1. Assuming that there is no appreciable time lag between the beginning of manufacture and the beginning of use owing to transport or other variables,

$$Ut_1 = Mt_1. \tag{20}$$

Assuming that discard begins when an appreciable quantity of the element is no longer found suitable for use, Dt_1 must be a function of Mt_1 and uselife (L):

$$Dt_1 = Mt_1 + L. \tag{21}$$

After manufacture activities are terminated (or procurement of a trade good ceases), some elements still remain in use; this increment of time also depends on the uselife:

$$Ut_2 = Mt_2 + L. \tag{22}$$

Summary 65

When these last elements cease to be used, they will be discarded (it is assumed that no S–S processes operate); therefore:

$$Dt_2 = Mt_2 + L. \tag{23}$$

We now can place the just-derived values of pt_1 and pt_2 into the equation for S_p. By definition, manufacture span is given by the equation

$$S_M = Mt_2 - Mt_1. \tag{24}$$

Using the values of Ut_1 and Ut_2 from Equations (20) and (22), respectively, yields S_U:

$$S_U = (Mt_2 + L) - Mt_1. \tag{25}$$

By a similar process, we arrive at the value of S_D:

$$S_D = (Mt_2 + L) - (Mt_1 + L).$$

This reduces to:

$$S_D = Mt_2 - Mt_1. \tag{26}$$

Therefore,

$$S_M = S_D. \tag{27}$$

And substitution of S_M for $Mt_2 - Mt_1$ in Equation (25) yields:

$$S_U = S_M + L. \tag{28}$$

In other words, use span is always the largest of the three quantities, whereas manufacture span and discard span are equal in magnitude. Quite clearly, as L/S_M approaches zero, the three quantities will tend toward equality. Whether or not there must be concern about variation in the duration of these processes depends, of course, on one's questions.

SUMMARY

The many formulas presented in this chapter as a first approximation to explicit c-transforms can be used judiciously to estimate many systemic context variables. It must always be kept in mind, however, that other processes take place after an artifact's discard, and thus $T_D \neq T_e$ in many instances. As a consequence, hasty and uncritical applications of these principles always should be guarded against.

6

Quantitative and
Spatial Transformations

The equations presented in the previous chapter are useful primarily for solving the quantitative transformation problem at the level of the site or community as a whole. To answer questions about intrasite behavioral variability, it is necessary to effect more detailed transformations—both quantitative and spatial. The purpose of this chapter is to formulate a set of transformation procedures useful in answering behavioral questions on an intrasite basis. The principles generated here are applied in Chapter 12 to derive systemic context statements about the chipped stone from the Joint Site. Besides providing principles that will be used later, this chapter indicates the utility of testing transformation procedures on simulated data (see also Schiffer 1975b).

The focus of intrasite c-transforms is the constituent activities of an activity area. Thus, the starting point for this exercise is the pathway transformation model presented in Chapter 4. The pathway model provides a quantitative expression relating activity performance to refuse production in an activity area:

$$Z = t(YF_{A_1} + YF_{A_2} \ldots + YF_{A_n})$$

where Z is the total refuse production, t is the duration of activity set performance, and YF_{A_n} is the product of the performance rate times the constituent elements. An important implication of this formula is that, regardless of the amount of time (t) over which an activity set is conducted, and as long as the relative performance rates of the activities do not change, the quantities of different elements produced are in constant proportion to one another. If this is so, correlational analysis of one form or another (such as multiple regression or factor analysis) might be useful to isolate from the archeological record elements discarded from the same activity set (assuming, also, that S—S and noncultural formation processes do not intervene significantly).

In short, the pathway transformation suggests that the archeological outputs of activity performance are produced in constant ratios. If other conditions are favorable, it should be possible analytically to detect these patterns of mutually correlated artifact types, determine the constituent elements of activity sets, and reconstruct past human behavior. It must be noted, however, that not all items of an activity set are discarded during any given time t (cf. Schiffer 1975c); thus, the constant ratios are not always so constant. For present purposes, it is assumed that this factor is negligible.

SPATIAL TRANSFORMATIONS

Unfortunately, cultural formation processes not only transform materials quantitatively, as described in the pathway model, but effect spatial transformations as well. When primary refuse, secondary refuse, or both were produced by a cultural system, the task of isolating clusters of artifacts that were used in the same activity set can become complicated. In order to cope with this behavioral variability, several models are presented which ascertain the consequences of pairing patterns of activity area structuring with different cultural formation processes. It then should be possible to state the conditions under which various transformation procedures based on correlational analysis can be expected to yield the elements of an activity set. For one situation, multiple activity areas and multiple secondary refuse deposits, simulated data are produced for testing with factor analysis. This transformation model is believed to replicate relevant conditions of the Joint Site. The models presented here do not begin to exhaust the possible combinations of activity structures and cultural formation processes; nevertheless, such models do provide a basis for the eventual construction of more encompassing formulations.

Single Activity Set

SINGLE PRIMARY OR SECONDARY REFUSE AREA

The simplest possible case is one activity set producing one primary or secondary refuse area. Under these conditions, the inventory of items in the refuse area provides the inventory of (preserved) elements used within the activity set. When the entire site is taken as the activity area, and all refuse is considered, coarse hypotheses about the activities conducted there can be examined, but fine-grained analyses of activity variability, change, and location are precluded. Archeologists sometimes are forced to operate at this general level, especially when using old data gathered with insufficient provenience information. The c-transforms developed in the preceding chapter are applied most usefully under these conditions (when the site as a whole is taken as the activity area).

MULTIPLE SECONDARY REFUSE AREAS

If an activity set contributes refuse differentially to two or more secondary refuse areas, different total quantities of various elements are produced which have the useful property of being proportional to one another among the secondary refuse areas. Elements of the activity set should be identifiable by their mutual correlations among the multiple secondary refuse locations.

Multiple Activity Sets

The situation is rarely so simple as portrayed in the two cases just cited. Multiple activity sets, multiple tool use within different activities of the same set, and sharing of the same activities and hence elements between sets, combine to make the task of activity set recognition more difficult. I now shall discuss several of these problems and assess the effect they might have on the production of the archeological record.

MULTIPLE PRIMARY REFUSE AREAS

A number of possibilities arise where multiple activity sets are concerned. We shall begin with the simplest case of total discreteness (that is, nonsharing of activities and elements) among activity sets. If each activity set forms a distinct primary refuse area, the classic paradigm of processual archeology, consisting of localized activity performance and localized artifacts in the archeological record, is approximated. Under these conditions, refuse within each area provides direct information about the elements used there in the past. From such information, more detailed and complete activity reconstructions can be made. It is necessary to point out, however, that the archeologist must identify the nature of the refuse areas (in this and the other cases) independently of other techniques applied to these data.

SINGLE SECONDARY REFUSE AREA

Multiple activity sets also can generate a single secondary refuse deposit. This situation is created when the entire refuse output of a community is gathered up and discarded in another location. The logistics of refuse removal, storage, transport, and discard subsystems determine in a complex fashion the kinds of artifact associations that occur in a secondary refuse area. Elsewhere, I have presented several hypotheses that describe some circumstances under which the elements of an activity set might be associated in a secondary refuse deposit (Schiffer 1972b:162). The ability to identify these association patterns would seem to require exceptionally fine excavation control to permit the recognition of individual discard episodes (Schiffer 1975a). Some secondary refuse, especially that subjected to additional processes such as burial of the dead and mounding, would not be amenable to controls on such a fine scale.

It is possible, however, to conceive of conditions that might lead to a more ready identification of the elements of activity sets from a secondary refuse area. If there is some variation in the rates at which the outputs of the activity areas are placed in the secondary refuse area, a nonhomogeneous deposit can result. It might be possible to record the artifacts of such a refuse area in arbitrary levels and sections and to combine these analytically in various ways as if they had formed multiple secondary refuse deposits. Dimensional analysis of variance (Whallon 1973) may prove to be a useful technique for identifying the scale or scales at which important patterns appear in the archeological context. Factor analysis or multiple regression then could be applied at the appropriate scale to identify covarying artifact types.

MULTIPLE SECONDARY REFUSE AREAS

When multiple activity areas generate multiple, independent secondary refuse deposits, the latter can be treated as if they were primary refuse. In other words, there is a one-to-one correspondence between activity area and refuse area. The artifact composition of refuse areas provides direct information on the element composition of activity sets. It should be apparent that this model is applied already by archeologists at a regional level. That is, the site as a whole is taken to be one activity area, and all refuse found therein is considered to be primary at a regional level—whether or not it is primary at a site level. This useful transformation underlies the Binfords' activity reconstruction for several Mousterian sites (Binford and Binford 1966).

Let us turn now to a more complicated case, in which multiple activity sets contributed differentially to multiple secondary refuse areas. Under these circumstances, it might be expected that activity areas contributed largely, but not exclusively, to the nearest secondary refuse area. In this instance (and when single secondary refuse areas are treated as multiple secondary), one would expect a uniform inventory of artifact types among all secondary refuse areas, but the differential contribution of each activity area produces variability in artifact frequencies that can be exploited by a factor analysis. It should be possible for a factor analysis to identify the elements of discrete activity sets on the basis of their constant proportionality among the secondary refuse locations.

A TEST WITH SIMULATED DATA

The models just presented can be set up as hypotheses. These hypotheses then can be tested on simulated data that are produced to represent closely the situation of interest. The recommended analytic techniques then can be applied to these data to determine if the results are as expected. I have examined only the case of multiple activity areas contributing differentially to multiple secondary refuse areas.

Nonoverlapping Activity Sets

Hypothesis 1: Factor analysis, when applied to secondary refuse areas that arose through the differential discards of multiple, but nonoverlapping, activity sets, will produce clusters of elements that were output from individual activity areas.

METHOD OF TEST

A simulated site was created containing 4 types of activity area and 36 secondary refuse locations. These numbers were chosen to approximate the activity structure and the cultural formation processes of the systemic context of the Joint Site. The activities conducted within each type of area employed 10 tool types. To simplify matters, it is assumed that the artifact types were discarded at the same rate. No sharing of activities or artifacts among the activity areas took place. Thus, in total, there were 40 different artifact types in clusters of 10 related to activity sets (corresponding to the 40 numbered variables of the factor analysis).

If the period of time that all activity sets were performed also is held constant, then, by the pathway model, all activity areas are producing the same quantity of artifacts. What remains to be specified is how the artifacts output from the activity areas are distributed among the secondary refuse areas. It is assumed that the quantity of artifacts that any activity area sends to a refuse area varies inversely with the distance between them. This being so, a coefficient can be assigned to each refuse area to simulate the contribution made to it by an activity area; a second set of coefficients determines refuse quantities for the second activity set; and so on. To facilitate assigning coefficients, a site was constructed on paper (Figure 6.1). The 36 secondary refuse areas were represented as the cells of a 6-by-6 grid. Four activity areas were placed just outside the corners of the grid. Using this grid, the easily perceived relative distance between any two points served as a guide in determining coefficient values.

The refuse contribution coefficients were simple integers, ranging in value

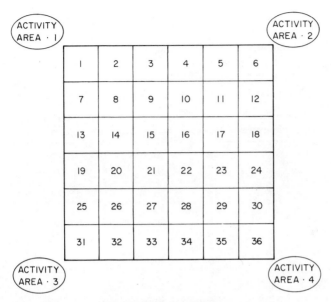

Figure 6.1 The abstract site.

from 20 to 60 (Table 6.1). These coefficients simply express the relative quantity of refuse contributed by the activity areas to any secondary refuse deposit. For example, Refuse Area 1 (Table 6.1) can be thought of as composed of 60 units of refuse from Activity Area 1, 10 from Activity Area 2, 5 from Activity Area 3, and 2 from Activity Area 4. If one examines the layout of the abstract site (Figure 6.1), it is seen that the coefficient values closely reflect the distance between the secondary refuse area and the activity areas.

It should be recalled that the discard rates of the artifact types from each activity area were constant and that all activity sets were performed over the same period of time. As a result of these assumptions, the task of assigning values to the artifact variables in the secondary refuse areas is simplified considerably. Because no refuse contribution coefficients are zero, all secondary refuse areas contain the same inventory of 40 artifact types, in varying relative frequencies. The frequencies of these artifact types are represented simply by the coefficients themselves. For example, in Refuse Area 1 (Table 6.1), there are 10 variables (artifact types), each with the value (type frequency) of 60, corresponding to the artifacts discarded from Activity Area 1. Variables 11–20 consist of the 10 artifact types used in Activity Area 2, each having a value of 10. The remaining variable assignments follow this pattern.

The technique applied to this set of simulated data was principal component factor analysis (without iteration), contained in the set of "canned" computer

Table 6.1 Coefficient Matrix for Simulated Secondary Refuse Data

Secondary refuse areas	Refuse contribution coefficients			
	Activity Area 1	Activity Area 2	Activity Area 3	Activity Area 4
1	60	10	5	2
2	50	20	4	10
3	35	30	5	7
4	19	40	3	8
5	15	50	2	9
6	5	60	2	10
7	50	9	15	2
8	50	15	20	20
9	40	30	15	22
10	30	42	18	17
11	20	50	20	15
12	4	50	10	20
13	40	8	19	3
14	42	17	30	18
15	45	32	30	35
16	30	45	35	32
17	15	40	22	30
18	5	35	7	30
19	30	7	35	5
20	30	22	40	15
21	32	35	45	30
22	35	30	32	45
23	18	30	17	42
24	3	19	8	40
25	20	10	50	4
26	15	20	50	20
27	17	18	42	30
28	22	15	30	40
29	20	20	15	50
30	2	15	9	50
31	10	2	60	5
32	9	2	50	15
33	8	3	40	19
34	7	5	30	35
35	10	4	20	50
36	2	5	10	60

programs known as SPSS (Nie, Bent, and Hull 1970). Varimax rotation and all default options were employed. Among the default options is the eigenvalue criterion of 1.00.

RESULTS

The results provide a complete confirmation of the model. Four factors were produced, each containing as the highest-loading variables the 10 different elements that were used in an activity area (see Table 6.2).

Overlapping Activity Sets

The results of testing Hypothesis 1 are encouraging, but one must introduce additional complications into the simulated data in order to take into account factors that reasonably can be expected to have operated in the past (at the Joint Site and elsewhere). To my knowledge, in few ongoing systems is the localization of activities among activity areas fully discrete. Some activities, especially those not requiring stationary facilities, can take place in a variety of locations, sometimes depending on the time of day, season, or other situational variables. It should be possible to determine the effect that activity sharing—and hence element sharing—between areas has on the application of factor analytic techniques to multiple secondary refuse locations.

Hypothesis 2. As the sharing of activities—and elements—among activity sets increases, it becomes more difficult to segregate by factor analysis the elements of different activity sets.

METHOD OF TEST

The data for this test were produced in the same manner as were the data for Hypothesis 1, except that the process was repeated 10 times. In each successive repetition, another element of the 10 in each activity set was held in common by all activity sets. For example, in the fifth repetition, individual activity areas used exclusively 5 elements, and the remaining 5 elements were employed in all activity areas. In this instance, a total of 25 variables, corresponding to the 25 elements, are required. Factor analyses were applied to each of the 10 groups of data in the same manner as in the testing of Hypothesis 1.

RESULTS

Binford and Binford (1966:245–246) predicted that element sharing (in an analogous situation) should be detectable because such elements will load equally on the factors (activity sets) that produced them. The results of testing Hypothesis 2 provide only partial support for this prediction. Up to and including the fifth run, common elements do have similar loadings on all 4 factors. The results of one analysis, where 5 elements were held in common, are

Table 6.2 Results of Factor Analyzing Simulated Secondary Refuse Data in a Test of Hypothesis 1[a]

Variable	Factor 1	Factor 2	Factor 3	Factor 4
1	−.207	.976	−.040	−.040
2	−.207	.976	−.040	−.040
3	−.207	.976	−.040	−.040
4	−.207	.976	−.040	−.040
5	−.207	.976	−.040	−.040
6	−.207	.976	−.040	−.040
7	−.207	.976	−.040	−.040
8	−.207	.976	−.040	−.040
9	−.207	.976	−.040	−.040
10	−.207	.976	−.040	−.040
11	−.040	−.040	−.207	.976
12	−.040	−.040	−.207	.976
13	−.040	−.040	−.207	.976
14	−.040	−.040	−.207	.976
15	−.040	−.040	−.207	.976
16	−.040	−.040	−.207	.976
17	−.040	−.040	−.207	.976
18	−.040	−.040	−.207	.976
19	−.040	−.040	−.207	.976
20	−.040	−.040	−.207	.976
21	−.040	−.040	.976	−.207
22	−.040	−.040	.976	−.207
23	−.040	−.040	.976	−.207
24	−.040	−.040	.976	−.207
25	−.040	−.040	.976	−.207
26	−.040	−.040	.976	−.207
27	−.040	−.040	.976	−.207
28	−.040	−.040	.976	−.207
29	−.040	−.040	.976	−.207
30	−.040	−.040	.976	−.207
31	.976	−.207	−.040	−.040
32	.976	−.207	−.040	−.040
33	.976	−.207	−.040	−.040
34	.976	−.207	−.040	−.040
35	.976	−.207	−.040	−.040
36	.976	−.207	−.040	−.040
37	.976	−.207	−.040	−.040
38	.976	−.207	−.040	−.040
39	.976	−.207	−.040	−.040
40	.976	−.207	−.040	−.040
Percentage of variance explained	35	35	18	12

[a]Varimax rotation.

shown (Table 6.3). However, after the fifth run, the patterns change radically. In the first place, bipolar factors become prevalent; in the second place, common elements cease to load on all factors but become concentrated in the first factor. Despite these additional complexities, consistent results were obtained. As an example, let us take the situation in which the same 7 elements were used in all activity sets, and 3 elements were unique to each (Table 6.4), making a total of 19 variables. In Factor 1, the last 7 variables form a high-loading cluster corresponding to the shared elements. Factor 2 is bipolar; the first 3 variables form one cluster of unique elements, and variables 10 through 12 form another. Both Factors 3 and 4 produced one high-loading cluster. These results support the belief that, if interpreted carefully, similar situations of high sharing could

Table 6.3 Results of Factor Analyzing Simulated Secondary Refuse Data in a Test of Hypothesis 2[a]

Variable	Factor 1	Factor 2	Factor 3	Factor 4
1	−.206	.976	−.039	−.040
2	−.206	.976	−.039	−.040
3	−.206	.976	−.039	−.040
4	−.206	.976	−.039	−.040
5	−.206	.976	−.039	−.040
6	−.039	−.040	.976	−.207
7	−.039	−.040	.976	−.207
8	−.039	−.040	.976	−.207
9	−.039	−.040	.976	−.207
10	−.039	−.040	.976	−.207
11	−.039	−.040	−.206	.976
12	−.039	−.040	−.206	.976
13	−.039	−.040	−.206	.976
14	−.039	−.040	−.206	.976
15	−.039	−.040	−.206	.976
16	.976	−.208	−.040	−.040
17	.976	−.208	−.040	−.040
18	.976	−.208	−.040	−.040
19	.976	−.208	−.040	−.040
20	.976	−.208	−.040	−.040
21	.503	.498	.499	.498
22	.503	.498	.499	.498
23	.503	.498	.499	.498
24	.503	.498	.499	.498
25	.503	.498	.499	.498
Percentage of variance explained	33	28	25	14

[a]Varimax rotation, five shared elements.

provide information on past activity patterning. The hypotheses generated to account for factor analysis results would need to be tested on additional data. For example, by developing further one's spatial transformation models, it should be possible to predict the behavior of the factor scores.

Even though high-sharing situations seem interpretable, the factor patternings are subtle. It would be desirable to find other techniques for discovering the elements—common and unique—of activity sets. Other rotations available within the SPSS package offered opportunities for experimentation. Oblique, equimax, and quartimax rotations were applied to all sets of stimulated data, again with the default options in effect. The resultant factor patterns largely replicated the previous results (see Table 6.5 for an example of oblique rotation), although some distortions were evident. Varimax rotation produced slightly better results than any other rotation throughout the entire range of simulated data, suggesting that the factor patterns built into the simulated data are highly orthogonal. Whether this orthogonal structure is a unique product of the

Table 6.4 Results of Factor Analyzing Simulated Secondary Refuse Data in a Test of Hypothesis 2[a]

Variable	Factor 1	Factor 2	Factor 3	Factor 4
1	.076	.200	−.129	−.129
2	.076	.200	−.129	−.129
3	.076	.200	−.129	−.129
4	.003	−.001	.282	.000
5	.003	−.001	.282	.000
6	.003	−.001	.282	.000
7	.003	−.001	.001	.282
8	.003	−.001	.001	.282
9	.003	−.001	.001	.282
10	.077	−.197	−.131	−.131
11	.077	−.197	−.131	−.131
12	.077	−.197	−.131	−.131
13	.116	.000	.015	.015
14	.116	.000	.015	.015
15	.116	.000	.015	.015
16	.116	.000	.015	.015
17	.116	.000	.015	.015
18	.116	.000	.015	.015
19	.116	.000	.015	.015
Percentage of variance explained	44	22	22	11

[a]Varimax rotation, seven shared elements.

Table 6.5 Rerun of Simulated Secondary Refuse Data in a Test of Hypothesis 2[a]

Variable	Factor 1	Factor 2	Factor 3	Factor 4
1	.332	−.000	.861	−.402
2	.332	−.000	.861	−.402
3	.332	−.000	.861	−.402
4	.332	−.000	.861	−.402
5	.332	−.000	.861	−.402
6	.343	.838	−.016	.424
7	.343	.838	−.016	.424
8	.343	.838	−.016	.424
9	.343	.838	−.016	.424
10	.343	.838	−.016	.424
11	.344	−.835	−.011	.427
12	.344	−.835	−.011	.427
13	.344	−.835	−.011	.427
14	.344	−.835	−.011	.427
15	.344	−.835	−.011	.427
16	.357	−.002	−.810	−.445
17	.357	−.002	−.810	−.445
18	.357	−.002	−.810	−.445
19	.357	−.002	−.810	−.445
20	.357	−.002	−.810	−.445
21	.999	.000	.014	.000
22	.999	.000	.014	.000
23	.999	.000	.014	.000
24	.999	.000	.014	.000
25	.999	.000	.014	.000
Percentage of variance explained	33	28	25	14

[a]Oblique rotation, five shared elements.

data-generating technique or a more general feature of all activity structures and secondary refuse production is not yet known. Further work is needed.

The results of testing Hypothesis 2 demonstrate that, under certain simplified conditions, activity sets containing common elements can be isolated by factor analysis of secondary refuse areas. Problems of interpretation arise when the number of shared elements exceeds the number of unique elements within all activity sets. This situation may occur more commonly than might be thought at first glance, because it requires that only 20% or more of the elements were used in all activity sets. The problem, then, is to determine which pattern (more or less than 20% sharing) is responsible; clearly, interpretations of the factors will vary considerably, depending on how the sharing problem is resolved. Another problem—not addressed—is the likely situation of some elements having been used in all areas, fewer elements used in some areas, and a few elements restricted in use to one area. This case deserves close study because it is probably the most realistic situation for many kinds of systems.

CONCLUSION

This chapter shows that the pathway model, when combined with spatial transformations, provides a powerful framework for considering the effects of various formation processes on hypothetical behavioral systems. Preliminary testing of factor analytic techniques on simulated secondary refuse data supports some of the models presented and provides insights into transformation procedures which may be of use in reconstructing activity sets and activity areas at the Joint Site.

The limited number of hypothesis tests conducted here also indicates the enormous potential of simulated data for examining methodological problems in archeology. I do not suggest that any are solved here; but some preliminary directions are indicated that can lead to eventual solutions. The future success of factor (and other) analytic techniques in archeology well may depend on whether or not the conditions for their applicability can be determined. By so doing, there is specified a range of activity structures and cultural formation processes that could be responsible for a given archeological pattern.

Testing of models on simulated data is a versatile technique for studying the numerous systemic patterns and cultural formation processes that can generate statistical patterns in archeological data. Studies of simulated data offer investigators what the best set of archeological data can never provide—complete knowledge of the conditions under which it was produced. The results of applying various pattern discovery techniques (factor analysis, cluster analysis, and so on) to archeological data can be interpreted with confidence only after many more studies on simulated data are conducted, taking into account a much wider range of variables in explicit models. Through such additional research, the effects of numerous cultural formation processes on systemic structures can be ascertained. By this process, a repertoire of sound transformation procedures can be accumulated and tests devised for identifying the most likely factors at work in specific cases.

7

An Introduction
to the Joint Site

In previous chapters, the stage was set for considering systemic context questions pertaining to actual archeological remains. In dealing with specific data from the Joint Site (N.S. 605), my principal aim is not that of illuminating the events that occurred at a particular location in eastern Arizona some seven centuries ago. Instead, I wish to show at which points in the process of archeological research the consideration of cultural formation processes by the application of explicit transformation procedures can lead to formulating better systemic context questions and provide paths for obtaining more definitive answers to those questions.

In addition to employing ideas presented earlier in this work, I shall develop in later chapters additional concepts and principles when the need for them arises. Topics such as the interpretation of absolute dates and the design of classificatory systems are discussed more conveniently within the chapters relating to the Joint Site than elsewhere.

BACKGROUND

The Hay Hollow Valley, in which the Joint Site is situated, is one of the best-known archeological regions of its size in the world. It is not necessary, therefore, to present discourses on topics, such as climate, vegetation, soils, culture history, and others, that customarily preface site descriptions. These topics have been treated in detail by my colleagues, and I shall refer the reader to the relevant, accessible publications.

The floral and faunal components of the environment, as it exists today, are discussed by Zubrow (1975) on the basis of a resource survey undertaken in the valley in 1970. Zubrow refers to other studies of past and present environments in the Hay Hollow Valley, with the exception of Dickey (1971). Fritz (1974) also provides useful environmental material. The reader interested in an inventory of usable plants and the uses made of them by the Hopi and Zuni should consult Hill (1970a). The geomorphology of the Hay Hollow Valley has received the recent attention of Bowman (1975).

A culture history of the "triangle area" of east central Arizona has been presented by Longacre (1970a) and revised with no significant modifications by Zubrow (1975), who erroneously applies the regional trends discerned by Longacre (1970a) to the Hay Hollow Valley, where many events took place at different times than in the region as a whole. For example, Zubrow (1975) presents population curves, using sites dated on the basis of associated pottery, that begin at A.D. 200. It is disconcerting to discover in the culture history section that pottery does not appear in the Hay Hollow Valley until A.D. 500, a statement apparently borrowed uncritically from Longacre (1970a:12). In fact, pottery occurs in the Hay Hollow Valley before A.D. 200 (Martin and Plog 1973). An up-to-date culture history of the valley remains to be written.

General processes of culture growth are discussed by Plog (1974) and by Martin and Plog (1973). Changes in the population of the Hay Hollow Valley occurring during prehistory have been measured by Schiffer (1968), Plog (1974), and Zubrow (1975). I now believe that many of the previously discerned trends, such as the early population peak in the years A.D. 300–600, may be artifacts of our measuring instruments, which have assigned an equal uselife to pithouses and pueblo rooms. The early population bulge, subsequent decline, and some other variations that have been the topic of considerable explanatory effort (e.g., Plog 1975) may disappear when proper attention is paid to this problem. Gregory (1975) has made a beginning in this direction by demonstrating that the one-room pueblos included in previous population estimates were, in fact, limited activity sites.

THE JOINT SITE

The Joint Site occupies an intermediate bench on the west side of the Hay Hollow Valley (Bowman 1975:12). From this location, the inhabitants had an impressive view of the entire valley, including most of its other major sites

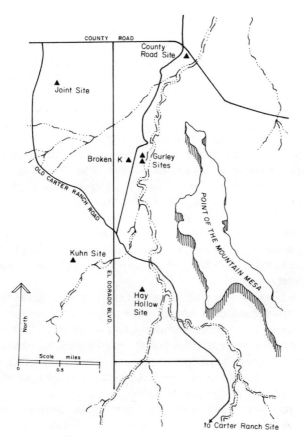

Figure 7.1 Map of the Hay Hollow Valley, showing the Joint Site in relation to other excavated sites and major physiographic features.

(Figure 7.1). Although this view may have been an important variable determining the original placement of the site, the decisions leading to its choice for excavations by the Field Museum of Natural History in the summers of 1970 and 1971 involved additional variables.

Three graduate students, John Hanson, Frederick Gorman, and myself, were hired by the late Paul S. Martin, Director of the Southwestern Expedition of the Field Museum of Natural History, to carry out archeological investigations of our own design within the anthropological laboratory of the Hay Hollow Valley. In exercising this unprecedented freedom, several logistic and labor allocation problems had to be solved. We had to find an equitable way of dividing the available resources, 2 field vehicles and 10 undergraduate research participants, among the field projects.

There were only three possibilities. The first required that one or two of us alter our research designs and apply them to data already gathered. The second was to scale down all projects to an extent and to be satisfied with securing less information from three independently conducted excavations. The third, and least plausible alternative, was to resolve somehow the conflicting data demands of our different problem orientations and utilize data from a single excavation. We chose the last alternative, in the hope that it also might serve as a unique experiment in the organization of archeological research (see Hanson and Schiffer 1975 for an evaluation of that experiment).

John Hanson's interests centered on the adaptive responses of community social organization to environmental change. Specifically, he desired to test hypotheses about social unit interaction under conditions of environmental stress (Hanson 1975). This interest required the excavation of a site large enough to contain at least two social units of the size demonstrated by Hill (1970a) to be about 20 rooms each. In short, we would have had to excavate at least part of a pueblo having over 40 rooms (Hanson and Schiffer 1975). In addition, burial data would have been needed for reconstructing various parameters of the past social system.

Frederick Gorman expressed interest in examining two sites in the Hay Hollow Valley occupied at different times, for the purpose of discovering the constants and variables in past systems of information processing (Hanson and Schiffer 1975). These were to be identified on the basis of attribute patternings in major artifact classes, especially chipped and ground stone. No specific requirements of site size were demanded by this problem focus, except that an adequate sample be obtained of floor provenience artifacts.

My research design was not developed in very great detail before excavation. I did know that I wished to provide behavioral explanations for the spatial and associational patterning of artifacts at a site, taking into account explicitly the cultural formation processes of the archeological record. I anticipated doing a comprehensive simulation to account for all major artifact and ecofact classes. This aim could be achieved most effectively by the complete excavation of a small site or by the recovery of a spatially and quantitatively representative sample of the various debris classes of a larger site. I preferred to work with a pueblo site of about 10 to 15 rooms.

Hanson's need to excavate a large pueblo understandably took precedence over my desire for a small site. I elected, rather, to deal with one major artifact class, chipped stone, and utilize other data as needed. Gorman did not object to the choice of a large site, although he realized that he would be unable to participate in the second season of its excavation if he were also to retrieve data from an earlier pithouse village.

Two previous surveys of the Hay Hollow Valley (reported in Schiffer 1968; Plog 1974; Zubrow 1975) had identified a number of possible sites meeting our requirements. Unfortunately, most of these pueblos had been potted extensively, sometimes with earth-moving equipment, rendering them useless for carefully controlled excavations. Of the remaining sites, most were inaccessible during the periods of rain that begin in early July and last throughout the summer, and had to be eliminated on that basis. What remained was a single site, N.S. 605, discovered during the 1968 survey of parts of the eastern and western sections of the Hay Hollow Valley (Plog 1974) and estimated to contain 35 to 40 rooms. Because of its proximity to the Carter Ranch house and its location on a bench as opposed to the valley floor or mesa top (where other pueblos of this size occur), it was insulated effectively against pot hunting. Since N.S. 605 was located conveniently near the County Road, it could be reached easily, even after heavy thundershowers. After visiting the site and finding it suitable for our joint purposes, as well as pleasantly located, we affectionately dubbed it the "Joint Site."

EXCAVATION PROCEDURES

The actual sampling procedures, excavation techniques, other background information, and the burial data are presented in the preliminary report (Hanson and Schiffer 1975). No purpose would be served by reproducing those accounts here. Instead, I shall provide only a brief summary of our data-gathering strategy and major results, and provide, wherever needed, corrections and additions relevant for using Joint Site data to illuminate the explicit use of transformation procedures.

Rooms

The Joint Site consists of two discontinuous blocks of 27 and 6 rooms each and 3 outlying semisubterranean rooms. Rooms were chosen for excavation on the basis of random sampling within 5 strata defined by variation in presumed floor area, as determined from the outline of the tops of walls. However, not all rooms were discovered during the wall-locating activity of the first season. As a result, several modifications of the site map were made in the second season, and the sampling strata were redefined, producing 6 instead of 5 strata. In general, the fewer the rooms in a stratum, the greater the percentage of rooms excavated. In all, 25 rooms were excavated to floor or below, and some testing was conducted in 5 others (2 more rooms were excavated in 1972 by John Hanson, but these data are not yet available). In Figure 7.2, one may examine the map of the roomblocks at the Joint Site; and, in Table 7.1, a summary of excavated rooms within the redefined sample strata is displayed.

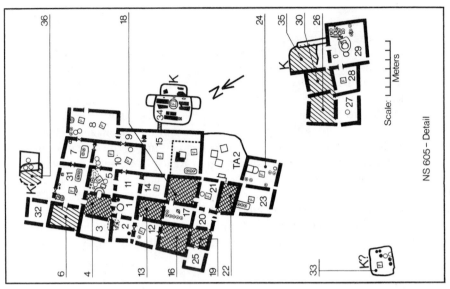

NS 605 – Detail

Scale: Meters

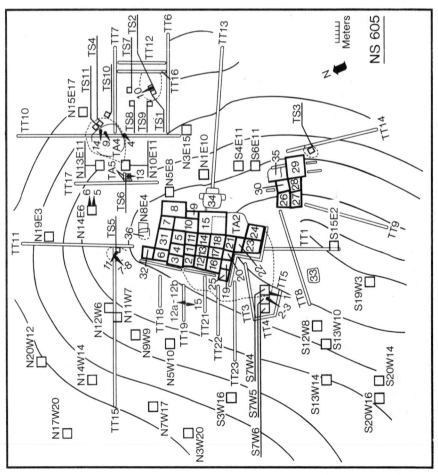

NS 605

Meters

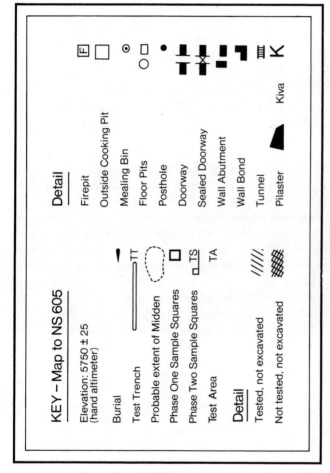

Figure 7.2 Map of the Joint Site, displaying major features and excavation units. (Modified slightly from Hanson and Schiffer 1975 to correct bond–abutment errors.)

Table 7.1 Final Stratification of the Joint Site Room Sample

	Excavated rooms			
Size class	1970	1971	Tested rooms	Unexcavated rooms
A (3.69–5.46 m²)	25, 32, 1, 2	20, 9		19
B (5.47–7.33 m²)	3, 17, 11, 21	12, 5	30	13, 4
	27, 28, 14			22, 16
C (7.34–9.38 m²)	33, 24		6	18
D (9.39–13.22 m²)	23, 7	31	26	
E (13.23–16.48 m²)	10, 8, 29			
F (>16.49 m²)	15			
Unknown			35, 36	

All rooms were excavated in arbitrary levels ranging in thickness from 10 to 20 cm, depending usually on artifact density. More control was maintained when more artifacts (in a grossly relative sense) were encountered (except for Room 17, which was excavated hastily in 20-cm levels at the end of the first season). Levels within each room were assigned a letter, beginning with A at the top, except for Rooms 1, 15, and 24. These latter rooms were investigated early in the first season before we had resolved the conflicts in excavation procedures between principal investigators and had imposed a modicum of uniformity on provenience designations.

During the 1971 season, Gorman commenced investigation of the Kuhn Site (N.S. 663), an early pithouse village (Figure 7.1). Hanson and I divided the authority and responsibility for decisions in the field at the Joint Site; Hanson continued excavating rooms, while I sampled extramural areas of the site.

Extramural Areas

SURFACE COLLECTION

In addition to excavating rooms, my research design required data from extramural areas of the site, principally secondary refuse areas. In order to provide a basis for deciding where to dig, a surface collection of lithics and ceramics was obtained during the first summer, in anticipation of constructing sampling strata based on the differential density of surface artifacts. At Cäyönu, Redman and Watson (1970) discovered a close relationship between surface and subsurface artifact distributions. That this was the case for a complexly stratified, multicomponent site encouraged us to identify strata on the basis of variations in the density of surface artifacts at the Joint Site. Regardless of whether or not there was a close correlation of the surface and subsurface artifact distributions, we at least could account explicitly for our excavation decisions. Later phases of the excavation (test trenches) were designed to test our assumptions about the nature of the subsurface site and allow us to construct explanations for the observed surface patterns (Hanson and Schiffer 1975; Schiffer and Rathje 1973; Reid, Schiffer, and Neff 1975).

The methods used for making the surface collections have been described before (Hanson and Schiffer 1975), but the general features will be reviewed. The original survey party, which discovered the site in 1968, made a grab sample of pottery. Paul S. Martin examined these sherds and assigned the Joint Site a probable occupation span of A.D. 1000–1300.

The controlled surface collection of 1970 was a stratified random sample, based on 16 arbitrary square strata of 400 m² each. A 32% sample of the area in each square was selected randomly, some by means of rows and columns, others by means of smaller squares. All observable lithics, ceramics, bone, and other artifacts and ecofacts were collected. However, no attempt was made to remove shrubbery—especially saltbush—growing on the site. The effects of grass and shrub distributions on our ability to collect the site with even intensity are probably negligible, owing to both even plant distribution and overall sparse occurrence.

All artifacts obtained from surface provenience units were counted and recorded within a system of coarse categories. John Rick and Eric Gritzmacher counted and recorded surface lithics, while I did the ceramics. These counts were lumped into gross lithic and ceramic frequencies for each unit of provenience, and a Pearson's r was computed to determine the extent that ceramic and lithic counts were correlated on the surface of the Joint Site. The value obtained was .91, significant at the .001 level. This made the derivation of excavation strata somewhat simpler, since no decisions had to be made concerning the importance of one or the other artifact category for reflecting what lies below. The artifact counts of the provenience units were divided into six density classes and displayed on a map by means of different colored crayons. The patterns that emerged from this simple technique formed the basis for defining the sampling strata. Subjective judgments applied to the distribution map yielded six strata and several substrata (Figure 7.3).

SAMPLE SQUARES–PHASE 1

At the suggestion of Dan Bowman, I decided to take an initial 2% sample of the extramural areas of the site. It was hoped that this initial material and data from trenching operations would provide adequate information to structure a second phase of test pits (see Binford 1964 and Redman 1973 for discussions of multiphase sampling procedures). The total number of 2-X-2-m squares contained within the strata and substrata was determined, and each square was given an arbitrary number. A table of random numbers was used to select

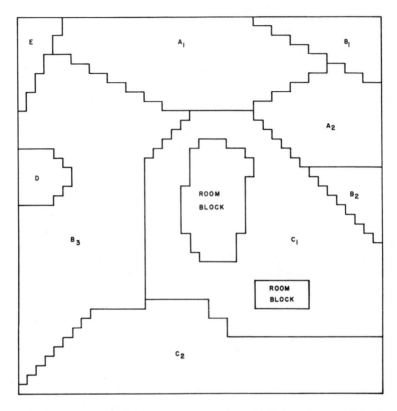

Figure 7.3 Sampling strata of Joint Site extramural areas based on differential density of surface lithics and ceramics. Order of decreasing artifact density: A_1, A_2, B_1, B_2, B_3, C_1, C_2, D, E.

Table 7.2 Phase 1 Sample Squares Chosen within Surface Strata[a]

Stratum	Stratum size[b]	Sample squares chosen for excavation
A_1	216	N19E3, N20W12, N12W6, N14E6
A_2	113	N13E11, N10E11
B_1	56	N15E17
B_2	36	N3E15
B_3	369	N14W14, N7W17, S3W16, N11W7, S13W14, N5W10, N9W9
C_1	378	N8E4, N1E10, S6E11, S7W6, S4E11, S7W4, N5E8, S7W5
C_2	278	S19W14, S19W16, S15E2, S13W8, S14W10, S19W3
D	30	N3W20
E	30	N17W20

[a]Roomblock areas (in 2-×-2-m squares) = 18, 77.
[b]In 2-×-2-m squares.

squares for excavation. These squares then were assigned a unique designation determined by their north–south and east–west distances from the centrally located datum point. For example, N8E4 is found to be eight squares north of datum and four squares east of datum (see Figure 7.2). Table 7.2 lists the excavation strata, the number of squares contained in each, and the squares chosen randomly for excavation. In a few cases in which a 2% sample of the squares within a substratum yielded only a fractional square, it was rounded upward to one, regardless of how small. In the remaining strata, rounding off conformed to normal mathematical procedures.

All sample squares were excavated in arbitrary 15-cm levels, within quarter sections. As in the rooms, levels were lettered, beginning with A at the top. Sections were numbered: SW = 1, NW = 2, SE = 3, NE = 4. Provenience control was maintained within squares to section and level. Occasional features encountered during sample square excavation, such as occupation surfaces or burials, necessitated the abandonment of arbitrary excavation units and provenience designations and their replacement with naturally defined units. Burials were recorded separately on standardized forms (Hanson and Schiffer 1975). Other features, such as a small reservoir encountered in S7W6, were treated on an ad hoc basis.

TEST TRENCHES

As an adjunct to Phase 1 sample square, a series of backhoe trenches were placed in various parts of the site to facilitate discovery of additional secondary refuse areas. A number of different criteria were used to select the locations of these excavation units. In some cases—for example, Test Trenches 7, 10, 12, and 16—we attempted to determine the subsurface boundaries of a refuse area (Figure 7.2). Other trenches—for example, Test Trenches 9 and 14—aided in locating the southeastern boundary of subsurface remains. In most cases, test trenches were placed in areas that were covered poorly by Phase 1 sample squares. Artifact collections from test trenches were made in some cases, the decisions to do so being largely arbitrary. In no case was collecting systematic, or aided by screening, except in the relatively few instances when a trench discovered a burial—scattering bones and grave goods (this occurred when Burial 11 was found in Test Trench 15 and Burial 12a was discovered in Test Trench 19). When a trench opened up a large area, the latter was termed a "test area." Several secondary refuse deposits, not located by sample squares, were discovered by the test trenches (see Figure 7.2). The test trenches also disclosed that subsurface deposits fell entirely within the boundaries of the sample-square grid.

SAMPLE SQUARES–PHASE 2

A total of 26 Phase 1 sample squares were excavated, and 6 more (N20W12, N14W14, N17W20, N3W20, N7W17, S3W16) were considered to have been

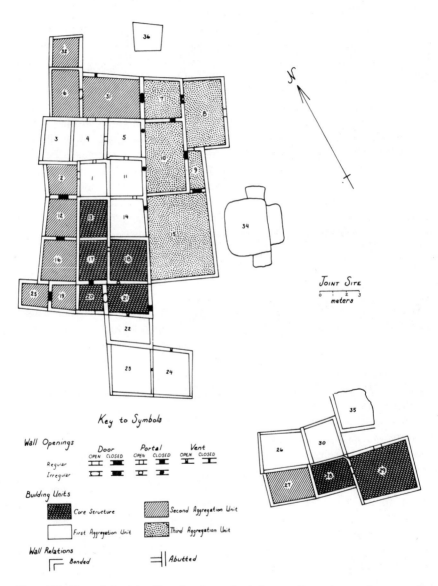

Key to Symbols

Wall Openings

	Door		Portal		Vent	
	OPEN	CLOSED	OPEN	CLOSED	OPEN	CLOSED
Regular						
Irregular						

Building Units

Core Structure   Second Aggregation Unit

First Aggregation Unit   Third Aggregation Unit

Wall Relations
    Bonded   Abutted

Figure 7.4 Map of the Joint Site, showing wall relations, wall openings, and construction sequence. (From Wilcox 1975.)

excavated because they contained no subsurface remains. The excavation of the Phase 1 sample squares plus 23 test trenches resulted in the discovery of most major secondary refuse deposits and a number of other features, including Rooms 34 and 36. The stage was set for the second phase of test squares, of which the purpose was the retrieval of information from secondary refuse locations that were not sampled or were sampled poorly during Phase 1. Phase 2 sample squares were placed in areas, undisturbed by backhoe trenches, within known secondary refuse deposits (Figure 7.2). No rigorous sampling technique was applied; any attempt to do so would have been ludicrous, given that only one, or at most two, test squares could be placed in any deposit. Phase 2 sample squares were excavated in the same arbitrary 15-cm levels as were Phase 1 squares, except when burials were encountered. The discovery of burials was a secondary aim of Phase 2 sample squares.

CONCLUDING REMARKS

We attempted to recover all macroscopic artifacts and ecofacts. This was facilitated by the use of a $\frac{1}{4}$-inch mesh screen applied to all provenience units in Phase 1 and Phase 2 sample squares and most provenience units within rooms, except for fill containing few artifacts. (This fill, sometimes removed with the backhoe, usually was examined by hand.) Pollen samples were collected from features, burials, room floors, and sample square levels, and an extensive series was obtained from the reservoir. Flotation samples were taken from the trash-fill levels of Rooms 1 and 17 and a few other scattered locations. A cornering project was undertaken by Tracz (1971), and, through her efforts, complete information of all bond–abutment relations for the large and small roomblocks was obtained. She also provided a preliminary construction sequence based only on bond–abut relations. Working with these data and others, Wilcox (1975) has ascertained the probable sequence in which Joint Site rooms were built (Figure 7.4). Hanson and Schiffer (1975) have assigned tentative functions to rooms, based largely on impressions from the field; later analyses, reported in Chapter 11, largely corroborate the subjective assessments.

8

General Considerations
of Artifact Classification

No cookbook exists from which an investigator can concoct classificatory devices to measure the variables of the past that interest him. However, I believe that it is both possible and useful to delineate several basic operations that ought to be approximated, to a greater or lesser extent, in all studies that generate and employ typologies. I have organized these operations into an ideal program of analysis, and present them here in the optimal order for efficient achievement of results. This order, because it more closely approximates the presentation of finished results than the actual conduct of research, is not the most important feature of the program.

DIMENSIONS OF MEASUREMENT AND
ATTRIBUTE SELECTION

All studies should begin with a statement of what dimensions (or set of related variables) from among the large potential number (Binford 1965) are to be measured by the system. These dimensions are determined by an investigator's wider problem focus and by the hypotheses to be tested. For example, an archeologist interested in technology might design a typology to measure the stages at which artifacts were produced in the manufacture process. Other questions may lead to measures of style—such as the different social units of manufacture. These are only some of the many possible dimensions that can be measured from a set of objects. In most studies, the investigator should have a set of types flexible enough to measure several dimensions. Such *multidimensional classifications* allow the same set of artifacts to be partitioned in several different ways, depending on the analytic task at hand (see also Faulkner and McCollough 1973). In the remainder of this chapter, only one dimension is discussed.

CORRELATES AND ATTRIBUTES

A clear statement of the dimension to be measured gives the archeologist a starting point from which to arrive at specific attributes and attribute states of his material. Bridging the gap between the properties of one's material and variables of interest within the dimension is a set of correlates. For example, assume that one is interested in measuring the different uses of the tools in a collection of chipped stone. In order to select the use-relevant attributes from among an infinite number of possibilities (Hill and Evans 1972), the archeologist applies several behavioral—material correlates. These correlates state the attributes an element must possess in order to perform a given task or the attributes an element acquires as the result of task performance (cf. Schiffer 1974). If one has prior hypotheses about specific tasks, it eventually should be possible, given further correlate development, to specify relevant attributes and attribute states. The usual case is that the investigator can only suggest in a very general way the attributes or general attribute classes that might be relevant—for example, edge angles.

At present, correlates for all variables of potential interest are poorly developed, with the exception of some manufacture activities. It is likely that an archeologist desiring to explain the variability in his artifacts for the purpose of measuring past variables will have to undertake experimental studies to derive and test correlates. This is really not as discouraging as it seems at first glance. Like all experimental laws, correlates, once established, can be used again and again in different studies without repetition of the experiments by which they were demonstrated initially. As these experimental studies are carried out on a wider scale, all archeologists will benefit through the development of a large set of correlates.

ORDERING OF ATTRIBUTES

Once the investigator has identified the attributes that are relevant to measuring the variables of interest, he must arrange the various attribute states into types. In the majority of cases, this still is done on an intuitive level. The archeologist orders his materials into sets of similar objects. Members of these object sets are more similar to other members of the same set than to members of other sets—on the basis of the attributes that are considered. This is the basic definition of set inclusion (Whallon 1972) and holds for both monothetic and polythetic types (Dunnell 1971; Thomas 1970; Clarke 1968). This arrangement process creates sets that appear to the investigator and many independent observers as "natural" subdivisions of the materials. It must be recognized, however, that an infinite number of divisions could be made that meet the definition of set inclusion. The intuitive recognition that an ordering is somehow "right" or "natural" results from the common possession by a number of investigators of a set of correlates that specify certain attributes and attribute combinations that inform on a past variable of shared interest, such as time. Individuals who have internalized these correlate sets recognize certain attribute clusters—types—as being the most meaningful and the most naturally appearing units.

Anyone who tries to break out of this closed system of type construction (based on the use of implicit correlates and often implicit attributes) will find it necessary to use various techniques of formal and multivariate analysis. For example, in one very promising study, Whallon (1972) demonstrates the utility of using the key or tree diagram as a model for ordering attribute discriminations to generate types.

The statistical approach, based mainly on demonstrable associations among attributes, now is enjoying a modest boom in activity. Multivariate analyses of many sorts, such as factor and cluster, offer the promise of clustering relevant attributes into types. It is necessary to point out, however, that some of these techniques, such as numerical taxonomy, derive from systematic biology (Sokal and Sneath 1963), where they are utilized in assessing "overall similarity." Sokal and Sneath discourage the selection of attributes on any relevance requirement basis. They counsel investigators to use many attributes—as many as 60—and allow the analytic technique to determine the relationships.

If the strict biostatistical approach is applied uncritically in archeology, it will hamper serious efforts at employing artifact variability to inform on variables of the past (see also Binford 1972b). I submit that the only variables that can be measured, if any, with uncritical "shotgun" attribute-selection procedures are relative time or gross size. And, although relative time is a useful measure, it is merely a summary dimension of all other kinds of variation.

The ability to measure relative time from artifacts is a by-product of the way human behavior changes and is reflected in material culture. Changes in behavioral subsystems, such as artifact use, manufacture techniques, and patterns of symbol recognition (style change), occur gradually or at least with continuity, probably independently and at different rates. The shotgun approach to attribute selection may cut across all three dimensions and more, with the useful result that overall similarity is measured. Gross similarity may be a function of evolutionary distance or some other composite measure of behavioral change as reflected in varying attribute combinations and changing type combinations. In short, uncritical attribute-selection procedures are useful for a limited range of problems, but their overzealous use in all areas of typology construction may lead to spurious results and the loss of potentially informative attribute and artifact combinations. Most American archeologists, it should be made clear, do not use this approach.

Perhaps the limited success to date of multivariate techniques results from its close coupling to shotgun attribute-selection procedures. As more archeologists come to appreciate that the attributes they incorporate into their statistical analysis determine to a large extent the dimension that can be measured by the resultant typology (Thomas 1970), more attention will be paid to the important process of selecting relevant attributes. The development of more useful statistical approaches depends on the concomitant development of better procedures for attribute selection.

EVALUATION OF TYPOLOGY

After one has arrived at intuitively or statistically adequate attribute clusters and has formed a set of types, there is a need to examine the resultant classes with respect to the body of correlates used to generate the constituent attributes and determine their correspondence. At present, this is still an intuitive procedure. The archeologist examines the types and asks: Do they measure the variable of interest? Are they the best measure of this variable that can be achieved on this collection of materials? There are no formulas by which to answer these and related questions. Ultimately, they are answered by how well the typology works in the study of which it is a part.

Other aspects of a typological system can be measured by performing tests of replicability (Thomas 1970). Another test that can be applied to determine the workability of a typology is to employ it directly on the actual collections. At this stage, the investigator should be looking for a close fit between the types and the materials.

A typology is *adequate* to the extent that it allows the unambiguous assignment of all specimens to the various types (Binford 1972b). Adequacy criteria are not met when there are increasing numbers of anomalous specimens or when there is increasing difficulty in choosing between types for any specimen. Adequacy, as defined here, usually is improved by one or more recycling steps. These changes are produced by adding or deleting attributes from the analysis, changing the technique of analysis, or making some other adjustment that results in a modification of the typology. These adjustments take place until the analyst is satisfied that the typology is adequate.

In some cases, it is possible to generate hypotheses about classificatory consistency that can be tested with distributional and correlational data. These independent tests may indicate the degree to which the typology is *accurate;* that is, they may indicate the extent to which it successfully measures the dimension of interest. Adequacy, it should be clear, does not ensure accuracy.

ATTRIBUTE AND TYPE DEFINITIONS

In the next stage of analysis, the investigator presents complete and rigorous definitions of the attributes and attribute-based definitions of the types. For each monothetic or polythetic type, the relevant attributes and their permissible states are listed. The attribute-based definitions of types can be used by independent investigators desiring to reclassify the artifacts. If the typology is adequate, the new arrangement of artifacts should approximate closely the first ordering.

To achieve full replicability, it is not sufficient merely to list the attributes and their states for each type; the analyst also must specify how each attribute is to be measured and how alternative states of each attribute can be identified (Thomas 1970). Usually, a discipline possesses standard methods of measuring its most frequently used variables; and so it is with some attributes of materials in archeology. But one must beware of ambiguities lurking in attribute definitions, even of attributes as commonly measured as "flake length." There are several ways to make this measurement (Jelinek 1972).

DECISION MODELS

Although complete attribute-based type definitions are sufficient to allow an independent investigator to apply a typology, there may be a way more efficient to acquire the necessary information than that of memorizing these definitions. Any set of types defined by attribute states can be represented as a decision-making model and can be used for assigning specimens to types. By this method, there is provided a sequence or key in which to examine the attributes of an artifact (Whallon 1972; Thomas 1970). If one state of an attribute is present, a type definition is met and the artifact is assigned to its proper place in the typology. If another state occurs, the analyst examines the next attribute in the sequence, and so on, until the attribute states of an artifact lead it along the decision paths to its proper type. Paradigm models also can be used in this manner (see Haury 1950 for an early example). The construction of decision-making models is an intuitive, trial-and-error process, much the same as writing solutions to componential analyses in cultural anthropology (Burling 1964). There is a large but finite number of decision models that can be generated for any set of type definitions.

At present, there is no set of rules that can be employed by an investigator for providing the most parsimonious model of the decision-making process. It should be possible eventually to elevate the process of model construction above the intuitive level by devising rules by which the distribution of attribute states among the attributes can be transformed into an ordering of the attribute discriminations. One possible objection to this procedure is that the most logically elegant solution may not be the most economical in terms of the time spent in classifying a set of artifacts. It might be supposed that the most efficient decision model, in archeological terms, would ensure that the fewest attribute discriminations are necessary to segregate the most frequently occurring types, thus reducing total sorting time. It is hoped that future experiments with decision model construction will shed light on the ways both to teach other investigators a typology and to allow the typology, once learned, to be applied efficiently. McCutcheon and Tamplin (1973) report several tests of a key-generating computer program the aim of which is to take these factors into account.

DISCUSSION OF ERRORS

The conclusion of any exercise in typology construction should include a discussion of several types of error that creep into the construction and use of any classificatory system. The first kind of error, resulting from differential recovery percentages, at first glance would seem misplaced in discussions of typology. This is not the case, however. Recovery percentages can be discussed only with respect to categories of artifacts employed in analyses, since some typologies might define unrecovered items out of existence. The basic question to be asked for each type is: What percentage of the artifacts of this type, originally present in the units excavated, are available for analysis?

The second kind of error occurs in all analyses and results from the assignment of artifacts to the wrong types. There are several basic causes of misassignment errors. The first is carelessness or accident. Errors from these sources are not likely to produce systematic skewing of the results, and their total contribution to any analysis is normally small, unless the personnel doing the typing are poorly trained.

A more serious cause of misassignments is related to the adequacy of the typology and results from ambiguities in the categories themselves. Although an attempt is made to provide the most rigorous attribute-based definitions possible for all types, this rigor of category exclusion is not always so apparent at the artifact level. Closely allied to this source of error are the errors introduced into the analysis by imprecise instruments for measuring attributes states. Errors produced by category ambiguity and imprecise measuring instruments are likely to be systematic. After an analysis has been completed, there should be some way to determine the possible effects these error sources have on the results. It would seem that the analyst is responsible for at least estimating their magnitude; after all, he is the only person, in the absence of replicability experiments, who can provide this information—however subjective it may be.

9

Chipped Stone from the Joint Site

PROBLEMS AND DIMENSIONS OF INTEREST

The purpose of classifying the chipped stone at the Joint Site was to facilitate a demonstration of explicit transformation procedures. Specifically, this demonstration will take place in the context of an attempt to reconstruct the activities and their locations and rates of performance within the systemic context of the chipped-stone artifacts from the Joint Site. Such a study raises the following questions:

1. What were the most frequent activities in which chipped-stone tools were used?
2. Where were various functionally distinguished chipped-stone tools used?
3. Why were tools made from different raw materials?
4. What were the manufacture rates of various tool types?

In order to answer these and related questions, a classificatory system was devised for measuring the dimensions of potential use and manufacture stage. A third dimension, raw material, also was measured since it relates to the other two. For example, two finished tools may be morphologically identical, but if they differ in the properties of the materials of which they were made, they could be used in different activities. Also, lithic materials, which differ in flaking qualities, might be manufactured by different activities in different locations.

And, finally, different materials may have been obtained from sources varying in their ease of accessibility. Scarce materials might be made into a restricted number of forms, used in fewer kinds of activities, or used in different locations. One might expect more recycling of the scarcer materials. (Several of these hypotheses are tested in Chapter 12.) Before discussing the three dimensions in greater detail, I present a brief account of the sorting and counting procedures.

PROCEDURE

The analysis of chipped-stone implements and debitage from the Joint Site began with a preliminary examination of approximately 50% of the A provenience units of the surface collection. The surface collection was thought to provide a usable, but not necessarily representative, sample of the range of formal variability in chipped-stone materials. I hoped that the surface sample would include most of the artifact types or at least those occurring in abundance.

The artifact bags were emptied onto a working area, and specimens of similar form were grouped together. The artifacts were grouped and regrouped until I was satisfied that types had been created which were based on attributes of manufacture stage, use potential, and raw-material type. The attributes I took into consideration included artifact size, edge angle, shape, relative placement of the working edge, use modification, retouch, and raw material. There was a constant interaction between the provisional types defined by the artifact sets and the equally tentative ideal types based on consideration of attributes relevant to the three dimensions.

After completing the sort and re-sort operation, I codified the types with preliminary attribute-based definitions. These definitions served for reference while the remainder of the collection was being classified. Because of the scarcity of manufacture-modified tools in the surface collection, I had to add types as I went along. As new types of unifacially chipped tools were encountered, they were added to the typology, as were their attribute-based definitions. All bifacially flaked tools were culled from the collection during sorting and were examined together at the end of the analysis. It was only at this terminal stage that bifacial tool types and attribute definitions were established.

All types were assigned a type number, and it is to these arbitrary numbers that reference is made throughout the remainder of this study. Sorting and counting were facilitated by the use of large cardboard charts on which a grid of 80 squares was drawn. Each grid square and number corresponded to a type or potential type. The type numbers in each square were duplicated on the

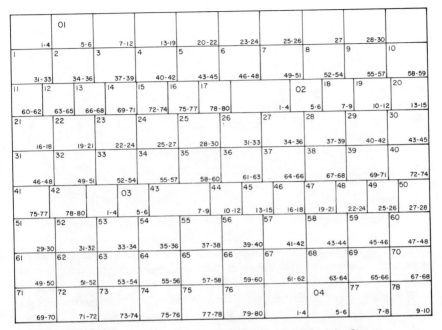

Figure 9.1 Recording form for chert artifacts from the Joint Site.

recording form, which was designed so that computer cards could be punched directly from it without the use of any intermediates. An example of the recording form for chert is presented as Figure 9.1.

Two sets of sorting charts were made, each consisting of one chart for each of the three kinds of raw material. While I sorted specimens on one set of cards, my wife Annette recorded the artifacts previously sorted on the other card set. To equalize sorting and counting times, Annette often made a preliminary division of the specimens by raw material and flake size and then discarded all unmodified stone that had been inadvertently collected. This procedure of sorting and recording worked extremely well—whether in operation by one or two persons. A recording form that corresponds in format and code numbers to the actual layout of the specimens (and is also geared to later keypunching) turned out to be efficient in terms of time spent, and also conducive to accuracy in counting and recording.

All artifacts were classified under uniform conditions of observation. Lighting was entirely artificial, consisting of fluorescent tubing of average intensity. No hand lens was ever used, despite the slight (corrected) farsightedness of the observer. In cases of doubtful use modification, the pink of the index finger served to place the contested edge into sharp contrast. The total time spent in sorting and recording amounted to 285 ± 25 person-hrs. I have no record of the time spent in designing the analysis and the typology.

Although many classes of artifacts were distinguished from similar classes on the basis of size or edge angle, no edge-angle measurements were made on any of the specimens by the use of a device other than the eye and the experience of the observer. Size occasionally was measured in borderline cases by means of a template within close reach of the sorting location.

RAW MATERIAL

Archeological classifications of stone material are usually straightforward applications of the system generally used in geology. These categories are based on attributes related to how a rock was formed, its most dominant mineral constituents, and occasionally the presence of trace compounds. Categories that grade rocks according to composition and genesis may or may not be useful for archeological purposes. In this study, the variables of fracturing and use properties are of primary interest, and accessibility of secondary importance.

The small body of literature reporting analyses of Hay Hollow Valley chipped stone was examined to learn if any categories of raw material usable in this study had been devised already. In describing materials from the Carter Ranch Site, Rinaldo (1964) identified the presence of several varieties of raw material, including chert, chalcedony, felsite, diabase, quartzite, basalt, and petrified wood. Rick and Gritzmacher (1970) tested several hypotheses dealing with spatial–temporal patterning in raw-material availability, desirability, and use. In doing so, five varieties of material were recognized and applied to surface collections from a spatially and temporally varied sample of sites. Their types were chert, agate, petrified wood, basalt, and quartzite. More recently, Garson (1972) distinguished three types of raw material—chalcedony, chert, and quartzite—in a study of the preferential selection of stone by color at N.S. 28.

Based on my field observations on the sources of lithic material in the Hay Hollow Valley during the summers of 1968–1971, I can state that the stone types identified by Rinaldo (1964) and by Rick and Gritzmacher (1970) cover the variability in materials as far as gross composition and locations of availability are concerned, with some exceptions that are discussed later. On the other hand, Garson's (1972) fewer categories commend his system to anyone who must prevent the unnecessary proliferation of categories, each of which has the effect of increasing by a sizable factor the magnitude of information-recording and punching time.

Unfortunately, Garson's types, useful for his own project, lack sufficient supplementary information about how other stone materials were included among them. It was possible, however, to examine each type of geologically identified stone in the valley and, based on considerations of fracturing and use qualities and locations of availability, to provide explicit criteria for including them within the threefold system of chert, quartzite, and chalcedony. The latter terms were kept as gross designations for raw-material categories.

Petrified wood comes in two varieties in the Hay Hollow Valley, differing in flaking qualities and locations of availability. Petrified wood originating north of County Road and east of the Hay Hollow Wash produces good conchoidal fractures. It is translucent and brightly colored by various oxide impurities. This material closely resembles the high-quality wood from the Petrified Forest, which lies about 20 miles to the north. Another form of petrified wood occurs in low density throughout the remainder of the valley. This material is opaque and comes in pink, white, red, gray, brown, or black. Wood of this type is highly variable in fracturing qualities—some of the red-brown wood has a good conchoidal fracture, but much of the rest produces splintering along well-defined cleavage planes.

According to Rick and Gritzmacher (1970:12), agate occurs in restricted locations on the west side of Point of the Mountain Mesa. I also have observed veins of this material cropping out along most of the west side of the mesa and in scattered locations along the east side. This material occurs in tabular form, is highly translucent, and blue, gray, brown, or black. The material is often lightly banded with a waxy appearance on fresh, sharply defined, conchoidal fractures.

The chert found in the valley occurs in browns, yellows, and reds, and varies greatly in chipping properties from extremely good to weakly conchoidal fracture. The surface texture varies from almost waxy in some specimens, to grainy and coarse in others. Chert (along with quartzite) is the most abundant stone material in the valley and also has the widest distribution, occurring primarily on the lower and middle benches and along the sides of the mesa. The Joint Site, located on a middle bench, rests squarely on soil containing many chert cobbles.

Quartzite is also an abundant material, occurring in approximately the same distribution as chert. It is found in various shades of white, gray, brown, and black, with occasional tints of red, green, and blue. Quartzite, like chert, varies greatly in its fracturing qualities from specimen to specimen; some fine-grained, highly metamorphosed varieties exhibit good fractures and sharp cutting edges, but large-grained incompletely metamorphosed examples often break irregularly. Quartzite is also abundant beneath and adjacent to the Joint Site.

Basalt occurs in a wide variety of forms in the valley and is abundant, especially in the vicinity of the Hay Hollow Wash and on the sides and top of the mesa. Fine-grained varieties fracture well and have been made into points on many sites in the valley. This material does not occur near the Joint Site, and none was procured or used there for chipped-stone artifacts, although grinding stones were occasionally made of vesicular basalt.

Obsidian does not occur in or near the Hay Hollow Valley, and only two pieces were found in the entire Joint Site collection. A volcanic rock containing prominent phenocrysts—probably felsite—was used infrequently at the Joint Site. This material fractures surprisingly well but is represented by fewer than 10 items. It occurs in the same locations as does basalt.

Because chalcedony (or agate) and the translucent petrified wood have similar chipping and use properties and occur at some distance from the site, they have been lumped together within the chalcedony category. Also included in this class are the two examples of obsidian.

In the chert category are included the few specimens of felsite. The opaque petrified wood that was chipped resembles grainy and coarse chert more than any other material. Because of similar chipping properties and nearby locations of availability, this material also is included in the chert category. The final category, quartzite, contains no other materials.

At best, the system employed for classifying Joint Site raw materials is a crude composite measure of the required variables. Arrangement by decreasing availability to the inhabitants of the site produces the following ordinal scale: quartzite, chert, chalcedony. Based on my observations, this ordering also corresponds to the decreasing roughness of fracture (see also Semenov 1964:34).

TECHNOLOGY AND STAGE OF MANUFACTURE

The ready availability of the raw materials used to make the majority of chipped-stone tools at the Joint Site had important effects on the technology of tool production. One might have expected an abundance of raw materials to lead to the use of a specialized set of techniques on materials meeting highly restrictive specifications of shape, size, and quality. This was not the case at the Joint Site. (Perhaps it is the case only when large quantities of artifacts are being made for export or when only some members of a community are engaged in the manufacturing activity.) The Joint Site technology of chipped-stone manufacture can be termed only "opportunistic." It was characterized by a marked indifference to quality control and standardization. Techniques were fitted to the chosen raw material, and vice versa.

Although the widespread split-cobble technique, reported in the Hay Hollow Valley at Broken K Pueblo (Longacre 1967:99), was used at the Joint Site, it was altered or abandoned when not suited to the piece of stone at hand. The split-cobble technique works most effectively on cobble-sized stones (10–15 cm in diameter and larger); at the Joint Site, chert and quartzite often occur in nodules smaller than cobble size, usually falling between 5 cm and 10 cm in the greatest dimension. One way the inhabitants of the site coped with flattened, pebble-sized nodules was to split them in half and, as if removing slices from a tangerine, strike off successive radial flakes, using the natural cortex as a striking platform until no more flakes could be removed (see Figure 9.2). Cores from this technique are not very distinctive, and many certainly were mislabeled as "shatter" in my tabulations. The most telling evidence for the widespread use of the *tangerine core technique* is the large number of small- and medium-size flakes that still retain cortex on three edges but lack it on the dorsal surface. The location of the bulb of percussion on these flakes clearly indicates that the striking platform was formed by one of the cortical edges. The tangerine core technique is one member of the larger family that Jelinek (personal communication, 1973) has termed "citrus core technology." Goodyear (1974:74), for example, has identified an orange core technique at the Brand Site.

Evidence for the lack of sophisticated core preparation techniques is also provided by the large number of utilized flakes displaying cortex on the dorsal surface and on one or more edges. These are termed "secondary decortication" flakes by White (1963:5), but, judging by their numbers, these flakes were the end product of flake production at the Joint Site, not a preliminary stage in the preparation of cores.

Despite the variability in chipping and use qualities of the chert and quartzite available at the Joint Site, very little raw material was rejected on the basis of unsuitability. The scant proof of material rejection comes from the relatively few nodules, usually of chert, from which only one to three flakes were removed. Cursory examination of these cores during counting led me to the conclusion that the material was simply too granular or irregular in fracture to

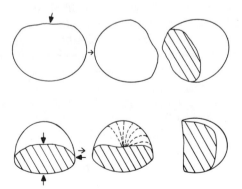

Figure 9.2 The tangerine core technique of flake production. Key: ▫ cortical surface; ▨ fracture surface; → direction of applied force; → results in; – – –future flakes.

produce flakes for the intended task. These "false start" cores were discarded without further modification. Compared to the size of the entire chipped-stone collection, these rejections were infrequent. Much use was made of lower grades of raw material.

There is no doubt that some makers of chipped-stone tools at the Joint Site had great control over their medium—but the control that was exercised was seldom greater than necessary to produce an adequate tool for the job at hand. Bifacially flaked tools, especially the small, triangular projectile point forms so characteristic of Pueblo III and IV occupations, often display remarkably controlled and regular patterns of secondary chipping and pressure retouch. On the other hand, "scrapers" made on flakes or shatter were almost never modified or retouched, and, if so, only the edge angle was steepened by applying highly variable techniques of pressure flaking.

Morphological blades—that is, flakes with a width-to-length ratio of about .3 to .5—did occur. There is no evidence to suggest that these flakes were produced by specialized core preparation techniques or pressure flaking. Furthermore, the dorsal surfaces of these flakes lack parallel flake scars. Their occurrence in low numbers, with no special modifications evident, suggest that they are simply one extreme in the normal range of variation in the dimensions of percussion-produced flakes. Lastly, no blade cores were recovered at the Joint Site. Heat treatment of some specimens was observed, but records of its incidence were not kept.

The Joint Site chipped-stone technology presented some problems in the construction of both useful and realistic categories relating to manufacture stage. In generating these categories, the variability in technique noted earlier—related to raw-material size variability—was largely glossed over. In order to cope adequately with the varieties of chipping technique, a large-scale technological analysis, probably involving experimentation with similar materials, is needed. From such a study, the varieties of technique could be inferred from attributes of the products and by-products. The magnitude of such an effort, an effect of which would have been an unnecessary proliferation of categories, forced the development of a more workable, compromise classificatory system.

In Figure 9.3, I have modeled what one might disparagingly call an "average" or "modal" path of chipped-stone production. This system evolved from an examination of existing typologies (Binford and Quimby 1963; White 1963; Collins 1971) and from familiarity with the Joint Site collection. It differs from its predecessors largely in its deliberate simplification, and in the way that behavior and material relations can be displayed economically. This model begins with the cobble-on-cobble technique to produce decortication flakes (White 1963:5), primary flakes, and shatter. These products may be used without further modification, subjected to percussion trimming that resulted in minishatter and trim flakes, or modified by pressure retouch that produced tools

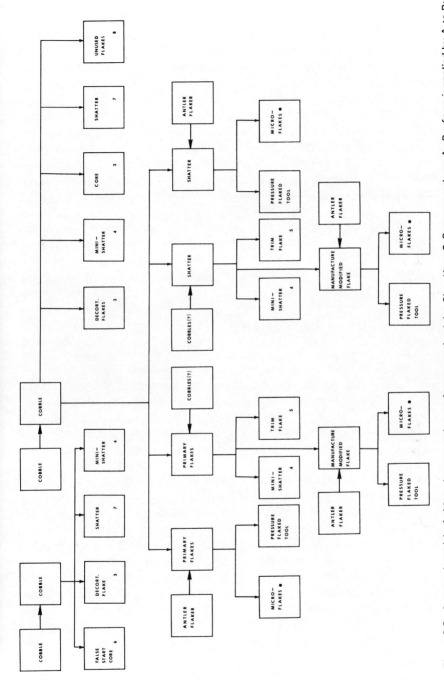

Figure 9.3 A general model of chipped-stone tool manufacture at the Joint Site. Key: 2–8, type numbers; A→B a force is applied by A to B; A→B the application of a force to A results in the production of B; ● not recovered in excavation at the Joint Site.

and microflakes. As noted in Figure 9.3, microflakes and other chipped-stone materials not captured by ¼-inch mesh screen were unavailable for analysis (Hanson and Schiffer 1975). The alternative behavior pattern, resulting in false start cores, also is diagrammed (Figure 9.3). In the same illustration, type numbers of unutilized by-products are noted.

The correlates from which specific attributes were selected to form, or allow the recognition of, the various technological classes are not presented here. The elaboration of what some readers would regard as obvious anyway has been avoided. Technological correlates generally are well-established; and the attributes they incorporate, such as bulb of percussion, hinge-fracture terminus, and striking platform, have a high degree of intersubjective recognition (cf. Crabtree 1972).

Although the simplified model and resultant typology obscure information that could reveal the specifics of past manufacturing behavior at the Joint Site, I believe it is suitable for indicating the approximate stage during which any given piece of stone emerged in the manufacturing process.

USE-POTENTIAL CATEGORIES

In marked contrast to the highly compressed and generalized categories of manufacture stage employed in this study is the large number of categories based on potential use. This deliberate proliferation of barely justifiable types is a consequence of the poorly developed state of use-relevant correlates and attributes. This condition has led me to overdiscriminate types in the hope that important varieties of use variability might be recognized in later stages of the study by combining categories. The technique of initial overdiscrimination in the face of overwhelming ignorance is useful only to a certain point, after which the returns fail to justify the extra effort spent on sorting, counting, and recording.

Unlike the manufacture stage categories presented before, no use could be made of extant chipped-stone typologies in the Southwest. These systems (e.g., Kidder 1931; Longacre 1967; Rinaldo 1964; Woodbury 1954) were devised to measure the variables of time, cultural affiliation, or use of extensively modified pieces. As such, they are based on a variety of attributes that are often inappropriate for identifying the potential use of all utilized artifacts. The degree of specialization of these typologies is illustrated by the following fairly typical examples. Longacre (1967) lists a total of 50 categories, 31 of which are applied to only 60 projectile points. All utilized flakes are lumped into a single class. Jelinek (1967:95–97) provides a similar example in which 211 projectile points fall within 94 of a possible 420 categories in the typology. Kidder (1931), Woodbury (1954), and many other investigators completely disregard unmodified but utilized pieces. But more than 90% of the chipped-stone artifacts made, used, and discarded at the Joint Site were unmodified! Although the other southwestern chipped-stone typologies may measure adequately the variables for which they were intended, the typology employed here must cover more evenly the morphological variations in all forms used as tools.

Four basic attribute sets were used to generate the use-potential types. These are:

1. *Size.* The size of a tool, all other attributes constant, is related to the variety of ways a tool can be grasped and used (cf. White and Thomas 1972). Size also affects the mechanical properties of inertia and momentum. One might suggest that, within limits, the larger the tool (all other variables constant), the greater the number of potential uses. Three arbitrarily defined size classes were used.

2. *Angle of the working edge.* Edge angle is related to penetrability and the kind of material on which a tool can be used. In general, specific edge angles on tools may facilitate the performance of certain tasks although precluding or making difficult the performance of others (Wilmsen 1968, 1970; Semenov 1964). Edge-angle classes, found useful by Wilmsen (1968), of less than 45°, of 45°–65°, and of greater than 65° are employed here. I now believe that these classes, derived from tools often heavily retouched, may be slightly weighted toward steeper edge angles.

3. *Specific modifications.* Tools that were modified differently in manufacture may have been intended to serve, or at least were suited to, different uses. In the Joint Site collection, denticulations of various size and quantity, notches, and several kinds of pressure retouch occurred. In addition to the regular retouch patterns forming both unifacially and bifacially modified tools, several infrequent and unusual kinds of modification were observed and built into the typology. I now believe that these forms received far more attention than they merit.

4. *Degree of modification and finishing.* Tools on which great effort was expended in manufacture were probably intended to have a relatively long uselife (Binford 1973) or a very specific use. Attributes relating to the extent of modification, such as extensive thinning or edge modification, were considered in building the types.

The presence of macroscopic use modification was a determining attribute for certain tool classes and served to differentiate use-modified from unmodified pieces. I did not attempt to identify different kinds of use modification—even at a macroscopic level—although it might have been possible to do so. Use modification was said to be present on an artifact if at least two or three small flakes or striations on the working edge were visible to the naked eye.

Rather than count utilized pieces, I chose to count utilized edges. This was my

Table 9.1 Type Numbers of Use-Modified Summary
Classes

Constituent utilized edge types	Summary utilized piece types
11, 12, 13	14
21, 22, 23	24
31, 32, 33	34
11, 21, 31	41
12, 22, 32	42
13, 23, 33	43
15, 16, 17	18
25, 26, 27	28
35, 36, 37	38
15, 25, 35	45
16, 26, 36	46
17, 27, 37	47

solution to the seemingly intractable problem of multiple uses of the same piece
(see also House 1975; Schiffer 1975d). Often two, sometimes even three or four,
edges of a flake had been used, and all combinations of edge angles were
observed on flakes and shatter that had been utilized. In order to get some idea
of the extent of multiple use and the actual number of used pieces, as opposed
to worked edges, a dual counting system was employed. For all flakes and
shatter, there were nine classes formed by the intersection of the three size
classes and the three edge-angle classes. Lima bean counters were placed on the
appropriate angle categories to indicate other utilized edges of a piece. The
placement of the piece itself among its possible angle classes was somewhat
arbitrary—there is probably no way to determine a "dominant" or most important edge of a use-modified, multi-edged tool. Row and column sums of worked
pieces were made of the 3-by-3 matrix to indicate the total number of artifacts
in any size or edge-angle class. Each summary class received its own type number
(Table 9.1).

Where use modification occurred on one or more unmodified edges of a
unifacially or bifacially modified tool, it was ignored and the tool was assigned
to the appropriate manufacture-modified category. This procedure is justifiable
because of the relatively low number of manufacture-modified tools compared
to the rather large quantity of use-modified tools.

A set of potential uses based on the attribute combinations embodied in each
type can be defined by the application of several very general correlates. In this
section, each type is given an explicit definition in terms of attributes, and
potential uses are suggested.

TYPE AND ATTRIBUTE DEFINITIONS, POTENTIAL USES, AND DECISION MODELS

The first division of Joint artifacts is into the four categories of unifacial retouch, bifacial retouch, use modified, and unmodified. Figure 9.4 indicates the relationship of these four categories and the sequence of attribute-based

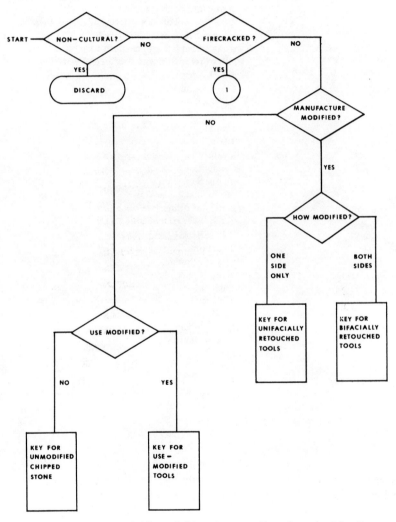

Figure 9.4   Primary divisions of chipped-stone artifacts from the Joint Site.

Table 9.2 Attributes of Unifacially Retouched Tools[a]

Attribute	Attribute state	Definitions
A		extent of retouch on margin of piece
	a_1	less than 180°
	a_2	greater than 180°
B		spacing of retouch flakes
	b_1	contiguous or overlapping
	b_2	2.0–6.9 mm between margins of adjacent flakes
	b_3	some contiguous, some spaced
	b_4	greater than 6.9 mm between each flake
C		width of retouch flakes measured at widest point
	c_1	1.0–3.9 mm
	c_2	4.0–6.9 mm
	c_3	7.0–11.9 mm
	c_4	greater than 11.9
D		length of retouch flakes
	d_1	1.0–6.9 mm
	d_2	greater than 6.9 mm
E		placement of retouch
	e_1	on distal edge only
	e_2	not on distal edge only
F		quantity of primary retouch flakes
	f_1	1
	f_2	2
	f_3	3 or more
G		stages of retouch
	g_1	composite retouch
	g_2	single retouch
H		area of tool when lying flat
	h_1	3.5–8.7 cm²
	h_2	8.8–17.4 cm²
	h_3	greater than 17.4 cm²
I		on core
	i_1	yes
	i_2	no

[a]Uppercase letters refer to attributes; lowercase letters with subscripts designate specific attribute states.

decisions that were made to determine the category into which a specimen falls. Keys are presented later for determining the specific type to which an artifact belongs within each of these four artifact divisions.

Tables 9.2 and 9.3 list, respectively, the attribute definitions and type definitions of all unifacially modified tools. Figure 9.5 presents an attribute-based key for assigning unifacial tools to the proper types.

Table 9.3 Attribute Definitions of Unifacially Retouched Tools

Type number	Attributes and permissible attribute states								
	A	B	C	D	E	F	G	H	I
73	a_3	b_1	c_1	d_1	e_2	f_3	g_2	h_3	i_2
74	a_3	b_1	c_1	d_1	e_2	f_3	g_2	h_1, h_2	i_2
67	a_3	b_1	c_2	d_1	e_2	f_3	g_2	h_3	i_2
68	a_3	b_3	c_2	d_1	e_2	f_3	g_2	h_2	i_2
69	a_3	b_3	c_2	d_1	e_2	f_3	g_2	h_1	i_2
75	a_3	b_3	c_3	d_3	e_2	f_3	g_2	h_3	i_2
76	a_3	b_3	c_3	d_3	e_2	f_3	g_2	h_1, h_2	i_2
77	a_1	b_5	c_4	d_2	e_2	f_1	g_2	h_2, h_3	i_2
78	a_1	b_5	c_3	d_2	e_2	f_1	g_2	h_1, h_2, h_3	i_2
40	a_1	b_5	c_3, c_4	d_2	e_2	f_1	g_2	h_2, h_3	i_1
62	a_1	b_1	c_2	d_2	e_2	f_3	g_2	h_1, h_2, h_3	i_2
64	a_2	b_3	c_3	d_2	e_2	f_3	g_2	h_3	i_2
66	a_1	b_2	c_2	d_1	e_2	f_2	g_1	h_1, h_2, h_3	i_2
63	a_2	b_2	c_1	d_1	e_2	f_3	g_2	h_1, h_2, h_3	i_2
65	a_1	b_1	c_1	d_1	e_1	f_3	g_2	h_1, h_2, h_3	i_2
61	a_1	b_4	c_2	d_2	e_2	f_2	g_2	h_2, h_3	i_2

Table 9.4 defines the attributes of bifacially modified tools, while Table 9.5 defines the bifacial tool types. Figure 9.6 is the bifacial tool key. In addition to the bifacial tool key, the single attribute of whole–fragmentary was employed to generate several other categories (Table 9.6). These types do not appear in the bifacial tool key (Figure 9.6).

Table 9.4 Attributes of Bifacially Retouched Tools

Attribute	Attribute state	Definition
A	yes/no	bifacial flaking on all edges
B	yes/no	bilateral symmetry of bifacially flaked portion
C	yes/no	bilateral symmetry of transverse cross section
D	yes/no	30 mm or less in length of longest dimension
E	yes/no	35° or less on the edge angle of the longest side
F	yes/no	triangular outline
G	yes/no	two lateral or basal notches

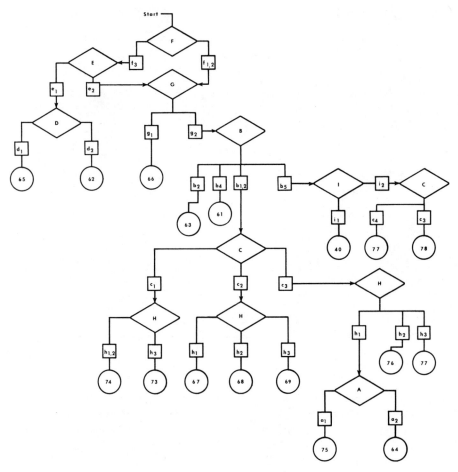

Figure 9.5 Attribute-based key for unifacially retouched tool types. Key: ◊ attribute letter; ▫ attribute state; ○ type number.

Use-modified tools are treated in the same manner. Table 9.7 contains attribute definitions and Table 9.8 displays the type definitions. Figure 9.7 is the key for use-modified types.

In Table 9.9, the potential uses of all tool types are presented. I admit with considerable embarrassment an inability to account rigorously for this list of potential uses. Many of them derive from the inferences proffered by Wilmsen (1970) and Semenov (1964) for tools having specified edge angles. Other potential uses were drawn from subjective applications of implicit correlates and from knowledge of what tasks, based on other evidence, took place at the Joint Site.

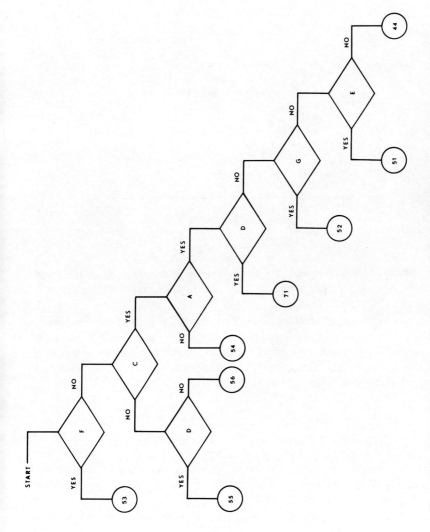

Figure 9.6 Attribute-based key for bifacially retouched tool types. Key: ○ type numbers; ◇ attributes.

Table 9.5 Attribute Definitions of Bifacially Retouched Tool Types

Type number	Attributes and permissible attribute states						
	A	B	C	D	E	F	G
51	yes	yes no	yes	no	yes	no	no
52	yes	yes	yes	no	yes no	no	yes
53	yes	yes	yes	yes	yes no	yes	yes
54	no	yes	yes	yes no	no	no	no
55	no	no	no	yes	no	no	no
56	no	no	no	no	no	no	no
71	yes	yes	yes	yes	yes no	no	yes no
44	yes	yes no	yes	no	no	no	no

The attribute definitions and type definitions of unmodified pieces are found in Tables 9.10 and 9.11, respectively, and the key for unmodified artifacts is illustrated in Figure 9.8.

As noted in an earlier section, the key presented for each of the four major artifact classes is only one of a large but finite number of possible keys. No claim is made that any of the models presented are the most parsimonious or efficient. Each key is simply an attempt to "mimic" (Thomas 1970) the decisions that were made in assigning specimens to types.

Table 9.6 Type Numbers of Whole and Fragmentary Bifacially Retouched Tool Types

Whole	Fragmentary
44	50
54	58
51	59
53	57
52	60
71	72

Table 9.7 Attributes of Use-Modified Tools[a]

Attribute	Attribute state	Definitions
A		edge angle of modified portion
	a_1	less than 45°
	a_2	46° to 65°
	a_3	greater than 66°
B		area of piece when lying flat
	b_1	less than 3.4 cm²
	b_2	3.5 to 8.7 cm²
	b_3	8.8 to 17.4 cm²
	b_4	greater than 17.5 cm²
C	yes/no	on cobble (no flakes removed)
D	yes/no	on core
E	yes/no	on shatter
F	yes/no	battering present

[a]Uppercase letters refer to attributes; lowercase letters with subscripts designate specific attribute states.

Table 9.8 Attribute Definitions of Use-Modified Tool Types

Type number	Attributes and permissible attribute states					
	A	B	C	D	E	F
49	a_3	b_2,b_3,b_4	yes	no	no	yes,no
30	a_1,a_2,a_3	b_2,b_3,b_4	no	yes	no	yes
20	a_1	b_1,b_3,b_4	no	yes	no	no
19	a_2	b_2,b_3,b_4	no	yes	no	no
29	a_3	b_2,b_3,b_4	no	yes	no	no
48	a_1	b_1	no	no	no	no
33	a_1	b_2	no	no	no	no
23	a_1	b_3	no	no	no	no
13	a_1	b_4	no	no	no	no
32	a_2	b_2	no	no	no	no
22	a_2	b_3	no	no	no	no
12	a_2	b_4	no	no	no	no
31	a_3	b_2	no	no	no	no
21	a_3	b_3	no	no	no	no
11	a_3	b_4	no	no	no	no
37	a_1	b_2	no	no	yes	no
27	a_1	b_3	no	no	yes	no
17	a_1	b_4	no	no	yes	no
36	a_2	b_2	no	no	yes	no
26	a_2	b_3	no	no	yes	no
16	a_2	b_4	no	no	yes	no
35	a_3	b_2	no	no	yes	no
25	a_3	b_3	no	no	yes	no
15	a_3	b_4	no	no	yes	no

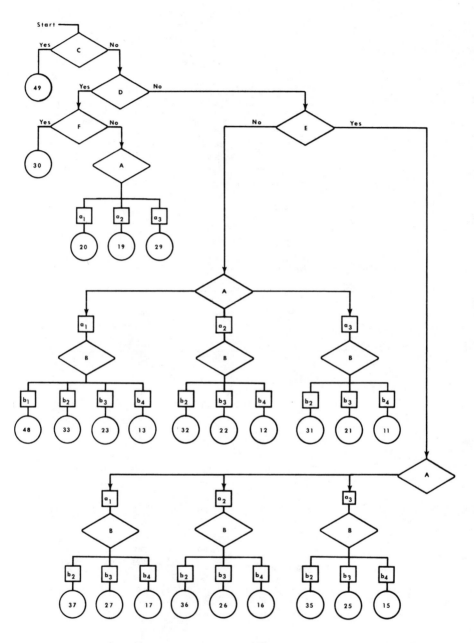

Figure 9.7 Attribute-based key for use-modified tool types. Key: ◇ attribute letter; ▢ attribute state; ○ type number.

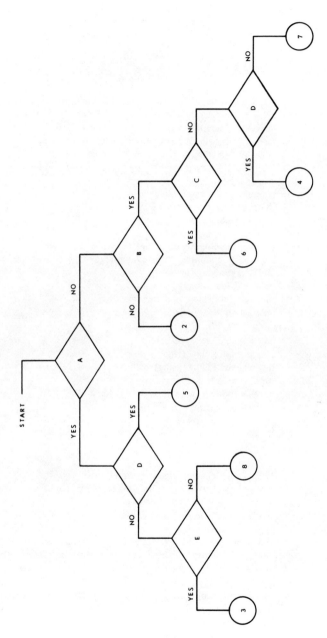

Figure 9.8 Attribute-based key for unmodified chipped-stone artifact types. Key: ◇ attributes; ○ type numbers.

119

Table 9.9 Potential Uses of Joint Site Chipped-Stone Tool Types

Type number	Potential uses
Unifacially retouched	
73	heavy-duty scraping, shredding (hides, wood, plant material)
74	medium-duty scraping, shredding (hides, wood, plant material)
67	heavy-duty scraping, shredding (hides, plant, wood)
68	medium-duty scraping, shredding (hides, plant, wood)
69	light-duty scraping, shredding (hides, plant, wood)
75	heavy-duty scraping, light chopping, digging (earth, hides, animal joints)
76	medium-duty scraping (hides)
77	shaving, scraping (wood, plant)
78	shaving, scraping (wood, plant)
40	shaving, scraping (wood, plant)
62	shaving, scraping (wood, bone)
64	heavy-duty chopping, cutting (animal joints, tendons)
66	incising, grooving (wood)
63	cutting (bone, wood)
65	medium-duty scraping (hides, wood)
61	enlarging holes (wood)
Bifacially retouched	
51	cutting (skin, meat, plant)
52	piercing and killing (large game)
53	piercing and killing (game)
54	drilling (wood, sherds)
55	incising (bone, wood)
56	heavy-duty cutting (animal joints)
71	piercing and killing (game)
44	medium-duty scraping, cutting (meat, plant, wood)
Use-modified	
49	hammer (stone)
30	hammer (chipped and ground stone, bone)
20	heavy-duty cutting, chopping (animal joints, tendons)
19	heavy-duty scraping, shaving (wood, bone)
29	heavy-duty chopping (animal joints)
48	fine, light-duty cutting (skin, meat, plant fiber, cordage)
33	fine, light-duty cutting (skin, meat, plant fiber, cordage)
23	fine, medium-duty cutting (skin, meat, plant fiber, cordage)
13	fine, heavy-duty cutting (skin, meat, plant fiber, cordage)
32	light scraping (hides, wood, plant fiber)
22	medium scraping (hides, wood, plant fiber)
12	heavy scraping (hides, wood, plant fiber)
31	light scraping, shredding (hides, wood, plant fiber)
21	medium scraping, shredding (hides, wood, plant fiber)
11	heavy-duty scraping, shredding (hides, wood, plant)
37	fine, lighty-duty cutting (skin, meat, plant fiber, cordage)

Table 9.9 *continued*

Type number	Potential uses
27	fine, medium-duty cutting (skin, meat, plant fiber, cordage)
17	fine, heavy-duty cutting (skin, meat, plant fiber, cordage)
36	light scraping (hides, wood, plant fiber)
26	medium scraping (hides, wood, plant fiber, cordage)
16	heavy scraping (hides, wood, plant fiber, cordage)
35	light scraping, shredding (hides, wood, plant fiber)
25	medium scraping, shredding (hides, wood, plant fiber)
15	heavy scraping, shredding (hides, wood, plant fiber)

Table 9.10 Attributes of Unmodified Chipped-Stone Artifacts

Attribute	Attribute state	Definition
A	yes/no	one or two positive bulbs of percussion
B	yes/no	three or fewer negative bulbs of percussion
C	yes/no	50% or more of surface is cortex
D	yes/no	area of piece when lying flat is less than 3.5 cm^2
E	yes/no	cortex covers at least 70% of one side

Table 9.11 Attribute Definitions of Unmodified Chipped-Stone Artifact Types

Type number	Attributes and permissible attribute states				
	A	B	C	E	F
2	no	no	no	no	no
3	yes	yes	no	no	yes
4	no	yes	no	yes	no
5	yes	yes	no	yes	no
6	no	yes	yes	no	yes, no
7	no	yes	no	no	no
8	yes	yes	no	no	no

RECOVERY PERCENTAGES AND MISASSIGNMENT ERRORS

Table 9.12 presents a percentage figure for all artifact types. This is the estimated minimum percentage at which artifacts of that type were recovered from all excavated units. No replicability tests were undertaken of the Joint Site chipped-stone typology. Instead, subjectively derived estimates of misassignment error are presented. What I have done is to examine each type and to ask the following questions:

1. What is the maximum percentage of wrongly classified artifacts? In other words, if every ambiguous item were placed in the wrong category, this percentage of misassigned pieces would result.

Table 9.12 Minimum Recovery Percentage of All Chipped-Stone Artifact Types

Type number	Minimum recovery (%)	Type number	Minimum recovery (%)	Type number	Minimum recovery (%)
1	80	30	85	58	60
2	90	31	95	59	95
3	80	32	95	60	95
4	75	33	95	61	95
5	75	34	–	62	95
6	50	35	95	63	95
7	90	36	95	64	95
8	90	37	95	65	99
11	95	38	–	66	99
12	95	40	90	67	99
13	95	41	–	68	99
14	–	42	–	69	95
15	95	43	–	70	–
16	95	44	99	71	99
17	95	45	–	72	95
18	–	46	–	73	99
19	90	47	–	74	99
20	90	48	85	75	99
21	99	49	60	76	99
22	99	50	95	77	99
23	99	51	99	78	95
24	–	52	99		
25	99	53	85		
26	99	54	85		
27	99	55	95		
28	–	56	95		
29	90	57	30		

2. Artifacts of which other types are likely to have been included in this category?
3. In what order of importance are these misassigned artifacts?

Table 9.13 lists the results of this exercise in introspection. For each type, 1–78, a percentage is listed corresponding to the maximum number of misassigned items in the category. The numbers of one or more artifact categories follow the percentage error. Artifacts from these classes contaminate the one of interest in decreasing frequency. Examples of some of the chipped-stone tool types are illustrated in Figures 9.9 through 9.12.

Table 9.13 Maximum Misassignment Errors for All Chipped-Stone Artifact Types[a]

Type number	Percentage error	Contaminating artifact types
1	25	80, 4
2	10	7, 56
3	20	80, 23, 33, 22, 32, 8
4	10	5, 7
5	10	33, 48, 8
6	25	80, 2
7	20	37, 36, 26, 27, 2, 15, 16, 17, 25, 35
8	20	33, 32, 23, 22, 11, 12, 13, 21, 22, 3
11	10	8, 21, 12
12	10	8, 22, 11, 13
13	10	8, 23, 12
14	–	
15	10	7, 25, 16
16	10	7, 26, 15, 17
17	10	7, 27, 16
18	–	
19	5	2, 29, 20
20	5	2, 19
21	10	8, 31, 11, 22
22	10	8, 32, 12, 21, 23, 3
23	10	8, 33, 13, 22, 3
24	–	
25	10	7, 35, 15, 26
26	10	7, 36, 16, 27, 25
27	10	7, 37, 17, 26
28	–	
29	5	2, 19
30	5	6
31	10	8, 21, 32
32	10	8, 22, 31, 33, 3
33	15	8, 23, 32, 5, 48, 3
34	–	
35	10	7, 25, 36

Table 9.13 *continued*

Type number	Percentage error	Contaminating artifact types
36	10	7, 26, 35, 37
37	10	7, 27, 36
38	–	
40	25	2, 20, 19, 29
41	–	
42	–	
43	–	
44	15	51
45	–	
46	–	
47	–	
48	25	4, 8, 33
49	5	80
50	10	59
51	15	44
52	10	51, 54
53	0	
54	10	53, 52, 55
55	20	54, 7, 4
56	15	2, 29
57	0	
58	0	
59	10	44, 52
60	15	51, 44, 53
61	50	7, 8, 54
62	20	68, 69, 67
63	15	33, 23
64	15	75, 76, 8
65	40	31, 21, 69, 68
66	15	55
67	5	68, 73
68	5	67, 69, 73, 74
69	5	68, 74
71	5	52
72	10	60, 50, 59
73	15	11, 12, 13, 74
74	15	21, 22, 23, 31, 32, 33, 73
75	10	64, 78, 76
76	19	75, 77
77	50	8, 78
78	30	8, 77

[a]Type 80 designates noncultural stone.

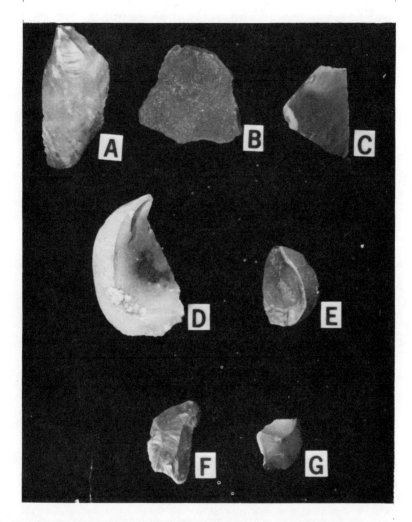

Figure 9.9 Use-modified chipped-stone flakes. (A) Type 23, chert; (B) Type 23, quartzite; (C) Type 21, chert; (D) Type 12, chert; (E) Type 33, chert; (F) Type 33, chert; (G) Type 48, chert. (D) and (E) are flakes from tangerine core. Height of letters is 1 cm.

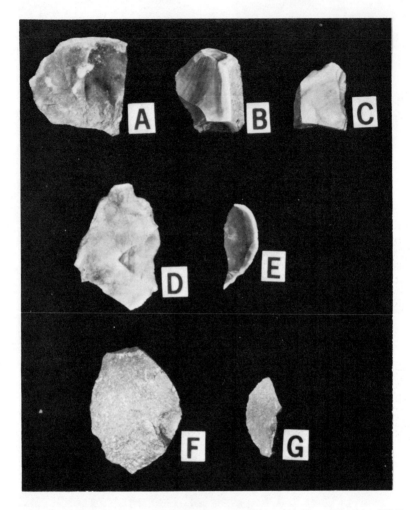

Figure 9.10 Additional use-modified chipped-stone flakes. (A) Type 25, chert; (B) Type 35, chert; (C) Type 37, chert; (D) Type 26, chalcedony; (E) Type 37, chert; (F) Type 23, quartzite; (G) Type 37, quartzite. Height of letters is 1 cm.

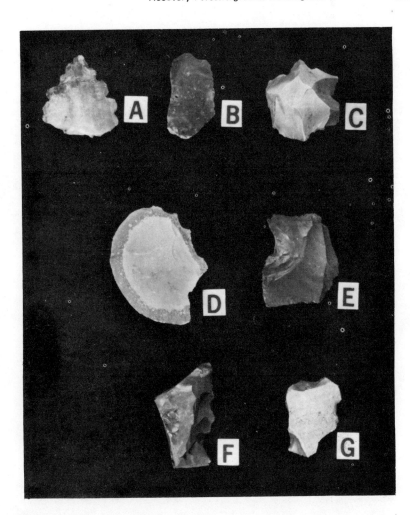

Figure 9.11 Unifacially retouched tools. (A) Type 63, chalcedony; (B) Type 74, chert; (C) Type 66, chert; (D) Type 76, chert; (E) Type 77, chert; (F) Type 68, chert; (G) Type 78, chert. Height of letters is 1 cm.

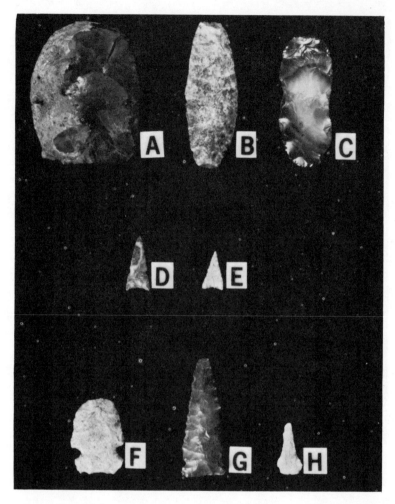

Figure 9.12 Bifacially retouched tools. (A) Type 56, chert; (B) Type 51, chert; (C) Type 44, chalcedony; (D) Type 53, chert; (E) Type 53, chert; (F) Type 71, quartzite; (G) Type 52, chert; (H) Type 60, chert. Height of letters is 1 cm.

10

Cultural Formation Processes of the Joint Site

The major transformation to be applied in the pursuit of activity sets operates entirely on secondary refuse. The identification transformations used to recognize secondary refuse areas were simple and straightforward. Such deposits possess the following properties: (1) predominantly worn-out, broken, or otherwise unusable materials, (2) a high diversity of materials (Haury 1936:56), and (3) a high relative density of materials. In most cases, the informal application of these criteria and judgments, based on field observations and notes, provided unambiguous assignments of deposits to the category of secondary refuse. Other transformations (the equations in Chapter 5) require data from the total normal outputs population. Additionally, it was hoped that activity and locational hypotheses could be tested on de facto and primary refuse. Unfortunately, identification of primary and de facto refuse types was not done during the excavation of the Joint Site, making it more difficult to segregate meaningful analytic units based on the refuse types within rooms and extramural areas.

THE RELATIVE ROOM ABANDONMENT MEASURE

In order to determine the nature of refuse within rooms, a new transformation, based on Reid's (1973; Reid and Shimada n.d.) measure of relative room abandonment, was used. If one assumes that every room follows approximately the same life cycle, while other rooms still are occupied (namely; use, abandon-

Table 10.1 Data for Applying Reid's Relative Room Abandonment Measure

Room number	Floor sherds	Fill sherds	Room area (in m²)	Restorable pots on floor	Floor sherds per m²	Fill sherds per m²
1	0	1046	4.9	0	0.0	213.4
2	6	154	5.5	0	1.1	28.0
3	1	85	6.1	0	.2	13.9
5	37	2097	6.8	0	5.4	308.4
7	21	1435	11.1	0	1.9	129.3
8	25	195	16.3	0	1.5	12.0
9	4	94	3.9	0	1.0	24.1
10	121	545	14.7	3	8.2	37.1
11	0	979	6.7	0	0.0	146.1
12	3	267	6.7	0	.4	39.9
14	46	138	7.2	0	6.4	19.2
15	222	2127	29.2	1+	7.6	72.9
17	0	3396	6.5	0	0.0	522.5
20	1	134	3.9	0	.3	34.4
21	67	217	7.1	3	9.4	30.6
23	95	1020	10.2	0	9.3	100.0
24	0	173	9.1	0	0.0	19.0
25	5	38	3.3	0	1.5	11.5
27	67	241	7.1	1	9.4	33.9
28	73	597	7.2	0	10.1	82.9
29	234	986	16.5	0	14.2	59.8
31	361	1462	13.2	4+	27.3	110.8
32	0	122	4.4	0	0.0	27.7
34	9	953	10.7	0	.8	89.1

ment, usable materials removed by scavenging, and, finally, use as a dump), one can predict that late-abandoned rooms containing de facto refuse will have a low density of sherds in the fill and a high number of whole pots on the floor. Rooms abandoned early and containing mostly secondary refuse will have a high density of fill sherds and a low number of whole or restorable pots on the floor.

I cannot apply the measure exactly as designed to the Joint Site, because we did not attempt to reconstruct whole vessels. In some cases, the pottery recording sheets (compiled by David Gregory in 1970 and John Hanson in 1971) contain some notations about reconstructable vessels, but these data are uneven. It should be possible, however, to use total floor sherds, rather than whole vessel counts, as an indicator of de facto refuse and to examine the reconstructable vessel estimates as confirmatory data. Total sherd frequencies of all "floor" proveniences (defined as the artifacts found resting directly on the archeological context floor) were divided by the room area to standardize the measure for variability in room size. Total sherds from the "fill" provenience (defined as all materials above the archeological context floor) were determined and the sherd densities for each room were calculated. In Table 10.1, these data are presented. Figure 10.1 is a scattergram of rooms plotted against the axes of fill sherd and floor sherd densities. By inspection, it would appear that three distinct clusters are present, which can be interpreted in terms of the refuse composition of rooms. An attempt was made by Morgan Tamplin to derive these clusters with the aid of a BCTRY cluster analysis. For reasons described by Reid (1973: 183–184), relating to the nature of the BCTRY technique, this attempt was unsuccessful. There are also a number of anomalies that required further explanation.

Cluster 1, with high fill density and low floor density, is composed of Rooms 1, 5, 7, 11, 17, and 34. Rooms 1, 5, 7, 11, and 17 clearly are dumps, as determined also by the earlier transformations. Room 34 falls within this cluster,

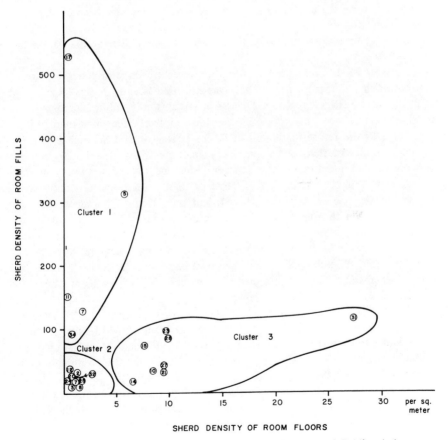

Figure 10.1 The clustering of rooms at the Joint Site in terms of Reid's relative room abandonment measure.

although it is known from stratigraphic evidence that the sherds in the fill of this room overlie the remains of the roof and once rested upon it. Because these materials probably were not dumped into the room, Room 34 really does not belong in the cluster and probably should be considered a member of Cluster 2. The rooms in Cluster 1 were the first to be abandoned.

Rooms falling within the second cluster (Rooms 2, 3, 8, 9, 12, 20, 24, 25, and 32) contain a low density of both floor and fill sherds. A strict interpretation by the abandonment measure is that, because these rooms contain little of each refuse type, they were abandoned after rooms in Cluster 1 but before those in Cluster 3. A number of anomalous cases suggest that the solution is not so simple. In the first place, the measure assumes that, during a room's systemic context, it had a likelihood of containing pots, the quantity depending only on room size. Clearly, gross differences in the activities performed within a room have an effect on the artifacts used there, of which some may become de facto refuse. Based on Hill's (1970a) study of space utilization at Broken K, one would expect the small rooms, used for storage, to contain little in the way of de facto refuse pots.

The effects of differentiation in room activities are discernible in Cluster 2, which contains all storage rooms that were not used later as dumps (Rooms 3, 9, 20, 25, and 32), except Room 27. Also in this cluster is Room 2, containing a small amount of secondary refuse on the floor, probably deposited there at the same time as the refuse in the fill of Room 1 (Hanson and Schiffer 1975). It should be apparent that rooms containing small quantities of secondary refuse and rooms that are functionally different must be treated separately in the interpretation of the room clusters. Most of these storerooms probably were abandoned late (see also Wilcox 1975), and one, Room 32, even contained burned maize on the floor, probably as de facto refuse. This finding makes it likely that other storerooms also contain primary and de facto floor refuse (other than pottery) which may be useful for testing behavioral hypotheses about the Joint Site chipped stone. The remaining rooms in Cluster 2 probably form a set abandoned at an intermediate time between the rooms of Cluster 1 and Cluster 3.

The last cluster, Cluster 3, consists of Rooms 10, 14, 15, 21, 23, 27, 28, and 29. These rooms, presumably abandoned late, contain a high density of floor sherds and a low density of fill sherds. All rooms in Cluster 3 were last used for habitation functions, with the exception of Rooms 27 and 29. Examination of Table 10.1 reveals that several of these rooms (Rooms 10, 15, 27, and 31) contain restorable vessels, tending to confirm their placement in the late-abandonment cluster. Again, however, there are several anomalies. Although Room 31 falls within this cluster, it has an inordinately high fill density, comparable to Room 7 in Cluster 1. The explanation of this anomaly relates to the kinds of provenience units defined at the Joint Site. In the case of Room 31, sherds from the same de facto refuse floor pots were encountered in the sand level above the floor and recorded within the arbitrary levels, C and B, of the fill. Sherds from a vessel that may have been intact at room abandonment were counted in different proveniences and used as measures of different kinds of refuse (secondary and de facto).

Resolving this paradox raises a larger issue that is worth discussing at some length. This concerns the relationship between analytic units (such as refuse types) and observational units (proveniences and their contents). Raising this issue allows further discussion of the vagaries in the use of the abandonment measure and leads to an evaluation of the likelihood that proper analytic units are definable at the Joint Site.

ANALYTIC UNITS AND PROVENIENCE DESIGNATION

In considering the problem of how to isolate relevant units of analysis at the Joint Site, I have been led to rethink the concept of provenience, along lines pioneered (in an explicit fashion) by Wilcox (1975, n.d.). Provenience usually is thought of as the spatial location of archeological remains. In a sense, every item present in the archeological structure has a unique provenience defined in terms of Euclidean three-dimensional space. In the field, however, it would be impractical to record the location of every artifact to, say, within 1 mm. And even if it were possible to do so, such unique provenience units would lend themselves to few analyses, except in terms of archeological context distributions. To overcome this problem, archeologists have devised other units of provenience, such as layers, levels, sections, and features. These more general units serve to summarize a set of locations in which archeological remains are found and to which these items are referred in one's analysis. A provenience, then, designates a set of materials that are related to one another on the basis of analytic criteria.

In the past, there has been some discussion about the use of "natural" versus "arbitrary" levels and proveniences (Drucker 1972). The term "natural level" most often is applied in Europe and the Near East, where it refers to a major episode of cultural deposition. These major units of cultural deposition often are identifiable as a result of the contrasting interstratification of various noncultural deposits. The identification of such units, dependent on sorting out cultural from noncultural formation processes, is not always a simple matter (Tamplin 1969; South 1974). A single-component site in North America or elsewhere does not have this kind of natural stratification, because, by definition, it was deposited during a single occupation. As a result, when Near Eastern archeologists, such as Wheeler (1956), complain about the use of arbitrary levels in American archeology, they have mixed analytical levels of stratification. The stratification that occurs in the major mounds of the Near East is not found in single-component sites (Drucker 1972).

Nevertheless, in single-component sites, stratification—albeit fine-grained—frequently is present. Often this stratification is considered to be quite minor, but only to the archeologist not requiring the data from such units. Take, for instance, a room at the Joint Site. If a room has been used as a dump, one can usually detect lenses of ash and other strata. Stratification, even in a small refuse area, may be extremely complex. These dumps usually are excavated and recorded in terms of arbitrary provenience units, which overwhelm or crosscut the natural strata. When the problem is to identify the major changes in artifact types that took place during the occupation of a site, these techniques are justifiable, because most of these small depositional units were laid down rapidly, and a succession of them rarely reveals typological change. The recording of materials within these dumps by relatively small, almost synchronous provenience units would not solve the problem of chronology any better than do the arbitrary strata presently used for the purpose.

If an archeologist were to ask other questions, different units of analysis might be required and proveniences would need to be discriminated at another level. For example, if one were interested in individual discard episodes—the items discarded together at the same time—one would strive to identify, if possible, proveniences that correspond to microstratigraphic variations. The identification of such provenience units would entail many practical problems of excavation; but, in the field, microstratigraphic variations that could inform on actual discard episodes are often perceivable, as in Room 5 at the Joint Site. For some problems, it might be crucial to record remains in this way.

Provenience units and profiles are simply models of a very complex reality. There is always much more variability of cultural and noncultural material in the archeological structure than is portrayed in the model. How much control is to be exercised in designating proveniences and recording remains at the site (assuming time and labor are constant) depends on the analytic units required for answering one's systemic-context questions. No method of provenience delineation is intrinsically better or worse than any other, except in reference to one's required analytic units.

Because one of my major analytic units at the Joint Site is secondary refuse deposits does not demand, however, that I treat every secondary refuse area as a single provenience. Archeologists have some responsibility to exercise as much control as possible in recording remains—if only because the remains are a scarce natural resource. At the Joint Site, we excavated in arbitrary levels, varying in thickness from 10 to 20 cm. To facilitate recombining provenience units into analytic units, suspected secondary refuse deposits were assigned unique numbers. In addition to midden numbers, all provenience units were given preliminary designations of refuse types. This information, along with other information, such as room number, room size class, and provenience type, provided a means by which arbitrarily defined proveniences could be grouped into various analytic units, such as discrete secondary refuse deposits within room fill or suspected de facto refuse in large rooms. A number of computer programs made this information readily accessible. These programs, the raw data, and the summary data are on file in the Arizona State Museum Library (Schiffer 1973b).

In coding these data according to provenience type and refuse type, serious problems emerged which illustrate the difficulty of using data that (although I gathered it) is inadequate for certain kinds of analyses. This results from our insufficient attention in the field to the problems of defining proveniences relevant to analytic units—which were not firmly in mind at the time. I now give several examples of this problem, couched in more general terms, to illustrate (*1*) the need for prior consideration of anticipated analytic units in terms of which proveniences must be referable, and (*2*) that the definition of such units requires the creative application of stratigraphic and nonstratigraphic transformation procedures in a continuous hypothesis-testing, multiphase program of field research (see Wilcox 1975, n.d.; South 1974).

Suppose one is interested in comparing the artifacts in several systemic-context analytic units within pueblo rooms. Three kinds of units are taken as examples. In the first place, refuse deposited on the floor while the room was in use, refuse in wall niches, and refuse hanging from the roof interior are of interest. The refuse may be primary or de facto. The second unit of concern is the (probably secondary) refuse deposited in the room after abandonment. The third unit consists of the materials that were deposited on the roof. These units are "provenience types," which may be related through various transformations to refuse types. A provenience type, such as "roof artifacts," is a culturally deposited assemblage of suspected analytic utility.

To illustrate some of the problems of identifying provenience types (not to mention refuse types), let us now invoke plausible cultural and noncultural formation processes, and transform the hypothetical room and the various systemic proveniences into archeological remains (see Beeson 1957). After the room is abandoned, additional refuse accumulates. The first secondary refuse may be expected to land on the floor; between events of secondary refuse discard, aeolian sand is also deposited. The next major event is the deterioration of the roof, which collapses, mixing materials from the wall niches and roof. If the roof collapses in this manner, many items will come into contact with the last deposited items of secondary refuse. The walls fall in and sand deposition continues on the rubble until weedy plants begin the formation of a soil horizon.

When a room formed under these conditions is examined in the archeological record, certain major natural strata are detectable. Roof clay and wall stones (CWS) often are found in a distinct layer. There may be a level of aeolian sand between the secondary refuse and the overlying wall–roof material. The CWS layer and the aeolian sand layer both contain artifacts. Continuing downward, one encounters the secondary refuse deposit and finally the floor. How can one interpret this archeological structure in order to arrive at the provenience types and systemic-context analytic units of interest? This is naturally a difficult problem, despite the obvious stratification. The "floor" in the archeological context (the provenience floor and what rests directly upon it) is not equivalent to the provenience type "floor" containing primary and de facto refuse. The archeological context floor contains several provenience and refuse types, mixing systemic-context analytic units.

The archeological-context provenience "fill" consists of secondary refuse introduced after room abandonment and of refuse that was on the roof as well as material contained in the roof and in the walls. Archeological context proveniences like "fill" mix provenience types and thus mix analytic units of the systemic context. Stratigraphic solutions may, in some cases, allow the recognition of what was once on the roof. Roof materials sometimes are contained within the CWS deposit and occasionally overlie the observable remnants of the roof beams, as in Room 34 of the Joint Site. But, in general, roof refuse or other provenience types may be very difficult to identify. This is so because there are not likely to be many straightforward stratigraphic solutions. And, further, there are no simple equivalences between systemic-context analytic units and archeological proveniences. Artifacts in the same observational unit (in archeological context) were not necessarily in the same depositional unit. And, conversely, artifacts in the same depositional unit are not necessarily contained within the same observational unit. Floor is not equal to floor, and fill is not equal to trash or roof.

Another example can be used to indicate the seriousness of the problem and to point the way to solutions that may be used under some circumstances. Let us take a room that was abandoned with various whole pots resting on the floor. After abandonment, aeolian sand began to accumulate around this de facto refuse; then the roof fell in, bring with it some wall stones and breaking the pots. This can be observed in the archeological context. One first encounters the CWS layer. At the base of this unit, a number of sherds from the same pot, some of which rest on the floor, are encountered as one trowels down, while other sherds, some from the roof, are mixed within the sandy level. What class of locations should be delineated in the archeological context which corresponds to the provenience type "floor (de facto) refuse?" There are three solutions to this problem.

The first solution is to allow "floor" (the analytic unit) to equal the assemblage on the archeological floor plus whatever is contained in an arbitrary level some designated distance (usually 10 cm) above it. In this solution, one would slice the pots in two: Some sherds are placed in the floor provenience also containing drift material in the sand, while other parts of the pot are in the next level above, corresponding to some kind of "fill" unit. If the "floor plus 10 cm above" provenience were applied to rooms containing secondary refuse, as it all too frequently is, one would cut into the secondary refuse deposit and group those materials with whatever refuse might have rested originally on the floor. The second solution is to have floor equal to floor alone; only the materials actually resting on the archeological context "floor" are included in this unit. When this solution is followed, the base sherds of the de facto refuse pots are placed within the unit "floor," and the remaining sherds are counted within the "fill." Certainly, this solution, which was applied at the Joint Site, is also unsatisfactory. Materials of the relevant analytic units are again either mixed or inappropriately divided.

Another solution, more consistent with the aim of providing meaningful analytic units, is possible. In order to derive (de facto) floor refuse or any units of interest, one applies a hypothesis-testing feedback technique of excavation and transformation. Encountering a number of sherds that are demonstrated to be from the same pot, one might entertain the hypothesis that parts of a de facto refuse vessel have been discovered. These sherds then are set aside and an attempt is made to test the hypothesis. If the base sherds of this pot are found on the floor, the hypothesis receives strong support. These latter sherds and the ones found earlier can be lumped safely into the provenience type "floor." Artifacts within the sand matrix surrounding the sherds would be in a different provenience, perhaps one corresponding to materials left on the roof. If the base sherds are not found or are not found on the floor, other explanations for this material should be considered and proveniences defined accordingly.

Archeological proveniences related to units of analysis can be achieved by applying in the field appropriate transformations in the absence of notions that provenience units must be horizontal, be of uniform volume or depth (unless that is important to one's systemic context interest), be mutually exclusive and exhaustive, or correspond to major strata produced by noncultural formation processes. Stratigraphy must be applied in new creative ways in order to identify the effects of cultural and noncultural formation processes. These problems really were not raised or resolved during the excavation of the Joint Site. As a consequence, I have had to pore over the site notes in an attempt, often in vain, to determine the probable analytic category of each provenience. This situation can be avoided by fieldwork oriented toward proposing and testing alternative hypotheses that account for what is observed in terms of cultural and noncultural formation processes. As Wilcox has informed me on a number of occasions, "The crucial question is, how did these materials get here?" Answers to this question require use of in-field transformation procedures to delineate proveniences that are relevant to one's systemic context questions and analytic units.

One by-product of this view of provenience determination is that fieldwork is not merely manual labor. An archeologist does not simply hire unskilled workers and expect them to "gather" or "collect" the data as if they were harvesting cherries or rhubarb. Fieldwork, conducted to acquire meaningful data for answering systemic context questions, is a complex process involving a knowledge of various kinds of transformation procedures and the ability to apply these in a multiple working hypothesis framework to account for the observations in the archeological context (Reid 1973). One must keep firmly in mind at all times the analytic units toward whose definition the fieldwork is directed. A good field archeologist has manual dexterity, to be sure, but such an individual also possesses an enormous body of proven transformation procedures and the ability to apply them flexibly and rapidly in the field. The view that fieldwork is a technical activity that can be divorced from systemic context concerns (Rouse 1972) should be discouraged, for it is based on erroneous notions about the nature of data retrieval in archeology.

Stratigraphy alone cannot solve the problems of defining meaningful proveniences. For the cases in which archeological provenience units crosscut different deposits, mixed proveniences will have to be designated. For example, in a room with secondary refuse on the floor, it is not yet possible to distinguish stratigraphically between the original floor materials and those deposited later as secondary refuse—unless whole vessels of de facto refuse are present. Such proveniences therefore are mixed. By pushing present transformation procedures to their operational limits and developing others, hopefully for in-field use, we will acquire gradually a broad body of principles and techniques for identifying relevant analytic units.

REFUSE TYPES AT THE JOINT SITE

I now return to the measure of relative abandonment as it is applied to rooms at the Joint Site, and attempt to assess the extent to which relevant proveniences and refuse types have been isolated. The results of applying the relative abandonment measure to pottery were employed in identifying an already defined provenience unit as one or another refuse type. For reasons just discussed, it is clear that sherds from the provenience "fill" may contain not only secondary room refuse but also roof refuse of various types as well as de facto floor refuse. Also, "floor" may contain a variety of refuse types, derived from several independent cultural deposits. The mixing of analytic units is illustrated clearly in Room 34, where arbitrary "fill" proveniences consist almost entirely of roof refuse and material carried in through the operation of noncultural formation processes. Similarly, Room 32, because of very late abandonment, should contain no secondary refuse. The fill sherds of this room must consist, then, entirely of roof materials.

If the refuse on the entire pueblo roof was not differentially distributed in terms of gross quantity, the relative abandonment measure is unaffected, because the fill density of all rooms is increased by a factor proportional, or nearly proportional, to room area. Although Wilcox (1975) believes that the materials on the roof of the pueblo were concentrated above Rooms 31, 7, 8, 10, 11, 9, 15, 21, 23, and 24, one still must account for the materials contained in the fill of rooms that Wilcox believes also were abandoned late (Rooms 32, 3, and 25). Returning to Table 10.1, one observes that the fill density of sherds in these rooms is low, but it is not out of line with the fill of other rooms, such as Rooms 8, 9, and 24, which did not contain secondary refuse and are believed to have had roof artifact deposits. The simplest way to account for these observations is to hypothesize that refuse of undetermined types occurred on all roofs.

Accepting this interpretation of the nature of the refuse contained within the fill of these rooms leads to a set of procedures for categorizing the proveniences in which chipped stone is found. In rooms containing no clear-cut secondary refuse deposits in their fills (all but Rooms 1, 2, 5, 7, 11, and 17), all chipped stone contained in levels above the floor is considered to have been on the roof and is of mixed or undetermined refuse type (primary, secondary, or de facto). Although all chipped stone lying directly on the floor of these rooms was labeled "primary" or "de facto" floor refuse, the possibility that some of these materials were once on the roof cannot be excluded. These units are mixed.

The rooms containing secondary refuse in the fill were treated differently. The probable roof assemblage of undetermined refuse type was taken to include all chipped stone in the low artifact density proveniences that overlay the major secondary refuse deposit. Where even these subjective judgments became uncomfortable, the label "mixed roof and trash fill" was applied. The trash fill of these rooms is assumed to correspond to the high density levels above floor. The artifacts from the floor were considered to be possible primary and de facto refuse units. That these also contain the first discards of secondary refuse from the fill and are mixed is readily conceded.

The criteria thus enumerated were applied as consistently as possible when designating a particular provenience as "roof" or "floor" or "trash fill." It is these units, crosscut by tentative assignments as to refuse type, that form the basis for analyzing the chipped stone. Materials within proveniences from the sample squares also were labeled by refuse type. For the most part, these transformations are considered to be fairly reliable where secondary refuse is concerned. It is possible that some primary refuse was uncovered in sample squares; those located at the north and west margins of the site often contained small amounts of material, usually of low variety. Such units were labeled "primary" refuse. It is likely, however, that much of this material simply washed down from secondary refuse areas, since, in most of these sample squares, the refuse was concentrated in the first level.

11

Systemic Context of the Joint Site

In this chapter, basic parameters of the human occupation at the Joint Site are reconstructed for later use in transformations of the chipped-stone assemblage. First of all, in order to estimate the duration of various processes, as required by c-transforms in Chapter 5, the occupation span of the site is inferred from consideration of tree-ring and radiocarbon dates. Discussion of the Joint Site dates is prefaced by a general consideration of the interpretation of absolute dates in the framework of behavioral archeology. Next, activity areas are treated briefly in an effort to distinguish basic types for use later in the secondary refuse transformation. And, finally, an effort is made to infer the occupational history of the site to supply for later uses an estimate of the average number of households present.

INTERPRETING ABSOLUTE DATES

The interpretation of an absolute date requires the careful consideration of two problems. The first is that of relating what is actually measured by a dating technique, such as radiocarbon content, to the event that is supposed to be measured, such as the death of an organism. Once the first problem is solved, which involves familiarity with the assumptions underlying the technique, the critical problem of archeological interpretation must be confronted. This problem is that of relating the dated event to a cultural event of interest.

In the past, archeologists interpreting absolute dates derived from a variety of techniques have displayed a remarkable reluctance to modify the obtained dates by adding or subtracting years based on their solutions to the two problems. Only recently have charts been constructed for taking into account the discrepancy between radiocarbon years and actual dates as determined through dating tree samples of known age (Stuiver and Suess 1966; Damon, Long, and Wallick 1972). These corrections slowly are being applied to archeological interpretations; and some have had far-reaching effects on the temporal relationship between major cultural events of the Old World (Renfrew 1970). While barriers to transforming "raw" dates, based on solutions to the first problem, are giving way slowly, almost no progress has been made in solving the second problem. Dean (1970:31) has stated the second problem succinctly:

> If it is assumed that the date, however derived, is correct, it is evident that the most critical factor in assessing the date is the nature of the relationship between the object from which it is derived and the event to which it is to be applied.

Although Dean is discussing the interpretation of tree-ring dates in particular, he has delineated the general problem that must be solved in using any absolute date. By considering cultural formation processes, it may be possible to offer some suggestions as to how one might modify a date by adding and subtracting years in order to transform it into the date of an event of interest.

An uninterpreted date obtained by an absolute technique is an archeological context date. In most cases, it is directly dating a noncultural event, such as the death of a tree or the eruption of a volcano, which has no intrinsic relationship to any past cultural system or event. To "interpret" a date, one must place the dated object within its systemic context, thus establishing a relationship between a noncultural and cultural event. In some cases, the relationship may be very direct, as when a tree is cut down and used the same year for constructing a roof; but even this requires a transformation. In most cases, the relationship cannot be established by the use of an equivalence transformation (that is, the time of the cultural event is the same as the time of the noncultural event that is dated); only by applying reasoned estimates of the intervening time between the absolute date and the date of the event of interest can the transformation problem be solved.

Many archeologists seem unaware of this transformation problem, fully blurring the archeological and systemic contexts of their dated materials. This approach is exemplified by the attempt to date "sites." A site, per se, cannot be dated in any meaningful sense of the term. However, *events* that took place during the occupation span or systemic context of a site, such as the initiation or termination of activity, can be dated (Dean 1969). Dates for other events that occurred during the occupation of a site are obtained by applying different transformations to the date. Thus, there need be no single interpretation of a date, just as there can be no date for a site. The transformation process involves arguing that one event or another relates by a certain amount of time to the date of the specimen.

Although the interpretation of tree-ring dates is more advanced in terms of achieved systemic context dates and some explicit transformation principles (Haury 1934; Bannister 1962; Dean 1969), I have chosen a recent application of tree-ring dating to illustrate my arguments, which are intended to apply to the interpretation of all absolute dates.

Breternitz (1966) has surveyed the literature of southwestern archeology in an attempt to determine the use span or manufacture span of the more commonly encountered pottery types (traditionally defined). His determinations are based on the association of pottery occurrences with materials dated by tree rings. Breternitz recognizes the two sources of error in the use of absolute dates, but his method does not provide satisfactory transformations of the archeological context dates. It is, therefore, difficult to evaluate how successfully he has estimated the use spans and manufacture spans of the pottery types.

Some hypothetical cases can illustrate this point. Suppose there is a pueblo room in which it has been established, using appropriate correlates (Bannister 1962), that the roof was constructed during the year 1247. In this room, an example of a St. Johns Polychrome bowl is found as secondary refuse. In other words, the room was constructed in 1247, used for domestic activities, then abandoned, and finally used as a dump. Although Breternitz (1966) considers dump material to provide a less reliable association with a dated roof than objects in other contexts, the date 1247 still would be used in constructing the manufacture span of the pottery type. Examining this case more closely, with an eye open to determining systemic context dates, leads to a different way of proceeding.

In the first place, one must make an estimate of the length of time the room was occupied (1). To that quantity must be added the length of time needed to accumulate the deposit up to the level where the bowl sherds occur. The discard date of the pot may be expressed in relation to the construction date of the room in which it occurs:

$$\text{discard date} = 1247 + 1_{\text{room}} + x$$

where x is the amount of time needed to accumulate the deposit to where the pottery occurs. The manufacture date of the pot can be determined by subtracting the uselife of the vessel from the discard date just produced. It should be noted that 1_{pot} will vary among the various shapes of any pottery type (Foster 1960; David and Hennig 1972; Pastron 1974), and this factor alone, if not taken into account, may introduce error into a systemic context date.

The reader will, of course, note that none of the above-mentioned quantities is measured easily. However, I submit that, unless reasoned estimates for these quantities are made explicitly, systematic error will be introduced by the implicit equivalence assumptions that are accepted instead. If the transformation problem is ignored, it is possible to build into our dates the following assumptions:

1. The length of time the room was in use is 0 years.
2. It took no time to accumulate the deposit in which the bowl was found.
3. The bowl was made, used, and discarded at the same time.

Although none of these assumptions is realistic, they underlie the use of every single date associated in the above-described manner or in a similar manner in secondary refuse. Labeling such materials as "indirect associations" (Breternitz 1966) does not eliminate the interpretive problem—it simply identifies it. We must strive to adjust our assumptions to the most probable formation processes that operated.

Primary or de facto refuse, even if found in floor context, provides similar problems of interpretation. Primary refuse can be related to the event of room construction, but this requires one to estimate the length of time a room was in use before the item was broken and discarded there. And, again, specific quantities must be added and subtracted from the roof date to yield the date of pottery manufacture—if that is the event of interest. De facto refuse must be treated similarly.

TREE-RING DATES

We were fortunate in uncovering at the Joint Site a number of wood and charcoal specimens amenable to dendrochronological analysis. The 47 dated samples obtained during the 1970–1971 excavations have been reported and interpreted by Wilcox (1975) and are presented here in Figure 11.1. I shall reexamine these dates for the purpose of estimating the probable occupation span of the Joint Site.

The earliest date from the site is 1188, obtained from a log fragment in the fill of Room 6; unfortunately, this is a noncutting date. The specimen, from a log very large in diameter, could have contained a number of additional rings. From this date, it can be inferred that construction of Room 6 began after 1188, if one is willing to assume that the log was a freshly cut roof beam. As a construction date, it would have to be considered an anomaly in light of the remainder of the evidence, which places construction of earlier rooms (in the building sequence) at a later date. The possibility that this single specimen may have been on, rather than a part of, the roof cannot be ruled out.

The next latest date is 1222, on a specimen presumed to be from a roof beam

PROVENIENCE					SPECIMEN	DATING	
SPACE	LEVEL	SEC-TION	ROOF BEAM	OTHER	NUMBER	INSIDE	OUTSIDE
6	FILL		PRIMARY		ULC-241	1020p	- 1188vv
9	SF·1	1		FLOOR CONTEXT	ULC-242	1192p	- 1238r comp.
10	A	2	PRIMARY		ULC-122	1203p	- 1235vv
			PRIMARY		ULC-123	1175p	- 1239r inc.
21	C	3	UNKNOWN		ULC-125	1159p	- 1222vv
31				FIREWOOD	ULC-238	1201fp	- 1245vv
	B	3	UNKNOWN		ULC-240	1204fp	- 1245vv
				FIREWOOD	ULC-239	1223fp	1255vv

34	A	2	UNKNOWN		ULC-154	1196p	1223vv
	A	1	UNKNOWN		ULC-185	1194fp	1229vv
			SECONDARY ?		ULC-193	1193p	1236r comp.
	FILL		SECONDARY ?		ULC-178	1203fp	1236r comp.
	B	2	PRIMARY		ULC-145	1203p	1238r inc.
	B	6	PRIMARY		ULC-200	1180p	1239vv
	A	1	UNKNOWN		ULC-184	1157p	1240r inc.
	B	1	PRIMARY		ULC-181	1159p	1240r inc.
	B	2	PRIMARY		ULC-217	1167p	1240r inc.
	B	5	PRIMARY		ULC-158	1172p	1240r inc.
	B	3	SECONDARY ?		ULC-204	1184p	1240r inc.
		6	SECONDARY		ULC-189	1191p	1240r inc.
	A	6	SUPPORT ?		ULC-220	1192p	1240r inc.
		6	SECONDARY		ULC-192	1191p	1240r inc.
	B	5	UNKNOWN		ULC-155	1198p	1240r inc.
	B	5	PRIMARY		ULC-133	1200p	1240r inc.
		6	SECONDARY		ULC-188	1207p	1240r inc.
	B	2	SECONDARY ?		ULC-139	1166p	1240rB inc.
	B	1	PRIMARY		ULC-183	1204p	1242vv
	A	1	UNKNOWN		ULC-186	1200fp	1243vv
	FILL		SECONDARY		ULC-177	1206fp	1244vv
	A	1	CLOSING MATERIAL		ULC-187	1207fp	1244vv
	B	2	UNKNOWN		ULC-160	1195fp	1244r inc.
	B	2	SECONDARY		ULC-140	1206	1244r inc.
	B	5	UNKNOWN		ULC-157	1095±p	1245r inc.
	A	6	SUPPORT ?		ULC-201	1203p	1246r comp.
	B	2	UNKNOWN		ULC-147	1207fp	1246r inc.
	B	1	SECONDARY		ULC-195	1202p	1247v
	B	2	PRIMARY		ULC-213	1192p	1247r inc
	B	1	UNKNOWN		ULC-171	1199p	1247r inc.
	B	1	PRIMARY		ULC-182	1199fp	1247r inc
	B	6	UNKNOWN		ULC-219	1203p	1247r inc
	B	6	PRIMARY		ULC-206	1216p	1247r inc
	B	2	PRIMARY		ULC-215	1194p	1247c inc.
		TT 13	UNKNOWN		ULC-223	1208fp	1237vv
		TT 13	UNKNOWN		ULC-224	1215	1240vv
		TT 13	SECONDARY		ULC-225	1131fp	1242vv
		TT 13	UNKNOWN		ULC-222	1163p	1244v
		TT 13	SECONDARY		ULC-226	1196fp	1244r inc.

Figure 11.1 The Joint Site tree-ring dates. The species of all specimens was Piñon. *Key:* ULC, Laboratory of Tree-Ring Research catalog numbers; fp, far from pith; p, pith ring present; v, variable; vv, very variable; c, complete outer ring circumference; r, partial outer ring circumference complete on specimen; B, bark present; comp., outer growth ring complete; inc., outer growth ring incomplete; SF, subfloor. See Robinson and Warren (1971) for full explanation of symbols. (From Wilcox 1975.)

of Room 21. Again, this is a noncutting date. If this is not a re-used beam, construction of the room began some time after 1222. And, if this room is, in fact, part of the core construction unit as Wilcox (1975) suggests, then initial construction, and thus occupation, of the Joint Site began some time after 1222, assuming that this material was not from a repair timber. Let us examine the evidence for whether or not Room 21 is within the core construction unit.

Bond and abutment patterns are ambiguous with respect to the placement of Room 21 within the core construction unit (Figure 7.4). Both Rooms 20 and 21 clearly abut core Rooms 17 and 18, and Room 19 of the second aggregation unit abuts Room 21, making the construction of Room 21 antecedent to the addition of the second aggregation unit. As evidence for the inclusion of Rooms 20 and 21 within the core unit, Wilcox (1975) cites the regular portal between Room 17 and Room 20, but he also cautions that such a portal may indicate only contemporary use, not necessarily contemporary construction.

If Rooms 20 and 21 were built at exactly the same time as core Rooms 13, 17, and 18, one would expect them all to have been built on an unmodified surface containing no refuse. In fact, some refuse is present below the floors of the three excavated rooms (Rooms 17, 20, and 21). Under Room 17, a total of 4 lithic and ceramic artifacts were found; whereas under Room 20, there were 20; and beneath Room 21 were found 4. This evidence is again ambiguous, but careful interpretation leads to reasonable doubt as to the inclusion of Rooms 20 and 21 within the core unit. Apparently, some refuse was present even under Room 17, one of undisputed core placement. This refuse, however, was all lithic, although a total of 9 sherds were found under Rooms 20 and 21. Because the site sits atop a deflated deposit that contains chert and quartzite cobbles suitable for quarrying activities, the presence of chipped stone under the earliest rooms can be explained as the result of activity conducted prior to site occupation. Based on this admittedly thin evidence, I suggest that Rooms 20 and 21 may not have been built at the same time as the other rooms of the core construction unit, since they are above several sherds that are more difficult to explain as the result of preconstruction activity. Thus, the date 1222 obtained for Room 21 may not relate to the earliest construction events at the site.

The third and last aggregation unit, consisting of Rooms 7, 8, 9, 10, and 15, probably was erected around 1239. A primary beam in Room 10 produced a cutting date of 1239, and another beam from the same room had a noncutting date of 1235—not inconsistent with the 1239 construction hypothesis. The other dated specimen (1238) from this aggregation unit occurred in association with the second floor of Room 9 (SF-1), not the lowest floor as Wilcox (1975) reports. This floor was very ashy and contained chipped stone that had been exposed to fire. In addition, adobe on the walls of the room was fired to a pinkish color. All of these observations can be explained by a fire that consumed the contents and original roof of the room some time after 1239. The remnants of the roof and other materials were floored over, and the room was re-used to suffer a less violent death at a later (but unknown) date.

Construction of the large kiva (Room 34) is the best-dated event at the Joint Site. Two major clusters of dates, at 1240 and 1247, suggest that stockpiling of beams had begun in 1240, well in advance of kiva construction during 1247. These inferences are based on correlates presented by Dean (1969). It is assumed that the latest dates from a roof are those of construction, unless remodeling or repair is suspected. Lack of burned walls in the kiva and the short time between 1240 and 1247 suggest stockpiling rather than repair as the more likely explanation of the two date clusters.

Three additional dates, all from Room 31 of the second aggregation unit, remain to be discussed. Two noncutting dates of 1245 and 1255, obtained from the firepit, demonstrate continued occupation of the room and the site to at least 1255. Another noncutting date, also 1245, is from a roof beam. If this date is taken as the construction date of the roof, at least this portion of Aggregation Unit 2 must have postdated the addition of Aggregation Unit 3. The bond–abut patterns do not preclude this possibility. Rooms 31, 6, and 32 could have been added after Room 7. There seems to be insufficient data to resolve the point, and, in any case, it does not bear on the problem of determining the occupation span of the site.

In order to provide more secure evidence for the dating of the initial construction events at the Joint Site, John Hanson returned there in the summer of 1972 to retrieve additional dendrochronological specimens from core Rooms 13 and 16. Unfortunately, the material he obtained was not datable.

In summary, construction at the Joint Site may have begun around 1222; but, depending on how one wishes to interpret a single noncutting date, it could have occurred before or after this time. It seems certain that construction activity ceased in 1247 with the building of Room 34, but site occupation continued to some unspecifiable year beyond 1255. In short, although major cultural activity occurring at the Joint Site can be firmly placed in the first two-thirds of the thirteenth century, the exact duration of the occupation span is not illuminated by the tree-ring evidence. A minimum occupation span of 33 years would be a warranted conclusion.

RADIOCARBON DATES

For a variety of reasons, dates obtained from the radiocarbon analysis of wood and charcoal samples did not provide much useful information for dating the earliest and latest events that took place at the Joint Site. In the first place, the standard deviation of a single sample is greater than the likely occupation span of the site, thus providing little power to discriminate events that occurred within a like interval of time. In the second place, radiocarbon samples were submitted to analysis before, not after, we received the results of the tree-ring study. Had we waited for the tree-ring dates, radiocarbon specimens could have been chosen very carefully for solving specific problems in determining events related to initial occupation and abandonment of the Joint Site.

In addition to the complete lack of problem guidance in the choice of specimens, no attempt was made to send only outside rings. This means, of course, that uninterpreted dates refer not to the date when the tree died but to an unknown date sometime during the life of the tree. This consistent source of error, present in all samples except the maize from Room 32, produces dates that are consistently older than the event that should be dated and thereby renders interpretation much more difficult.

A partial solution to this problem is possible. If it is assumed that any portion of the cross section of a tree branch had an equal chance of being chosen as a radiocarbon sample, a large number of samples will approximate a date equal to 75% of the life span of the tree. This was determined by drawing a facsimile cross section of a branch with rings of equal width and imposing a regular grid over them to simulate the selection of samples. The ring whose length was the greatest for each square was recorded as the date for that square. Using this technique, I determined that the average of all samples from a branch is equal to three-fourths of the total number of rings (ignoring the additional problem of sap diffusion). The two basic assumptions of ring width equality and equal opportunity of selection are both unreasonable, and their probable effects should be noted.

Because ring width increases toward the center of a limb, there would be a greater chance of selecting earlier material on a random selection basis than if all rings were of the same width. Because outer rings decay first on roof beams and are burned to ash first in fires, it is likely that all specimens would tend to favor the earlier portions of the tree disproportionately. Given both sources of systematic error, tending toward earlier dates, the correction factor of $\frac{3}{4}$ must be altered. Without further justification, I shall employ the value of $\frac{1}{2}$. In other words, I assume that the death date of the tree from which a radiocarbon sample was selected without consideration for sending outside rings is approximated by the following equation:

$$D_c = D_o - \tfrac{1}{2}l$$

where

D_c = the corrected date in years B.P.;
D_o = the uncorrected date in years B.P.;
l = the age at death of the tree.

Table 11.1 Radiocarbon Dates from the Joint Site

Joint Site date number	Geochron laboratory number	Provenience	Material	Date
1	GX-1975	Room 32, Level C, associated with floor	charred maize	655 ± 95 B.P.
2	GX-1976	Room 29, Level A, Section 4 (10 cm above floor)	charcoal	1020 ± 95 B.P.
3	GX-1977	Test Area 2, Firepit 2	charcoal	960 ± 95 B.P.
4	GX-1978	Room 15, fill, 40–50 cm above floor	wood	515 ± 100 B.P.
5	GX-1979	Room 10, fill (Beam 5)	wood	795 ± 95 B.P.
6	GX-1980	Room 8, firepit, Section 3	charcoal	1145 ± 85 B.P.
7	GX-1981	Room 2, fill, roof beam	wood	1390 ± 100 B.P.
8	GX-1982	Room 24, in pit (m-4)	charcoal	460 ± 105 B.P.
9	GX-1983	Room 25, Level A (22 cm above floor)	charcoal	1280 ± 95 B.P.
10	GX-1984	Room 14, Level A, Section 2 (4 cm above floor)	charcoal	1100 ± 120 B.P.

The age at death of a tree is, of course, a difficult variable to estimate and will vary with species of tree, cause of death, and other factors. When used with care, however, this formula can provide a basis for taking into account the error introduced by a failure to select only outside rings from a sample.

In Table 11.1, a complete list of radiocarbon dates derived from Joint Site materials is presented. It is to their interpretation that I now turn.

Sample 1 is of particular relevance in determining the date at which human activity ceased at the Joint Site. One might suppose that this maize found stacked on the floor of Room 32 was a part of the last crop harvested by the inhabitants of the Joint Site. Using the correction curve for radiocarbon dates based on the dating of known-age specimens produces the dates of 1252 or 1355 (Ralph and Michael 1970), or of 1280 (Stuiver and Suess 1966). The date of 1355 is clearly at odds with the ceramic evidence, which indicates a complete lack of fourteenth-century White Mountain redwares, and should be discounted. The range of 1252–1280 ± 95 is a reasonable date for the abandonment of the Joint Site. If additional funds were available, it certainly would be worthwhile to submit several more samples of this maize for dating. It is possible that a very precise date of abandonment could be determined.

The second date is from a specimen found in the fill of Room 29 and is presumed to be from a roof beam. If an age at death for juniper is taken to be 200–300 years, an application of the tree-ring correction and the formula presented earlier yields a date of 1040–1090 ± 95. This falls slightly before the tree-ring date for early site occupation, but is not really aberrant.

Correcting the third date in the same manner produces 1100–1150 ± 95, which is not anomalous for an outdoor firepit that probably was fueled by dead wood.

Date 4, when corrected, proves to be 1500–1550 ± 100, a substantial anomaly, which is perhaps best explained as material deposited after site occupation. Given that this specimen was not found very far below present ground surface, it well might have been part of a root or an old fence post.

Date 5 requires a different correction procedure, because, to my knowledge, it was the only pine specimen submitted to radiocarbon analysis. The site records indicate that this sample is not from either of the logs that yielded the tree-ring dates from Room 10. It is necessary, therefore, to make an independent estimate of the tree's age. An average age at death of dated pine logs from the Joint Site is about 55 years. The corrected date, using 55 as the value for 1, is determined to be 1238, 1203, or 1168 (Ralph and Michael 1970). It should be apparent that the first date missed by only a year the date at which the room is inferred, on the basis of the tree-ring evidence, to have been constructed.

There is no need to spend time on the interpretation of Specimens 6–10, for they provide no new information with respect to the events of interest during the systemic context of the Joint Site. Based on the interpreted radiocarbon dates, the end of occupation of the Joint Site might be tentatively placed between A.D. 1252 and 1280. Taken with the tree-ring dates, the probable occupation span of the Joint Site is A.D. 1220–1270.

ACTIVITY AREAS

At Broken K Pueblo, Hill (1968, 1970a) found an association between large rooms, mealing bins, and firepits; rooms with these features are said to have been the location of habitation activities. Smaller rooms which lack these features are considered to have been storage rooms. A similar pattern of room size and feature association, possibly representing the same functional room classes, is found at the Joint Site (Hanson and Schiffer 1975). Based on a χ^2 test, rooms with a floor area greater than 7.5 m^2 tend to occur with firepits; those below this figure do not ($p < .05$). Although the cutoff point between the two classes differs slightly from the 6.6 m^2 found at Broken K (Hill 1968), it is likely that gross patterns of space utilization were similar.

Habitation activities, such as cooking and some others involved in food preparation, most likely would occur in close proximity to a hearth. Therefore, I assume that the presence of a firepit in a room indicates that habitation activities took place there, unless the room is also semisubterranean. In the latter case, it served a special function as a kiva. The absence of a firepit indicates that a room functioned primarily as storage, although, in Rooms 17, 7, and 29, mealing

Table 11.2 Frequency of "on Floor" Materials in a Test of the Room Use Differentiation Hypothesis

				Material or feature				
Room	Marine shell	Unworked bone	Bone awls	Miscellaneous worked bone	Sherds	Chipped stone	Fire-cracked rock	Mealing bins
Rooms with firepits								
10	1	55	2	0	121	36	7	0
15	0	55	1	4	222	21	42	3
21	0	0	0	0	67	14	1	0
23	0	0	0	0	95	5	3	3
28	0	76	2	0	73	30	0	0
31	1	15	0	0	361	5	207	5
Total	2	201	5	4	939	111	260	11
Mean	.33	33.5	.83	.66	156.5	18.5	43.3	1.83
Rooms without firepits								
3	0	0	0	0	1	0	0	0
9	0	0	0	0	4	0	0	0
20	0	1	0	0	1	1	0	0
25	0	73	0	0	5	0	0	0
27	0	0	0	0	67	3	0	0
29	0	5	1	1	234	30	2	7
32	0	0	0	0	0	0	0	0
Total	0	79	1	1	312	34	2	7
Mean	0	11.3	.14	.14	44.6	4.9	.29	1.0

activities also were performed (see Figure 7.4). Despite the crudeness of these room-use divisions, they seem adequate to define major variations in the use of interior space at the Joint Site.

Comparison of the room classes in terms of de facto floor refuse provides additional support for the inferred differences in function. As shown previously (Chapter 10), not all room floors have comparable refuse types present; early-abandoned rooms, for example, doubtless contain secondary refuse on their floors. To control for this likelihood, only rooms were considered which, by available evidence, seem to contain little or no secondary refuse in the fill. This selection is based on the assumption that, if there is no secondary refuse in the fill, there is likely to be none on the floor. Rooms meeting this criterion were grouped into two classes, depending on the presence or absence of a firepit. Rooms with firepits are 10, 15, 21, 23, 28, and 31; and those without are 3, 9, 20, 25, 27, 29, and 32.

Table 11.2 displays the frequencies and means for each class of several types of artifacts, ecofacts, and features found on the room floors. These figures consistently indicate that more items and more kinds of items are found on the floors of hypothesized habitation rooms. These data strongly support the division of rooms into type on the basis of the occurrence of firepits. It should be noted that, in terms of the storage class, Room 29 is clearly an anomaly, which tends to inflate drastically the means of that class. However, the anomaly is less so when conditions of Room 29's use are considered. Because this room is inordinately large for a storage room and because it is the only storage room connected by an open doorway to an adjacent habitation room, one would expect a greater overlap of activities (that is, an intrusion of nonstorage, nonprocessing activities into the large, often empty space). In any event, whether or not one retains Room 29 within the storage class, a clear pattern of differentiation in room use is apparent, closely paralleling that found by Hill (1970a:48–56) at Broken K Pueblo.

Elsewhere, Hanson and Schiffer (1975:59–77) tentatively have assigned functions to rooms at the Joint Site; those assignments can now be updated. Table 11.3 displays the sequence of inferred uses I presently favor for all excavated rooms. Some discussion of the three discrepancies between entries in Table 11.3 and the earlier formulations is necessary. In all three instances, there is a change in interpretation of the initial use of the room. In Room 1 was found a small, floored-over firepit of a type not discovered elsewhere at the site. To Hanson and Schiffer (1975:59), this firepit indicated habitation activities. However, its small size suggests that it could not have been used in the same range of domestic activities as that of the larger firepits present in demonstrable habitation rooms. Further, the firepit could have been in use contemporary with the pre-room occupation surface that underlies Room 1. For these reasons, I see no need to postulate for Room 1 an early habitation function.

For Room 5, Hanson and Schiffer (1975) infer a sequence of four uses: storage, habitation, storage, and dump. The evidence for an early storage function consists of a floored-over, bell-shaped pit, similar to one found in the plaza at the Carter Ranch Site (Martin et al. 1964:46). Unfortunately, there is no justification for the inference that the pit was used prior to construction of the firepit in this room, nor is there unambiguous evidence that the firepit was constructed after, rather than at the same time, the room itself came into use. Because of these uncertainties, it is perhaps best to discount the early storage use of Room 5.

Room 29, previously assigned a storage function, is the second largest room at the site; it contains a variety of habitation debris and features, yet it has no firepit. In closely studying the floor photograph of this room (Hanson and Schiffer 1975:73), I noticed that there is a squarish depression in the large and shallow, amorphous pit occupying the center of the room. Such a depression could have occurred when an earlier firepit, perhaps constructed with the room, had been disassembled. On the basis of this admittedly slim evidence, I infer that Room 29 was used first for habitation activities. Overall, none of these changed

Table 11.3 Inferred Patterns of Room Use at the Joint Site[a]

Room	Use(s)	Room	Use(s)
1*	storage, dump	20	storage
2	storage, dump	21	habitation
3	storage	23	habitation
5*	habitation, storage, dump	24	habitation
7	storage, dump	25	storage
8	habitation	27	storage
9	storage	28	habitation
10	habitation	29*	habitation, storage
11	storage, dump	31	habitation
12	storage, habitation	32	storage
14	habitation	33	kiva
15	habitation	34	kiva
17	storage, dump	35	kiva, dump
		36	kiva, dump

[a]Multiple uses are listed early to late. An asterisk indicates a conflict in interpretation with room-use inferences in Hanson and Schiffer (1975).

interpretations has any far-reaching implications for inferring the occupational history of the site or for activity reconstruction.

In addition to habitation rooms, storage rooms, and kivas, several other major kinds of activity space are found at the Joint Site. Because many rooms were entered by the roof only (Wilcox 1975), the roof of the pueblo almost automatically would have become an activity area. Extramural areas of the site also contain past activity surfaces, as indicated by the firepits in Test Area 2 (Figure 7.4). In attempting to apply various transformations to the assemblage of chipped stone from the Joint Site, I consider the following kinds of activity areas to be of interest: roofs, habitation rooms, storerooms, kivas, and extramural areas.

OCCUPATIONAL HISTORY

Like most southwestern pueblos, the Joint Site was neither built nor abandoned in an instant. Using the information on abandonment sequence, presented in Chapter 10, and Wilcox's inferred sequence of room construction events, it is possible to approximate the occupational history of the site. My aim is to estimate when all habitation rooms were founded and abandoned. This exercise should provide data for determining the average number of households resident at the Joint Site, a figure that will be used repeatedly in the quantitative transformations presented in the following chapter.

At the outset, it is assumed that habitation rooms, those with firepits, correspond directly to the past locations of households. Although later habitation rooms may have sheltered larger, perhaps multifamily, households (Hanson 1975), that possibility will be ruled out of present calculations.

The first task at hand is to identify the habitation rooms among the unexcavated rooms (4, 6, 13, 16, 18, 22, 26, and 30). This determination can be made by applying to unexcavated rooms an established predictor, such as (inferred) floor area. Unfortunately, the previously derived cutoff point of 7.5 m^2 between habitation and storage rooms creates room classes with some anomalies. For example, Room 14, with floor area of only 7.2 m^2 would be identified as a storage room by area, yet it has a firepit. These anomalies result from an increase in floor area among late-constructed habitation rooms. A better predictor of room use is obtained by treating separately early- and late-constructed rooms. Only data from the large roomblock is used, since limited testing revealed that Room 26 has a firepit and Room 30 does not (Hanson and Schiffer 1975).

Included within the early-constructed class are all rooms except those in the northern second aggregation unit (6, 31, and 32) and the third aggregation unit (7, 8, 9, 10, and 15). The latter two sets of rooms comprise the late-constructed set. The southwestern second aggregation unit has been included in the early set because of a similarity in the shapes and sizes of rooms. When early-constructed rooms are plotted by measurements of floor area (or inferred floor area), a unimodal distribution with outliers is obtained. Despite the lack of multi-modality, some gratifying consistencies emerge when the presence or absence of firepits is noted:

at > 6.7 m^2, all excavated rooms have firepits;

at < 6.7 m^2, all excavated rooms do not have firepits;

at 6.7 m^2, one room has a firepit and one does not.

On the basis of these findings, I assign Rooms 4, 13, and 19 (< 6.7 m^2) to the storage class, and Rooms 16, 18, and 22 (> 6.7 m^2) to the habitation class.

A floor area plot of late-constructed rooms shows no marked modal tendencies. Again, however, regularities appear in the distribution when firepits are considered: Excavated rooms greater than 12 m^2 in floor area have firepits, but those below that figure do not. On the basis of this finding, Room 6, the only unexcavated room in the late-constructed set, is placed in the storage category.

One other habitation room needs to be accounted for. When Room 15 was subfloored, there were discovered the remains of a smaller room containing a firepit. For most purposes, this room, which was poorly excavated in the waning moments of the 1970 season, has not been taken into account. However, to obtain a reasonably accurate occupational history of the site, it is necessary to consider this additional habitation room, which I now label Room 37.

The second major task is determining the date when each habitation room was founded. From previous information, it was inferred that, in the large room-block, the core construction unit was founded in 1220 and the third aggregation unit was founded in 1239. On the average, then, approximately 6 years intervened between the construction of successive aggregation units. Assuming that the use of this 6-year average figure minimizes error, I estimate that the first aggregation units were built in 1226 and the second in 1232. Room 37 is grouped with the first aggregation unit. Room 17 of the second aggregation unit changed function from storage to habitation; it is assumed that this change occurred midway during the use of this room. No tree-ring dates were obtained from the small roomblock, nor does any other evidence illuminate the date of construction events there. It seems likely, though, that the large roomblock was already in existence when the smaller one was built; perhaps construction of the core unit of the latter was around 1226. Using the value of 6 years between construction units yields an estimated construction date of 1232 for the first aggregation unit of the small roomblock. It should be evident that this estimating procedure is not based on sound argument or evidence, although the magnitude of the error is probably not great.

The third and last major task is determining the abandonment dates of habitation rooms. This can be accomplished readily by setting up more definitive classes for habitation room abandonment than was done in Chapter 10, and assigning dates to them. Using the variables of fill sherd density, floor sherd density, presence or absence of reconstructable floor vessels, and evidence for change in function or disuse by superpositioning, four room abandonment classes (RAC) can be set up (data are presented in Table 10.1). From early to late abandonment, they are:

RAC I (Rooms 5, 29, and 37)
By stratigraphic and other evidence, it can be concluded that these rooms or their habitation functions had been abandoned early. In no case were reconstructable vessels present on the floors.

RAC II (Rooms 8, 12, 14, and 24)
By all evidence, it appears that these rooms were the next to be abandoned. They contain a fill sherd density greater than $125/m^2$, a floor sherd density of less than $7.6/m^2$, and have no reconstructable floor vessels.

RAC III (Rooms 23 and 28)
These rooms, with little evidence of secondary refuse in the fill and some evidence of de facto refuse, were next abandoned. They contain a fill sherd density of less than $125/m^2$, a floor sherd density greater than or equal to $7.6/m^2$, but there are no reconstructable vessels.

RAC IV (Rooms 10, 15, 21, and 31)

In these rooms, abundant de facto floor refuse and little secondary fill refuse indicate that they were the last to be abandoned. They have a fill sherd density of less than $125/m^2$ and a floor sherd density greater than $7.6/m^2$. In addition, restorable vessels were found on the floors.

A crude measure of abandonment rate, based on refuse production, can be used to derive the abandonment dates for RACs II–IV. (Rooms within RAC I are treated individually later.) It is assumed that, once abandonment of several rooms had occurred, secondary refuse was dumped in them in preference to the extramural secondary refuse areas. If this assumption holds even approximately, the ratio of total extramural to intramural secondary refuse should yield a measure of when, during the period of occupation, the change to intramural secondary refuse areas took place (assuming a constant rate of refuse production). For example, if room abandonment began at 1230, one would expect a large portion of the total secondary refuse generated by the community to be concentrated in room fills. However, if abandonment did not begin until 1260, the pattern should be reversed. This relationship between intramural and extramural secondary refuse and the date when room abandonments began can be expressed in equation form:

$$d = F + (F-A)\frac{E}{T}$$

where

d = date when room abandonments began;
F = date when site was founded (1220);
A = date when site was abandoned (1270);
E = total extramural secondary refuse;
T = total secondary refuse.

The techniques used to estimate E and T for chipped-stone artifacts are described in the next chapter. The values obtained are: $E = 393,158$ and $T = 406,974$. It must be noted that these totals include all refuse types. However, errors introduced by this procedure are likely to be relatively small, owing to the dearth of primary and de facto refuse. When these quantities are plugged into the equation, a date of 1268.3 is obtained. This result suggests that the abandonment of the Joint Site was quite rapid.

This estimate, it should be pointed out, is a limit and not a most probable date. It is quite likely that the dumping of some secondary refuse continued in extramural areas, even when intramural dumps were available. Further, since fewer households were contributing refuse during the last part of the occupation, it is likely that abandonment had begun before 1268, if we are to allow for the production of that quantity of refuse. To take into account both of these factors, which bias the obtained date to values nearer site abandonment, I

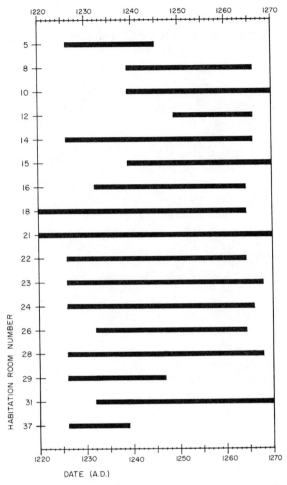

Figure 11.2 Estimated occupation span of all habitation rooms at the Joint Site.

assume that abandonment of rooms in RAC II began as early as 1266. This would allow a 2-year interval between RACs, such that the abandonment of RAC III was at 1268, and RAC IV at 1270.

The previous procedure permits one to estimate a date for the abandonment of all excavated habitation rooms in RACs II–IV; unexcavated rooms and rooms that changed function during occupation in RAC I call for special treatment. It has been inferred that the first uses of Rooms 5 and 29 and the last use of Room 12 were for habitation. A reasonable estimate of the abandonment date is obtained by assuming that habitation use accounts for one-half of each room's occupation period. For unexcavated rooms, the mean abandonment date of all rooms (except 37) was used (1264.3). It is assumed that Room 37 was abandoned at 1239, the year when Aggregation Unit 3 was constructed above its remains.

In Figure 11.2, the estimated occupation span of each habitation room (or habitation use of a room) has been plotted against the occupation span of the site. From that plot, it is possible to determine the average number of habitation rooms and, by extension, households present during the systemic context of the Joint Site: This is obtained by comparing the total number of household years represented by the occupation spans of all habitation rooms (575.2) with the maximum number possible (17 habitation rooms times 50 years). This is expressed as:

$$\frac{558.2}{850} = \frac{x}{17}.$$

Solving for x yields an average of 11.2 households present at the Joint Site. Many sources of error inhere in this estimate, although it is likely that some are cancelled out. At any rate, this figure represents a probable value, and is not likely to be biased strongly in one direction or the other.

SUMMARY

Compared to many of the Southwest's better-known pueblos, the Joint Site seems to have been occupied only briefly. Although the initial founding of the site is poorly dated, and abandonment is not securely dated, most evidence points to occupation during the 50-year period between A.D. 1220 and 1270. The pattern of space use appears to have been similar to the nearby and largely contemporary Broken K Pueblo; storage rooms, habitation rooms, and kivas were present, and other activities were carried out on roofs and in extramural areas. The community that occupied the pueblo was founded by 2 households in 1220, and grew during the following two decades by several large spurts until the peak population of 15 households was reached in the 1240s. Community size remained fairly constant until large-scale abandonments began around 1266. During the entire period of occupation, the average number of households present was 11.2.

12

Systemic Context
of the Chipped Stone

The purpose of this lengthy chapter is to describe the results of applying to the chipped stone from the Joint Site many of the principles and models developed in earlier chapters. The exercises should be considered as extended illustrations of the use of principles, since illumination of the systemic context of the chipped stone is the secondary, not primary, aim. Had the substantive aim received top priority, I would have examined many more lines of evidence and conducted numerous ancillary studies. Our journey into the systemic context begins with a qualitative examination of the differential use of chert, chalcedony, and quartzite. Differential usage is then examined quantitatively, in terms of flow rates, by using c-transforms from Chapter 5. Estimates of uselife for utility flake tools also are derived. An inferred increase in the flow rate of chalcedony during the end of occupation serves as a basis for explanation; quantitative c-transforms are used to generate multiple working hypotheses and their test implications. The final exercise focuses on identifying locations of activity performance by means of the secondary refuse transformation constructed in Chapter 6.

DIFFERENTIAL USE OF RAW MATERIALS

Hypothesis 1

In Chapter 9, I suggested the hypothesis that materials that are costlier in terms of procurement effort are used more economically than the accessible,

Table 12.1 Test Results for Hypothesis 1

	Flakes			Shatter			Flakes plus shatter		
	Utilized edges	Utilized pieces	Use-intensity index	Utilized edges	Utilized pieces	Use-intensity index	Utilized edges	Utilized pieces	Use-intensity index
Chert	5190	4199	1.24	1996	1819	1.10	7186	6018	1.19
Quartzite	515	434	1.19	248	240	1.03	763	674	1.13
Chalcedony	310	213	1.46	167	139	1.20	477	352	1.36

inexpensive materials. If raw materials are used more economically, they may be used more intensively. This will be revealed in the ratio of utilized edges to utilized pieces. With more intensive use, a higher index is obtained. The values for chert, chalcedony, and quartzite should vary, with chalcedony, the rarer material, having the highest use-intensity index value. In testing this hypothesis, site totals for all types were examined. These data are presented elsewhere (Schiffer 1973a: 270–273). The composite data on which the indices were based and the index values themselves are presented in Table 12.1. The results confirm the differential use hypothesis. In terms of flakes, shatter, and totals for both, the use-intensity index is considerably higher for chalcedony than for chert or quartzite. A χ^2 test of the raw counts is significant ($p < .05$).

Hypothesis 2

Earlier in this study, I discussed the variation in chipping properties of the three raw material types used at the Joint Site. If these differences were marked enough to affect the suitability of a material for use as one or another tool type, this should be reflected directly in the proportions of raw materials used for each type. Before testing this hypothesis, it should be remembered that the raw-material types discerned are only a coarse measure of the underlying variables of interest—flaking and use qualities. Fine-grained quartzite did occur, and granular chert was abundant. Chalcedony, however, was of consistently high quality.

To examine the differential use hypothesis, a series of *chi*-square tests was run. The raw counts of each material for a type were used as the observed values. The expected values were computed by multiplying the total tools of a type by the percentage of each raw material used in all tools at the site. The latter frequencies do not include fire-cracked rock (Type 1) or unutilized chipped stone

(Types 2–8). At the Joint Site, the following percentages of raw materials occur as tools:

chert	83.47%
quartzite	10.43%
chalcedony	6.10%

χ^2 tests were computed only when the total frequency of a tool type exceeded 50. This requirement was met by 34 types; of these, 28 tests were found to be significant at the .05 level or less. Before these results are interpreted further, a word of caution is in order. When large raw frequencies on the order of several hundred are dealt with, as is the case for many of the types examined, a statistically significant pattern can be generated by relatively minor differences in the percentage of raw materials. Thus, what is statistically significant may not be behaviorally significant. To reduce the possible importance of this factor, the following procedure was employed. In all cases of statistically demonstrated patterning, the contribution of each raw material to the χ^2 value was examined. If $(E-O)^2/O$ was greater than 3.0, then that raw material was being preferred or not preferred for the manufacture of that type, depending on whether the observed frequency (O) was greater or less than the expected (E). Also calculated were composite tool categories based on the frequencies of two or more types. In Table 12.2, the results of these determinations are presented.

Close examination of Table 12.2 reveals a number of general patterns of raw-material usage. There is a tendency for larger tools, such as large utilized flakes and shatter, to be made from quartzite. Quartzite also seems to have been less amenable to fine flaking of one sort or another. It was used only rarely for bifacial tools and was almost never retouched. Chalcedony, on the other hand, was highly favored for use in bifacially retouched tools, especially the small triangular projectile points. Chert and chalcedony are the most generalized materials in the sense that they seem to have been appropriate for almost all tool types (see also Rick and Gritzmacher 1970:13). As might be expected, when bifacial flaking or small tool manufacture was anticipated, the Joint Site artisans were more selective in the materials they used, preferring chert and especially chalcedony. On the other hand, when heavy-duty butchering or battering was anticipated, quartzite, a material less likely to shatter or fracture while under heavy stress, more often was used. Similar patterns of raw-material usage were observed by Rick and Gritzmacher (1970:18) for the Hay Hollow Valley through time.

When one considers the assemblage taken as a whole, however, it is seen that most of the commonest tool types—the small- and medium-size utilized flakes and shatter—were made of all raw materials. Although there is some variation, it seems that, for generalized cutting, scraping, and shredding tasks, all raw materials were suitable. These usage patterns accord well with the "opportunistic"

Table 12.2 Differential Use of Raw Materials at the Joint Site

	Preferred		Not preferred
Chert	31	11	28
	33	12	30
	34	13	49
	43	14	18 + 14
	All bifaces	18	
	(except 56)		
	34 + 38	26	
Quartzite	11	21	74
	12	31	All bifaces
	13	32	(except 56)
	14	33	34 + 38
	18	34	41 + 45
	26	35	43 + 47
	27	36	78
	28	38	
	30	41	
	49	43	
	18 + 14	45	
	24 + 28	48	
Chalcedony	25	22	
	26	24	
	28	34	
	48	41	
	74	42	
	43	49	
	24 + 28	All bifaces	
	34 + 38	(except 56)	
	42 + 46		
	43 + 47		

technology employed at the Joint Site. Nevertheless, a number of behaviorally significant patterns of differential raw-material usage have been identified. These seem to be related to constraints imposed by the nature of the material on manufacture or use qualities.

FLOW RATES

Archeologists are accustomed to comparing the occurrence of artifacts at different sites in terms of relative frequency. A more powerful measure of *behavioral* variability can be based on flow rate. Comparisons of flow rate not only overcome problems inherent in the use of relative frequencies, but also are amenable to a variety of more refined studies requiring standardized systemic context units.

Flow rate is measured with respect to a social unit, such as household or community. The flow rate of an artifact type for households in a community is given by the following equation, the derivation of which is presented as Equation (4) in Chapter 5:

$$T_D = f_D tc$$

where

T_D = total quantity of artifacts (of a type) discarded by the community;
f_D = rate at which artifacts are discarded by households;
t = duration of the discard process;
c = number of households.

By transposing terms, the variable of interest, f_D, can be isolated on the left side of the equation:

$$f_D = \frac{T_D}{tc}.$$

In subsequent calculations, the values for c and t (derived in Chapter 11) of 11.2 households and 50 years are used.

Calculations

In order to apply this equation, one must estimate T_D, the total artifacts of a type discarded at the Joint Site. Because chert, quartzite, and chalcedony do not decay in the Hay Hollow Valley, and other postdepositional disturbances would have had minimal quantitative effects, it is assumed that $T_D = T_e$ (T_e is the total present archeologically at the Joint Site). The use of probability sampling techniques makes it possible to estimate T_e from the recovered artifact samples. Total recovered artifacts, by type, from the large roomblock, small roomblock, and Phase I sample squares were multiplied by the reciprocal of the sampling fraction. (For example, a .5 sampling fraction requires that the sample be multiplied by a *correction factor* of 1/.5 or 2.0 to create an estimate of the total population.) In the large roomblock (including Room 34), 21 rooms were excavated from a total of 28, yielding a sampling fraction of .75. Artifact totals were multiplied by the correction factor of 1.33. The sampling fraction for the small roomblock (including Room 33) is .57, and the correction factor is 1.75. Because at least one sample square was excavated in each extramural stratum, the sampling fraction is actually 1/47, not 1/50; as a consequence, the correction factor is 47. The quantities produced by correction-factor treatment of the three samples were summed to obtain an estimated site total for each artifact type (see Appendix, Tables A.1–A.3).

Two composite artifact types, cores and use-modified flakes, can provide, respectively, approximations of manufacturing rates and utilization rates of each material type. Let us begin with cores. All recovered cores, whether or not they were modified by uses unrelated to flake detachment (for example, pounding, chopping), enter into this calculation. Thus, estimated site totals of artifact Types 2, 19, 20, 29, 30, 39 and 40 were summed to give an estimated total of recovered cores (T_e). For chert, this figure is 8073. When that quantity is introduced into the equation along with the previously determined values of t and c, we obtain:

$$f_D = \frac{8073 \text{ chert cores}}{(50 \text{ years})(11.2 \text{ households})}.$$

This equation reduces to 14.4 chert cores per household per year. The corresponding values of T_e for quartzite and chalcedony are 1277 and 277. Inserting these numbers into the formula produces an annual flow rate of 2.3 for quartzite and .5 for chalcedony.

The procedure applied to cores can be applied also to flakes. To perform this calculation, estimated site totals of use-modified flakes (Types 14, 24, 34, and 48 for each lithic material) were summed and plugged into the formula. The respective values of T_e for chert, quartzite, and chalcedony are 51,230, 4893, and 2503. The discard rates, expressed as use-modified flakes per household per year, prove to be 91.5, 8.7, and 4.5. It is likely that some flakes would have been removed from the Joint Site and used and discarded elsewhere; as a consequence, the flow rates are probably slight underestimates. In conjunction with the flow rates for cores, these results have several important implications for assessing the nature of the chipped-stone industry at the Joint Site and articulating it with other cultural subsystems.

Discussion

The present approach to measuring flow rates dovetails neatly with the recent emphasis on energetics in experimental archeology (e.g., Saraydar and Shimada 1973; Shimada n.d.), especially as these considerations relate to testing evolutionary–ecological models of behavioral change. In order to test such models, data are required on the energy expended in the performance of various activities. When coupled to flow rates of various artifact types, experimental data on task performance can provide a fairly accurate reflection of the properties of a past behavioral system. Although relevant experimental data are not available, I shall illustrate the process by dealing with the lithic procurement and manufacture subsystems. In the following discussion, it is assumed that the time devoted to a task accurately reflects the amount of energy invested in it.

In the first place, it reasonably can be inferred that the amount of effort spent in manufacturing unmodified chipped-stone tools was slight. The 17 cores (of all materials) used annually by a household easily could have been reduced to 105 flakes and assorted debitage by one person in less than an hour (J. Jeffrey Flenniken, personal communication, 1975). The only chipped-stone tools in which considerable effort was invested during manufacture were bifaces, especially arrow points. Flenniken's (personal communication, 1975) experimental research suggests that 10–20 minutes were required to modify flakes into arrow points. Thus, the annual manufacture of just 3–6 arrow points by a household would have equaled the effort spent in producing all unmodified tools. Because of the multiple discard and loss loci for bifacial tools (especially arrow points), of which the Joint Site is only one, more precise estimates of energy expended in biface manufacture will not be proffered. It is likely, however, that relative to simple reduction of cores to usable flakes, manufacture of bifacial tools required more of a household's annual energy budget.

Also noteworthy in these flow rates is the effort devoted to procurement. Clearly, the procurement of chert and quartzite required a negligible expenditure of energy, since these materials occur abundantly in the gravels that ring the pueblo. Even though the chalcedony was obtained from a distance of at least 1.5 miles, a household's yearly consumption could have been quarried and transported by one person in considerably less than an afternoon's work. Even more interesting is the inference that chalcedony sufficient for the annual consumption of the community also could have been procured with the same effort. This is so because the major effort involved was simply getting to and from the quarries.

If one is willing to accept the basic cultural–materialist principle that the nature of an organization is determined by (or at least is closely related to) the tasks it carries out (see Sanders and Price 1968; Harris 1968), then the above findings are relevant to identifying the type of organization responsible for procuring chalcedony; unfortunately, a lack of explicit, relevant correlates reduces considerably the rigor of this part of the exercise. Nevertheless, because the flow rate of chalcedony is so low, one would not expect chalcedony to have been obtained through a formal, multivillage trade network. (It should be noted that the simple presence of a material not locally available does not in itself provide evidence of trade, despite G. Wright's (1974:3) statement implying otherwise.) The possibility of trade also can be excluded on the basis of independent evidence. If a trade network distributed chalcedony (and, presumably, circulated other items), one would expect a gradual decrease of the consumption rate as the distance from the source increases, but that rate should not reach zero until other comparable resource loci or trade network boundaries are encountered. Rick and Gritzmacher (1970) provide some evidence bearing on this discussion. In surface samples from nine spatially and temporally varied sites in the Hay Hollow Valley (including the Joint Site), they found that the variable most closely related to the relative frequency of chalcedony was distance from the source. Their regression formula predicts, however, that the frequency of chalcedony drops to zero at about 2 miles, in locations where no outcrops of comparable material are found. Not only is this decrease in the consumption rate rapid when compared to the distribution of demonstrable trade items in the prehistoric Southwest—for example, Jeddito Polychrome, marine shell, and turquoise—but the apparent constancy of this pattern through time in the Hay Hollow Valley indicates that a more casual procurement mechanism was in operation, one that could be practiced by a variety of cultural systems (compare G. Wright 1974:4). The low volume of chalcedony moved and the scant distance it traveled suggest that the procurement system was no more complex than periodic visits to outcrops along Point of the Mountain by one or more individuals residing at the Joint Site.

Given the low flow rate of chalcedony and the fact that tools made of chert would suffice in the same tasks, one might ask why chalcedony was used at all. The answer seems to be that it was preferred for the manufacture of certain tool types, perhaps because of slightly better flaking qualities than those of chert or because its properties are more uniform and predictable. In the previous section (Table 12.2), it was shown that both chert and chalcedony are preferred for biface manufacture. A closer look at these data indicates that chalcedony was used in especially high rates for the manufacture of Types 53 and 57 (unbroken and broken arrow points): Of 51 total specimens, 19 were made of chalcedony. When flow rates based on estimated site totals are calculated, the pattern of preference stands out even more sharply: .54 chert points per household per year and .51 chalcedony points per household per year. For reasons mentioned earlier (multiple discard loci), these rates are far too low; nevertheless, they do indicate relative flow rates if it is assumed that loss or discard probability varied independently of material type. It would seem that chalcedony was procured primarily for the manufacture of arrow points; it may have been easier to pressure flake (Albert Goodyear, personal communication, 1975), or perhaps its homogeneous composition (compared to the available chert) lowered the probability of failure during the final stages of manufacture. Naturally, many other tool types were made from the waste products.

If chalcedony was the material preferred for making arrow points, one can reverse the previous question and ask why any were made of chert. An hypothesis to explain this, consistent with the inferred procurement behavior, is that points were made from chert when no chalcedony was on hand. This could have been a frequent occurrence if chalcedony were not stored in large quantities and especially if chalcedony were procured only when other activities brought an individual close to Point of the Mountain. The de facto refuse from late-abandoned habitation rooms can provide information about the extent that chalcedony was stored, assuming that it was stored (between procurement and manufacture and between episodes of use) in habitation rooms and that the de facto refuse there reflects approximately quantities stored. On the floors of Rooms 8, 10, 12, 14, 15, 21, 23, 28, and 31 (all in RACs II, III, and IV) there was recovered a total of only three chalcedony flakes and not a single core. (Room 24 was deleted from this analysis owing to the difficulty in identifying the floor; see Hanson and Schiffer 1975:71.) This finding of negligible chalcedony storage supports the hypothesis that chalcedony was procured intermittently in small amounts and, perhaps, during much of the time in any year, little of it was available for manufacture into tools. That chalcedony supplies were allowed to decrease in all habitation rooms to nearly zero supports the inference that other variables influenced the timing for procurement; for example, it may have occurred only when another activity, such as hunting, brought individuals near Point of the Mountain.

Another bit of information may be contained in the inferred low storage levels relevant to defining precisely the chalcedony procurement organization. If procurement were carried out independently by households, one might expect there to have been considerable variability in the amount of chalcedony in the de facto refuse in the last-abandoned habitation rooms, reflecting different times since procurement last took place. The contrary finding supports the inference that procurement ordinarily was simultaneous. This could have been the case if only one individual had the responsibility to procure and distribute the material of if the activity whose performance facilitated chalcedony procurement was participated in widely by members of the community. The latter possibility would be compatible with the hypothesis of group hunting activities. Another explanation is that the use of chalcedony simply had ceased during the Abandonment period; however, evidence is presented in the last section which shows that the use of chalcedony actually increased. For purposes of continued analysis, the inferences that chalcedony was procured by groups of males during hunting trips, primarily for the manufacture of projectile points, are retained.

USELIFE

The aim of the present analysis is to discover how long, on the average, tools of a given type were in the use process. This variable has been termed "uselife" (L), and will be estimated by applying Chapter 5's Equation (9) ($S = kc$) to de facto refuse in late-abandoned habitation rooms to derive a value for S. This quantity then will be plugged into Equation (5) ($T_D = St/L$) to yield an estimate of L. The reader may note that application of Equation (10) ($T_D = kct/L$) will yield L directly. There is, however, value in taking the more circuitous route in order to illustrate the derivation of intermediate variables.

Quite clearly, in order for this exercise to produce credible results, it must make use of tool types not likely to have been scavenged or curated. Although one cannot rule out the possibility that use-modified or potentially usable flakes were scavenged, especially in the case of chalcedony, it does seem reasonable to suppose that unmodified flakes would not have been curated. This inference is based on the c-transform stating that easily replaced, portable objects are probably not curated, when the means of transportation is limited to human energy and the distance to the next site is great. Of all the tool types, then, usable and use-modified flakes probably come closest to meeting the assumptions of this analysis. Also assumed, with somewhat less justification, is that all tools in use were stored in habitation rooms. Although this assumption is shaky, it is the only one possible on the basis of the limited evidence from de facto refuse on hand. However, it will be possible to assess the direction in which the results are skewed by this, and other, assumptions.

The de facto refuse examined came from the floors of Rooms 8, 10, 12, 14, 15, 21, 23, 28, and 31, all of which are contained in RACs II, III, and IV (Room 24, with its problematic floor, again has been deleted). Summary counts were made of Types 3, 8, 14, 24, 34, and 48 for all rooms, and then these tools were added to yield a new artifact class, that of use-modified or potentially usable flakes. Throughout the remainder of this section, they are referred to as *utility flakes.*

In the 9 habitation rooms containing de facto refuse, there was a total of 40 chert utility flakes. The number in use by a household (k) is simply equivalent to the mean number in de facto refuse, or 40/9, which equals 4.44. Use of this value (and 11.2 for c) in Equation (20) allows the derivation of S:

$$S = (11.2 \text{ households})(4.44 \text{ chert utility flakes/household})$$
$$S = 49.73 \text{ chert utility flakes.}$$

The estimated total of discarded chert utility flakes (T_D) is 80,601. When this value (and 50 for t) are entered into Equation (5), all the requisite information is present to solve for L:

$$80,601 \text{ chert utility flakes} = \frac{(49.73 \text{ chert utility flakes})(50 \text{ years})}{L}.$$

Transposing terms, we arrive at:

$$L = \frac{(49.73 \text{ chert utility flakes})(50 \text{ years})}{80,601 \text{ chert utility flakes}}$$

$$L = .031 \text{ years.}$$

Multiplying the latter quantity by 365 days per year yields an estimated uselife for chert utility flakes of 11 days.

The same procedure was followed in deriving L for quartzite and chalcedony artifacts. With values of 12.43 for S and 7081 for T_D, the uselife of quartzite utility flakes is estimated at 32 days; that of chalcedony is 21 days when $S = 3.70$ and $T_D = 3182$. In these calculations, it also has been assumed that no postabandonment collecting took place.

One should not build too many inferences on these fragile quantities. Nevertheless, the estimates of uselife for chert and quartzite are probably within an order of magnitude, and give some indication, however coarse, of the average time a utility flake was in the use process. The uniformly sparse distribution of chalcedony utility flakes among rooms within all abandonment classes suggests that the de facto refuse was not scavenged, on the assumption that the very latest rooms could not have been scavenged and would, therefore, contain appreciably more artifacts. However, it is also possible to interpret this pattern as resulting from both extensive scavenging and a lack of chalcedony procurement during the *very* latest use of the site. This latter explanation is consistent with previous inferences. Thus, the uselife of chalcedony utility flakes should be considered the most suspect of the three estimates.

The likelihood that utility flakes also were stored outside habitation rooms has not been taken into account in the present analysis because de facto refuse could not be isolated in other activity areas (except in storage rooms and kivas, which had few floor artifacts and were not placed in room-abandonment classes). The effects of additional storage on uselife can be determined by examining Equation (5). As S increases, which would be the case when other artifacts are in use, L decreases proportionately. Quite clearly, scavenging, curate behavior, postabandonment collecting, and other, uncounted de facto refuse artifacts all tend to yield values of S that are too low, thus overestimating uselife. It also should be pointed out that these estimates of uselife clearly do not take into account the possibility that many activities would have occurred more frequently during certain seasons. This factor, too, would bias estimates of uselife upward. A warranted conclusion from the present analysis is that the uselives of chert, quartzite, and chalcedony utility flakes were on the order of several weeks, probably less. Variations between uselives for the different materials cannot be evaluated meaningfully.

EXPLAINING CHANGE IN CHALCEDONY USE

An explanatory challenge that often confronts the archeologist is quantitative variability in the relative frequency of artifact types through space or time. In

Chapter 5, it was pointed out that explanations for these phenomena usually have been couched in vague terms like differences in "popularity," which convey no behaviorally meaningful information about the determinants of variability. In the following analysis, one instance of variability, an increase in the flow rate of chalcedony relative to chert and quartzite during the Abandonment period (ca. 1266–1270), serves as a focus for explanatory attempts. With Equation (12) of Chapter 5 ($F_D = kcf_U/b$), it is shown how quantitative c-transforms can generate multiple working hypotheses to explain variability. Testing of the hypotheses, although not definitive in any sense, does yield interesting information about changes in behavior during the last years of occupation at the Joint Site.

Changes in Flow Rate of Chalcedony

An obvious place to look for change is in patterns of use of the three raw materials (see also Osborne 1965). Quite clearly, because secondary refuse areas at the Joint Site cannot be precisely dated, we can hope only to document and explain *relative* change in material usage. In order to carry out this study, it is first necessary to associate secondary refuse deposits with the gross occupation periods of the site. This can be achieved, in a coarse way, by making several assumptions about depositional patterns:

1. During the Main Occupation period, when all rooms were still occupied (except 37), secondary refuse was deposited only in extramural areas.
2. During the Abandonment period, which began after the first rooms were abandoned and lasted until the site was vacated totally, secondary refuse was deposited mainly in empty rooms.

From these assumptions, the following conclusions can be drawn: Extramural deposits contain secondary refuse primarily from the Main Occupation period, but secondary refuse in room fill consists exclusively of Abandonment period refuse. (This model of refuse disposal should apply to all pueblo sites that had a single occupation.) Because the Abandonment period at the Joint Site probably lasted fewer than 4 years, extramural deposits contain relatively little Abandonment period refuse. One factor overlooked in this model is the contribution that primary refuse of the Abandonment period from extramural areas can make to the inferred early totals. It is likely that this would cause negligible skewing in the case of the Joint Site, in view of the limited amount of primary refuse likely to be contained in the extramural sample units. Thus, we have an excellent opportunity to study the use of material during two major periods of site occupation.

To obtain an artifact sample for the Main Occupation period, materials from Phase I and II sample squares were combined by type. The trash fill from Rooms 1, 2, 5, 7, 11, and 17 comprise the sample of Abandonment period refuse. When

Table 12.3 Changes in Use of Raw Materials at the Joint Site

Material	Count per period		Percentage per period (of total artifacts)	
	Main Occupation	Abandonment	Main Occupation	Abandonment
Chert	11,692	3,696	88.42	82.52
Quartzite	1,084	499	8.20	11.14
Chalcedony	447	284	3.38	6.34

the two periods are compared by artifact percentage of each material, a striking trend emerges: Relative to chert and quartzite, the flow rate of chalcedony increases by a factor of nearly 2 during the Abandonment period (Table 12.3). Also apparent is a trend toward the increasing use of quartzite. For purposes of continued analysis, it is assumed that the household flow rate of all chipped-stone artifacts was approximately constant during the two occupation periods. This assumption cannot be tested presently without circular uses of the data, given the latter's previously mentioned limitations. Nevertheless, of the assumptions that can be made, constant household flow rate of total chipped stone is probably the least objectionable.

The reader may have noted that the procedures used until now suggest only that a change took place in the relative amounts of chalcedony used and discarded; at no time has it been shown that an increase occurred in the rate of procurement. This is an important point, for it does not follow that a higher rate of use and discard necessarily leads to a higher rate of procurement. That would be true only if the occurrence of scavenging and re-use could be ruled out. It is to that task that we now turn.

If chalcedony were being scavenged during the Abandonment period from Main Occupation secondary refuse deposits, one would expect the following:

1. Less procurement would be reflected directly in less manufacture; there-fore, there should be a decrease in the relative amount of unused chalcedony debitage.
2. There should be an increase in the ratio of chalcedony tools to all chipped-stone artifacts, assuming that scavenged artifacts would have a greater likelihood of being used in tasks.
3. If used artifacts as well as unused debitage were being scavenged, there would be expected a dramatic increase in the use-intensity index of chalcedony.
4. If scavenged artifacts were selected for potential suitability in various tasks, it would be expected that flakes would have been preferred over shatter, and, thus, the ratio of chalcedony flakes to shatter should increase.

These implications can be examined readily with available data.

The evidence strongly contradicts the first test implication. The ratio of unutilized debitage to all chipped-stone artifacts increases from 2.21 to 3.26. When that index is divided into large and small debitage, the pattern remains the same, thereby excluding the possibility that scavenging had depleted the extramural deposits of unused debitage (one would not expect minishatter and trim flakes to have been scavenged). This finding suggests that there was an actual increase in chalcedony procurement.

The second implication is confirmed by an increase in the ratio of chalcedony tools to all artifacts from 1.17 to 3.08. This is not unexpected, since it is consistent with either the scavenging or procurement hypothesis; although, in conjunction with the previous index, it does indicate that more tools were being discarded during the Abandonment period than can be accounted for by the debitage present. This is based on the assumption that the ratio of tools to unutilized debitage ought to remain approximately constant.

Evidence for the third test implication is presented in Table 12.4, and it suggests a more intensive use of the material, which would be consistent with the hypothesis that some scavenging took place. An increase in the intensity of use of the other materials, although very slight, is also observable. The last implication provides definitive evidence for the occurrence of scavenging: The ratio of utilized flakes to utilized shatter increases from 1.11 to 1.84. (It also should be mentioned that similar patterns were observed, in attenuated form, for the other two materials, suggesting that they too were being scavenged to some extent.) In conclusion, it appears that, although there was an increase in chalcedony procurement during the Abandonment period, considerable use was made of previously discarded artifacts.

Explanations of Change in Flow Rate

The terms in Equation (12) directly suggest possible explanations for a change in the flow rate of chalcedony, with one exception: Change in flow rate is independent of c, since the measure of change already has been standardized with respect to c. Let us take each variable in turn and generate several hypotheses.

1. If k increased (more chalcedony tools in use per household), then F_D would increase. A change in k could be brought about by use of chalcedony in a wider range of tasks by most households, or by a more widespread use of chalcedony among households.

2. If f_U increased (higher use rate of chalcedony by households), then F_D would increase. A change in f_U might arise from a higher rate of task performance, or by the use of chalcedony tools in a larger variety of tasks.

Table 12.4 Changes in the Use-Intensity Index from the Main Occupation to Abandonment Period

	Flakes				Shatter				Total	
	Main Occupation		Abandonment		Main Occupation		Abandonment			
Material	Flakes	Index	Flakes	Index	Shatter	Index	Shatter	Index	Main Occupation	Abandonment
Chert	1506	1.23	939	1.25	820	1.07	316	1.16	1.18	1.23
Quartzite	153	1.16	124	1.23	104	1.07	51	1.02	1.12	1.17
Chalcedony	59	1.36	59	1.63	53	1.09	32	1.31	1.23	1.52

3. If b decreased (fewer uses per tool), then F_D would rise. A decrease in b could be caused by a change in the tasks in which chalcedony tools were used, or by a decrease in the efficiency of tool use.

The possible explanations that are implied by changes in the variables k, f_U, and b can be reduced to a set of four testable hypotheses:

1. The efficiency of the use of chalcedony tools decreased.
2. Chalcedony tools were in more widespread use among households.
3. The range of tasks involving chalcedony tools increased.
4. Chalcedony tools were used for the same tasks, but the rate of task performance increased.

It should be noted that none of these explanations are excluded on an a priori basis by any of the others. It is certainly conceivable that more than one factor contributed to a change in the flow rate of chalcedony, and the present exercise allows us to examine this possibility and to appreciate the complex linkages between systemic variables.

Tests and Test Implications

HYPOTHESIS 1

Of all the hypotheses, the first is most easily subjected to test. A less efficient use of tools should be reflected readily in the use-intensity index, since, as the number of uses per tool decreased, so too would the number of utilized edges per tool. It is assumed that the efficiency of use would have been more or less constant among the range of tool types. In Table 12.4, use-intensity indices for the Main Occupation and Abandonment periods have been presented. The index demonstrates that, contrary to the expectations of Hypothesis 1, chalcedony use (both flakes and shatter) appears to have become more efficient during the Abandonment period. Of course, the scavenging that occurred also raises this index; nevertheless, the occurrence of scavenging itself suggests, if anything, a trend toward more efficient use of chalcedony tools. Hypothesis 1 is rejected.

HYPOTHESIS 2

This hypothesis is least amenable to direct archeological test, so an indirect method is used. Direct testing would require, for each period, comparable sets of de facto refuse. Such data are not available, and test implications are not formulated easily for secondary refuse deposits. However, previous discussion on the nature of chalcedony procurement suggests that, although k was at a high value during the Abandonment period, the pattern of procurement and, thus, distribution probably was no different in the two periods. Even so, it is possible to show how slight shifts in other variables might lead, in effect, to an increase in k. This could occur, for example, if there were a change in the probability that members of a given household would join in a group hunt and procure chalcedony during the year. This scenario is consistent with earlier inferences, and cannot be excluded, given the available evidence.

If it is assumed that the amount of chalcedony procured throughout the year depended only on the number of adult males present in the village, but chert and quartzite procurement depended, in part, on the number of adult females present, then a change in the adult sex ratio would affect k, perhaps only to a very small extent. An alteration in k also could be effected by a change in the sexual composition of households (for example, polygynous to monogamous) or by short-term, essentially stochastic fluctuations in the developmental cycle of domestic groups (and marital residence patterns). It is interesting to note here that variability in k can reflect both organizational change and stochastic, nonchange processes.

Some evidence is at hand by which to assess the organizational hypothesis. As noted in Chapter 11, there seems to be an increase through time in the size of habitation rooms. Even though the change in habitation rooms begins considerably before the onset of the Abandonment period, it may have been a contributory factor. Hanson (1975:99) has noted the trend toward construction of habitation rooms with two firepits, and suggests that they reflect occupation by "more than one nuclear family." In that event, it is unlikely that the ratio of males to females would increase. A test of this hypothesis on male- and female-associated tools is precluded by the lack of comparable de facto refuse from the Main Occupation and Abandonment periods.

Using several methods of population estimation (cf. Hill 1970a: 75–77) reveals that the community that occupied the Joint Site always consisted of fewer than 150 people; therefore, it would have been exogamous (Tuggle 1970)—especially during the Abandonment period. Thus, any sexual bias in the exchange of males and females, particularly when the population was declining, could lead to a relative increase in the number of males and, thus, more chalcedony use. On the other hand, one can imagine a situation in which, during much of the Main Occupation period, there may have been a bias in favor of one sex which was reduced or reversed when growth ceased during the Abandonment period. Quite clearly, this process, and random fluctuations in sex ratios at birth or preferential infanticide, would have had delayed effects on patterns of chalcedony use. Although none of these explanations can be tested presently, they are included here to indicate the broad range of social processes that can influence patterns of chipped-stone procurement and use (see also Rock n.d.). Although Hypothesis 2 cannot be excluded, the contribution that any of these variables might make to changes in chalcedony flow rate is likely to be small in the present case.

HYPOTHESIS 3

If chalcedony tools were being used in more and different tasks, one would expect them to occur in a greater variety of types. Since most tool types were

Table 12.5 Changes in the Variety of Tools Made
from Chalcedony

	Period	
Tools	Main Occupation	Abandonment
Use-modified	14	19
Manufacture-modified	16	9
Total	30	28

probably multipurpose to begin with, this test implication is weak, but worth examining. Table 12.5 displays the number of different tool types, use-modified and manufacture-modified, from the two periods. The totals reveal no marked trend in either direction, but the subtotals provide a glimpse of change, not easily interpreted. It appears that, although chalcedony was being funneled into fewer manufacture-modified types, flakes and cores were used in a wider variety of tasks. One explanation for these seemingly contradictory results is that the greater number of utility flakes and exhausted cores generated during the latter period would have been used opportunistically, in preference to other materials, in the range of tasks for which they were suited by size, morphology, and use qualities. Given the increase in the use-intensity index, this explanation—which presupposes no change in tasks carried out—is certainly plausible. Thus, it seems that there was an increased use of chalcedony for fewer types of manufacture-modified tools. This finding, of course, tends to eliminate Hypothesis 3.

HYPOTHESIS 4

The last hypothesis requires that there be found evidence of an increase in the performance rate of the various tasks in which chalcedony tools were used. The results obtained from testing Hypothesis 3 suggest, however, that only the tasks involving manufacture-modified tool types, those for which the chalcedony specifically was procured, ought to be considered. Based on all previous information, then, Hypothesis 4 states essentially that there was an increase in the rate of hunting by groups of males.

If hunting increased, assuming that more hunting means retrieval of more animals, the ratio of food species to total chipped-stone tools should increase appreciably between the Main Occupation and Abandonment periods. In Table 12.6, the ratio of the total number of identifiable bones (of the five most common food species) to the total number of stone tools is presented for the two periods. Quite clearly, the ratio increases by a factor of at least 10 for all species. On the basis of this evidence, one might be justified in accepting Hypothesis 4 without further ado. Unfortunately, there is at least one questionable assumption inherent in the previous test which renders the results somewhat

Table 12.6 Ratios of Bone to Chipped Stone in Main Occupation and Abandonment Period Refuse

	Period	
Species	*Main Occupation*	*Abandonment*
Antilocapra americana	.0054	.0480
Odocoileus hemionus	.0028	.0831
Lepus californicus	.0146	.6030
Sylvilagus auduboni	.0781	2.0951
Cynomys gunnisoni	.0093	.2393

less definitive: Conditions of preservation were the same in extramural and intramural deposits.

The occurrence of many different large and small bones in both kinds of deposits suggests that the soils themselves clearly are conducive to bone preservation; otherwise, only fragments of the most durable elements (for instance, mandibles) would have remained in the extramural deposits. One variable in which the extramural and intramural deposits do differ is the amount of exposure to the environment, including scavenging animals. It is probable that the only bone preserved in extramural deposits was covered over quickly by additional refuse. Bone left on the surface, even in an arid environment, will deteriorate. At the Hay Hollow Site, Fritz (1974:412–413) reports that few bones were found, and he postulates a similar mechanism of exposure and deterioration. At present, there seems to be no way of correcting for this decay process. The apparently positive test results must be considered suspect until additional evidence is evaluated.

If hunting had increased, one also might expect there to have been a corresponding increase in the gathering of plant resources. At Broken K Pueblo, for example, Hill found evidence that, under the stress of less reliable agricultural inputs (induced by a slight environmental shift), the inhabitants had expanded their dependence on wild plant foods (Hill 1970a:90–91). It is likely that, at the Joint Site, a similar behavioral change may have followed the onset of subsistence stresses at about the same time. Hill's (1970a:92) inference of increasing difficulty in hunting at late Broken K should be noted but cannot be evaluated, owing to a possible lack of comparability in analytic units. Hevly (personal communication) has adduced some evidence suggesting that, during the late stages of Joint Site occupation, there was an increased dependence on wild plant foods. Unfortunately, most of the refuse analyzed by Hevly probably belongs to the Abandonment period, and, thus, the inference of change in dependence is not demonstrated. Even so, he has shown that there was reliance during the

Abandonment period on a considerable variety of wild plants for food, many of whose use (for instance, *Opuntia*) suggest that secondary subsistence resources were being exploited. It is also noteworthy that more species of animal are represented in the Abandonment period refuse than in that from the Main Occupation (16 to 12). Although some of the former are more likely to have been introduced nonculturally, this finding is consistent with the inferred pattern of a diversified, stress-related exploitive regime.

By now, it should be apparent that a test to exclude decisively Hypothesis 4 cannot be performed for lack of comparable analytic units (see Reid's [1973] telling discussion of a similar dilemma with data from the Grasshopper Ruin). However, it is possible to predict that, if hunting increased, so too did butchering and, consequently, the tools associated with processing of animals and their by-products. One then might expect a corresponding increase in the flow rate of tools used in those activities. It has been observed already that the flow rate of quartzite, a material preferred for large flake and cobble tools, increased during the Abandonment period. The latter tool types have been interpreted as possibly serving in heavy-duty butchering or battering tasks. Although this evidence could be questioned because of the chronic imprecision in identifying uses, it does provide tantalizing, if tentative, support for Hypothesis 4.

On the basis of all lines of evidence considered, it seems judicious to retain Hypothesis 4. As mentioned earlier, however, more than one factor could have caused a change in the flow rate of chalcedony. It is to a consideration of the linkages between causal variables that I now turn, in an attempt to summarize tidily what has been learned thus far.

Summary

It seems as though the environmental conditions conducive to subsistence agriculture in the Hay Hollow Valley deteriorated considerably during the second half of the thirteenth century. In response to the stresses created by a high rate of crop failure or by reductions in available agricultural products, the inhabitants of the Joint Site diversified their procurement strategies to include more species of wild foods, and a greater dependence on the wild foods ordinarily consumed. The heavier emphasis on hunting brought with it a greater demand for arrow points and other hunting and butchering tools. Because the increased rate of hunting by groups of males resulted in more trips to the vicinity of Point of the Mountain, chalcedony, a material favored for the manufacture of arrow points, was retrieved more frequently. Often, however, chalcedony was unavailable and secondary refuse areas were searched for flakes that could be manufactured into tools. This activity frequently turned up usable flakes of chert and quartzite, and these, too, were scavenged. With more cooperative hunting by groups of males, probably for antelope, deer, and rabbit (see Fritz 1974), the toolkit for manufacture and maintenance of hunting and butchering gear became more standardized and streamlined, resulting in a slight reduction in the range of modified tools. On the other hand, more abundant chalcedony at some times meant a greater availability of utility flakes and cores, which found use in a wider range of tasks. The increased usage of butchering tools caused an increase in the flow rate of quartzite, out of which some butchering tools probably were made. It is likely also that, because of the increased rate of hunting, more households had some chalcedony in use than at earlier times.

No claim is made that the preceding account is an accurate description of the causes for the change in flow rate of chalcedony at the Joint Site. It is simply a synthesis of the available inferences, consistent with the evidence presented. The primary purpose of this exercise has been, after all, simply to illustrate the use of quantitative c-transforms in generating multiple working hypotheses. That purpose has been served admirably and, one hopes, something has been learned also about the circumstances surrounding change in the flow rate of chalcedony at the Joint Site.

ACTIVITY LOCATIONS

In Chapter 6, a transformation model was developed for use on deposits of secondary refuse. Its aim is to identify the sets of artifacts used in the same type of activity area. If different types of activity areas contributed refuse differentially to the secondary refuse deposits, clusters of artifacts related to activity sets will be detectable by factor analysis of artifact counts in the secondary refuse samples. Information obtained from the previous analyses on the systemic context of the chipped stone can guide interpretation of the results.

The number of deposits of unquestionable secondary refuse at the Joint Site is somewhat small, on the order of 13. These areas include the trash fills of Rooms 1, 2, 5, 7, 11, and 17, although there is really very little material in Room 2. Also included as secondary refuse areas are the extramural middens depicted on the site map (Figure 7.2). In order to increase the number of cases for input to the SPSS factor analysis (Nie, Bent, and Hull 1970), the following set of procedures was employed.

The total type counts for each sample square, both Phases 1 and 2, were tallied by computer. The total counts of each provenience type within rooms was calculated likewise. These provenience types include: roof artifacts, trash fill, roof and trash mix, above floor but not secondary refuse fill or roof artifacts, on floor, subfloor level, on subfloor occupation surface, and unknown but above floor. The computer then was programmed to cull from the sample square and room data only those cases for which the total number of artifact Types 4 and 34 exceeded 10. The 73 cases thus produced formed the preliminary body of data.

Quite clearly, many of these cases may not be secondary refuse. To reduce this set to certain and suspected secondary refuse proveniences, the criterion of case inclusion was made more stringent. By increasing the requisite total of artifact Types 4 and 34 to greater than 50, the case number was lowered to 33, still considerably greater than 13, however. These case reduction procedures were effected by use of the *select if* statements built into the SPSS program package (Nie, Bent, and Hull 1970).

The question, then, is: With how much confidence may these 20 additional proveniences be considered to contain secondary refuse? A listing of the cases (Table 12.7) reveals some gratifying consistencies. With the exception of Room 5, only two provenience types, trash fill and roof, are represented. The demonstration that ceramics and now lithics were deposited on roofs suggests that the outputs of a wide variety of activities are being dealt with. This increases the probability that such refuse is secondary but really does not demonstrate it.

As for the sample squares, several patterns emerge. A number of squares fall within the same secondary refuse area (for example, S7W4, S7W5, and S7W6), but others fall within areas of less concentrated refuse. It is not possible to

Table 12.7 Proveniences Used as the Thirty-Three Cases for the SPSS Factor Analysis

Rooms	Sample squares, Phase 1	Sample squares, Phase 2
R5, trash fill	S7W4	Sq. 1
R5, subfloor levels	S7W5	Sq. 2
R7, trash fill	S7W6	Sq. 3
R8, roof	S12W8	Sq. 4
R10, roof	S4E11	Sq. 5
R11, trash fill	S6E11	Sq. 8
R15, roof	N9W9	Sq. 9
R17, trash fill	N11W7	
R29, roof	N12W6	
R31, roof	N1E10	
	N8E4	
	N10E11	
	N13E11	
	N14E6	
	N15E17	
	N19E3	

demonstrate unequivocally that these deposits too are secondary refuse, but the fact that they occur in extramural areas suggests that at least some of them may be. If they are primary refuse, the transformation model should be largely unaffected, unless certain specialized activities were conducted in highly restricted locations that produced only primary refuse.

In choosing the variables to include in the analysis, one finds that the number of possible chipped-stone type combinations in a minimum of 200 factorial. Given this large number of variable combinations, plus the additional possibility of variable modifications, there could be demonstrated pretty well whatever one desires—if one had the time to experiment. In order to illustrate use of the secondary refuse transformation, I shall not have to bore the reader with a description of the trials and tribulations and programming errors that accompanied the early runs; instead, I shall summarize briefly the few patterns that did emerge from these preliminary analyses, to provide a background to the final factor analysis reported here in detail.

On the basis of about a dozen SPSS factor analyses, many of them differing only trivially in the variables chosen, three or four interpretable factors usually emerged, although sometimes as many as six total factors were produced. The "interpretable" factors tended to indicate that the unutilized by-products of tool manufacture behaved differently with regard to raw-material type. In addition, some runs showed that many large tool types behaved differently from the mass of small tool types. In short, a case could be made that elements of activity sets had been isolated on the basis of the secondary refuse transformation. I now report the results of perhaps the simplest analysis conducted. It is simple because it requires the fewest assumptions to justify the variables that were included, only some of which were modified.

The variables examined are composed primarily of utilized flakes and shatter, unutilized by-products of tool manufacture, and other tool types that occur in relative abundance. The counts of flakes and shatter within edge-angle size classes were combined for each type of raw material. The chert and chalcedony totals then were summed. Quartzite tools, have slightly different use qualities, were kept separate in the analysis. The unutilized by-products of chipping activities were kept segregated by raw material, but several infrequently occurring debitage types were deleted. In Table 12.8, the variables used in the analysis and their SPSS factor analysis labels are listed; the modifications used to generate composite variables also are shown. The raw data input to the factor analysis are presented elsewhere (Schiffer 1973a: 285–291).

The specific technique applied was principal component factor analysis (PA2), with all default options in effect, from the SPSS repertoire (Nie, Bent, and Hull 1970). Varimax rotation was employed. The results of this analysis, which yielded five factors, are displayed in Table 12.9.

The results of this analysis can be presented in a simpler form. This is achieved by determining a minimum value of factor loading below which variables are

Table 12.8 Chipped-Stone Variables Used in the SPSS Factor Analysis[a]

SPSS variable label	Joint Site chipped-stone type number		
	Chert	Quartzite	Chalcedony
VAR008	2		
VAR009	3		
VAR010	4		
VAR011	5		
VAR012	6		
VAR013	7		
VAR014	8		
VAR082	78		78
VAR086		2	
VAR087		3	
VAR088		4	
VAR089		5	
VAR091		7	
VAR092		8	
VAR164			2
VAR166			4
VAR167			5
VAR169			7
VAR170			8
LGHI	11, 15		11, 15
LGMED	12, 16		12, 16
LGLO	13, 17		13, 17
MEDHI	21, 25		21, 25
MEDMED	22, 26		22, 26
MEDLO	23, 27		23, 27
SMHI	31, 35		31, 35
SMMED	32, 36		32, 36
SMLO	33, 37		33, 37
QLGHI		11, 15	
QLGMED		12, 16	
QLGLO		13, 17	
QMEDHI		21, 25	
QMEDMED		22, 26	
QMEDLO		23, 27	
QSMHI		31, 35	
QSMMED		32, 36	
QSMLO		33, 37	
HAMCOB	49	49	
HAMCOR	30	30	30
RETSCR	74		74
SMNOTCH	78		78
SAW	63		63

[a]When two or more Joint Site types appear in the same row, they have been added to yield the corresponding SPSS variable.

Table 12.9 Results of Factor Analysis of Joint Site Chipped Stone

Variable	Factor 1	Factor 2	Factor 3	Factor 4	Factor 5
VAR008	.149	.287	.797	.081	.325
VAR009	.224	.303	.884	.128	.010
VAR010	.345	.467	.764	.024	−.233
VAR011	.230	.655	.656	.185	−.063
VAR012	.411	−.124	.671	.425	.284
VAR013	.285	.486	.737	.193	.041
VAR014	.257	.660	.570	.369	.094
VAR082	.865	.064	−.015	−.087	.050
VAR086	.005	.277	.463	.715	.113
VAR087	.211	.530	.318	.067	−.205
VAR088	.509	.351	.617	.192	−.309
VAR089	.189	−.135	.454	.461	−.083
VAR091	.606	.419	.624	.011	−.112
VAR092	.357	.511	.521	.426	.000
VAR164	.168	.809	.001	.228	.025
VAR166	.372	.823	.316	.127	−.160
VAR167	.223	.856	.276	.055	−.022
VAR169	.469	.732	.277	−.165	.202
VAR170	.191	.792	.160	.357	−.105
LGHI	.503	.745	.135	.144	.116
LGMED	.844	.264	.066	.358	−.052
LGLO	.769	.230	.213	.237	.037
MEDHI	.494	.699	.372	.220	−.056
MEDLO	.894	.305	.199	.186	.078
SMHI	.486	.568	.584	−.039	−.186
SMMED	.763	.469	.362	−.001	−.016
SMLO	.829	.355	.391	.089	.007
QLGHI	.543	.604	.038	.153	.047
QLGMED	.604	.462	.380	.439	−.076
QLGLO	.612	.178	.160	.584	−.020
QMEDHI	.532	.134	.593	−.203	.112
QMEDMED	.866	.319	.256	.042	.021
QMEDLO	.718	.319	.356	.428	.092
QSMHI	−.071	−.009	.659	.218	−.053
QSMMED	.787	.292	.214	−.031	−.087
QSMLO	.816	.329	.359	.094	−.169
HAMCOB	.509	.678	.049	.249	.168
HAMCOR	.695	.461	.077	.117	.242
RETSCR	.232	.883	.230	−.089	.085
SMNOTCH	.381	.269	.434	.260	.380
SAW	.167	.775	.099	.233	.077
Percentage of variance explained	72.2	10.3	9.9	5.1	2.5

Table 12.10 The SPSS Variables That Load at .60 or above on Each of the Five Factors

Factor 1	Factor 2	Factor 3	Factor 4	Factor 5
VAR082	VAR011	VAR008	VAR086	none
VAR091	VAR014	VAR009		
LGMED	VAR164	VAR010		
LGLO	VAR166	VAR011		
MEDLO	VAR167	VAR012		
SMMED	VAR169	VAR013		
SMLO	VAR170	VAR088		
QLGMED	LGHI	VAR091		
QLGLO	MEDHI	QSMHI		
QMEDMED	QLGHI			
QMEDLO	HAMCOB			
QSMMED	RETSCR			
QSMLO	SAW			
HAMCOR				

excluded from factors. The remaining variables then can be listed with the factors on which they load above this specified value. Setting this cutoff factor loading at .60 reveals some rather definite patterns in the first three factors but also results in the loss of Factors 4 and 5 (Table 12.10).

Factor 1 contains a large sampling of utilized flakes and utilized shatter of all sizes and all except the steepest edge angles. Also included are a single unifacially retouched tool, battered cores, and quartzite waste shatter. In short, all but one of these types has been used. If one refers back to Chapter 9, where the use potentials of the Joint Site tool types are presented (Table 9.9), some general inferences about the activities in which these artifacts took part can be proffered.

Most of these tools may have been used for light-, medium-, and heavy-duty cutting and scraping, possibly on skin, meat, hides, wood, and plant fiber. Battered cores could have been used to roughen the grinding surface of metates or to break bone. Clearly, these activities probably comprise most of the major tasks that would have been performed within a sedentary community practicing a mixed subsistence strategy. For this reason and because Factor 1 accounts for the lion's share of the variance (72.2%), I suggest that these activities were performed in most activity areas. This is in accordance with the results of transforming simulated secondary refuse data (Chapter 6). In that analysis, it was learned that, when more than 20% of an assemblage was used in all activity areas, the first factor contains all of the elements held in common by the activity areas. This would seem to be a parsimonious as well as plausible explanation for the observed patterns.

Factor 2 consists primarily of the unutilized waste products of chalcedony tool manufacture and some of the unutilized waste products of chert tool manufacture. In addition, three tool types with steep edge angles, a hammerstone, a saw, and a retouched scraper, are found within this factor. These results suggest a set of tools used to make other tools, such as projectile points, arrows, bows, and other hunting equipment. Steep-edged scrapers would be useful for shaving and scraping wood or other dense material; saws would come in handy to work plant and wood materials. It should be recalled that the tools isolated in Factor 1 also may have been used in this activity set.

I suggest that these activities were performed primarily in rooms and on the roof of the pueblo. This inference rests on the assumption that, in order to use the scarce chalcedony as economically as possible, it would have been desirable to have a great deal of control over all by-products of tool manufacture. This would have been facilitated by performing these activities close to where this material was stored, presumably in rooms or on roofs.

Factor 3 consists of the waste products of chert and quartzite tool manufacture activities. The only exception is a small utilized quartzite flake or piece of shatter with a high edge angle. One might interpret the inclusion of this tool type within Factor 3 in the following way. It is possible that, on small pieces of quartzite waste material having a steep edge angle, the normal fracturing pattern produces a texture resembling use wear. Thus, such artifacts would be classified consistently as utilized flakes and shatter instead of as waste flakes and waste shatter. In any case, this factor can be interpreted as the waste products of chert and quartzite tool manufacture. Such activities may have occurred in the extramural areas of the site in close proximity to the sources of the raw materials. This inference is supported by the presence of false start cores in this factor, many of which would have been discarded from the quarry location. Again, the activities identified within Factor 1 also may have taken place in this area.

Attempts to test these activity area hypotheses in light of the de facto refuse from room floors proved to be inconclusive (Schiffer 1973a:296–299), for reasons that should be evident already. Unfortunately, we are left with considerable uncertainty as to where the activity sets isolated by the secondary refuse transformation were conducted. What is important in the context of this presentation, however, is that grossly interpretable factors were produced with a minimum of fiddling and fudging. The inferences generated here suggest that the structuring of activities in space at the Joint Site may not have been very specialized. That most of the variation can be explained by one factor lends strong support to this conclusion. Thus, in addition to an opportunistic technology, the occupants of the Joint Site may have opportunistically used their activity areas; that is, most activities were performed in most areas. This is not, of course, to deny the importance of activity patterning in space, but only to suggest that the patterns may have been very general. It is also possible that activity patterning varied seasonally, so that, at any given time, activity areas were fairly discrete; although, during an entire cycle, almost all activities would have been performed in a given area.

13

Prospects for a Behavioral Archeology

Having come this far, the exasperated reader may be wondering how the seemingly endless series of digressions that form this study are related. There are two basic themes that integrate the preceding discussions into a coherent program for conducting studies in behavioral archeology. The first and major theme of this work concerns the effects of cultural formation processes on the archeological record and how various transformations must be performed in order to use archeological remains to measure behavioral and organizational variables of the past. I have shown that knowledge of the past is accessible only when laws or assumptions pertaining to the formation processes of the archeological record are employed. I have argued also that cultural formation processes must be considered when deducing test implications, interpreting absolute dates, and designating proveniences (see also Reid 1973). Many of these points have been illustrated with examples drawn from the Joint Site, a Pueblo III ruin in the Hay Hollow Valley. Although the inferences about the systemic context of Joint Site chipped stone hardly qualify as revelations, they nonetheless have been accomplished in a more rigorous fashion than in comparable studies, through the explicit consideration of cultural formation processes.

The second theme of this work is that studies in behavioral archeology can succeed only to the extent that we are able to increase the corpus of laws that comprise archeological knowledge—correlates, c-transforms, n-transforms—and those which explain cultural variability and change. I have argued that some of these laws already are extant and many are in current use by archeologists who often are unaware of their lawlike character. In Chapter 5, I have attempted to formalize a number of these principles, those dealing with the coarser aspects of the relationship between quantitative characteristics of the systemic context and of the archeological context. Formalization and systematization of extant principles can go a long way toward providing behavioral archeologists with the laws necessary for operating successfully within Strategy 1. Unfortunately, this process has only just begun.

In combing the literature for laws, I have come to the conclusion that, for many subjects now receiving attention, such as cultural formation processes, a more efficient approach to law acquisition lies in Strategy 2 of behavioral archeology. By using this strategy, archeologists can test various laws using one or another kind of experimental design on data from ongoing cultural systems. As mentioned in Chapter 1, past studies in Strategy 2 have been unnecessarily narrow in the scope of problems conceived, variables examined, and test situations chosen. However, once the significance of laws to archeology is appreciated more widely, the way is prepared for the expansion of modern material culture studies into heretofore unexplored domains. The only legitimate boundary of such studies is that one or more of the variables under examination be potentially measurable in the archeological record. Our minds are challenged to comprehend the diversity of subject matter thus delimited. Clearly, the archeological study of the present has barely begun.

The purpose of this final chapter is to illustrate the promise held for behavioral archeology by the study of modern material culture in systemic context. Here, I attempt to demonstrate the ease with which lawlike statements can be devised and tested if appropriate questions are asked within Strategy 2. The key to increasing the repertoire of laws useful for studying the past is in the proper formulation of general questions: Without general questions, there can be no general answers (laws). Although no cookbook is available for formulating such questions, I shall illustrate the process with a number of examples drawn from several recent studies of modern material culture.

I also point out that modern material culture studies not only can increase the body of laws useful for carrying out research in Strategy 1, but they offer archeologists the potential of increasing the understanding of modern human behavior within Strategy 4, thus contributing to anthropology as a whole. Projects such as these, which deal with the interaction of etically defined variables in ongoing systems, perhaps are better able to bring to fruition the cultural materialist strategy (Harris 1968) than any other approach, with the exception of cultural ecology, in modern anthropology. In presenting examples drawn from undergraduate student projects, I do not hesitate to suggest how their results might be applied to understanding modern human behavior.

Since the early 1970s, William Rathje, J. Jefferson Reid, and I (sporadically) have taught undergraduate courses in archeological theory and method at the

University of Arizona (Reid, Rathje, and Schiffer 1974). In using these courses as a laboratory for testing ways of teaching the basic concepts of archeology, we have found that modern material culture provides a readily accessible data source of limitless dimensions (see also Salwen 1973). Students can use such data for carrying out projects that treat important topics, such as seriation, classification, sampling, and the explanation of distributions. These data also can be used for acquiring and testing lawlike statements of utility to archeological research within Strategies 1 and 4.

If undergraduates are to conduct studies that aim to produce laws, they must possess—in addition to creativity—a well-developed context of questioning for discerning areas to investigate. We acquainted all students with scientific methods and a generalized framework of archeological question asking. Under this system, specific research projects are obtained in several ways: Students can be assigned problems or questions, be given hypotheses ready for testing, or be left to their own devices to find a problem area and appropriate hypotheses. The best results are obtained when students are free to choose among these options according to their interests and abilities.

I shall now discuss a number of these undergraduate projects to illustrate the expanded range of problem areas and subject matter available to archeologists who are interested in learning the laws of human behavior.

Although pedestrians in major United States cities are not yet knee-deep in garbage, the amount of refuse indiscriminantly discarded in streets and other inappropriate places is considerable. McKellar (1973) has provided a hypothesis to explain the discard locations of at least some of this refuse. She suggests that, regardless of the availability of trash receptacles, items less than 4 inches in overall dimensions are discarded in outdoor areas whenever and wherever they cease to be useful. McKellar tested this hypothesis on refuse from the campus of the University of Arizona. Holding constant the intensity of use of sampled areas, she examined 30 lots of trash both near and far from refuse containers. Her results, based on this limited test, provide a tentative confirmation of the hypothesis. Small items are discarded almost independently of the location of trash cans, but larger items find their way into trash cans if these containers are handy.

If these preliminary findings are accepted for the purpose of discussion, some interesting implications emerge for designing policies for the control of litter. Unless the probability of being caught and sent to jail for littering increases radically, putting us all in the company of Arlo Guthrie, these behavior patterns are not likely to be changed by increasing the intensity of threats and exhortations emanating from high places. The soft sell is also a noticeable failure. In order to bring about a change in behavior, the results of this project might be fed into the American system at the level of packaging design. Items that can be crushed easily—hence, made smaller—or items that are intrinsically small, such as pop-tops and matchbooks, should not be used in packaging. For cases in which this is not practical, the value or recyclability of small items should be increased artificially. Beer companies might offer a six-pack of beer for 200 pop-tops, thus assigning a coupon function to an otherwise worthless object. I suspect that, within a week after initiating such a program, not a single beer can pop-top would be visible on any United States campus. As another example, cigarette coupons should be printed on the package, thus increasing its value, rather than simply being tucked loosely inside the cellophane cover. The use of cellophane, a prime offender, should be discouraged altogether. McKellar's hypothesis probably has cross-cultural applicability and can function to explain the occurrence of primary refuse in outdoor areas of any community's activity space.

Several modifications of the hypothesis should be made before it is examined in the light of other data. In the first place, the factors affecting the size threshold should be investigated. One might suggest that, as the use intensity of an activity area increases, the size threshold of tolerable primary refuse will decrease; this hypothesis might apply to both indoor and outdoor areas. In the second place, variables relating to techniques of refuse removal and transport should be considered. Even so, this example suggests that, by studying the refuse produced in an urban setting, archeologists can acquire important generalizations about discarding behavior. In conjunction with other information, these generalizations can be used to devise noncoercive means for altering behavior.

A pervasive quality of modern American culture is the widespread quest for upward mobility and higher status. Fortunately for archeologists, statuses are in part actualized in, and symbolized by, material objects. In attempting to explain the phenomenon of rapid status symbol change and other aspects of status symbol distribution in the United States, Swan (1972) tested a hypothesis that has implications for understanding system disequilibrium and technological growth.

Specifically, the hypothesis states that, if the availability of a status symbol increases, occupants of lower statuses will begin to acquire the symbol, disrupting the equilibrium distribution of status symbols. To maintain the system of status grading and the appropriate patterns of social interaction that it reflects and facilitates, the symbol of the higher status will be replaced. Using data from the 1960–1970 U.S. census statistical abstracts, Swan examined changes through time in the distribution among income classes of cars per household, black-and-white televisions, color televisions, washing machines, clothes dryers, refrigerators, and dishwashers. These changes in distribution through time were compared with changes in cost relative to the 1958 dollar. By the early 1960s, most of these objects already had become middle- and low-income status symbols; thus, the test was not conducted under the best of conditions. A further complication is the increased availability of all durable consumer goods owing both to cost decreases and to income increases. Nevertheless, Swan found that, in the early

1960s, clothes dryers and two or more cars appear to have been middle-class status symbols. Later in the decade, as these items increased among lower income groups, dishwashers and color televisions seem to have taken their place as middle-class status symbols.

These are tentative results. Even so, I can amplify this model of status symbol distribution and change and discuss several of its implications. In a complexly stratified, highly mobile society, quantity and diversity of household material objects vary directly with status. This implies that a Guttman scaling or even a seriation of households by material objects provides a ranking of statuses. In other words, all statuses have couches, plates, and glasses, but, at each successively higher level, new items are added until, at the top, where the highest statuses are reached, there are found material objects that have limited distributions. The items that define or symbolize a high status do not appear in appreciable quantities among lower status categories. Low-status items also can be restricted in distribution of those classes, but they occur in much higher overall frequencies. On the basis of Rathje's (1973) social mobility model, totally discrete distributions would not be expected among any classes.

In order to maintain the system of status grading, this differential distribution of status symbols should be approximated closely. Each status should have symbols that are not shared to a significant extent by lower status groups. It follows that, if the frequency of a status symbol increases among lower statuses, it can no longer function to discriminate one status group from another. Thus, the higher status group must find a new symbol, which it can do by either increasing the demand for symbols of the next higher status or by creating demand for an entirely new symbol.

The maintenance of the sytem of status grading by changes in status symbols constitutes a negative feedback or deviation-counteracting mechanism. New status symbols are acquired to replace old ones that have become devalued by more widespread distribution. But the status grading system does not operate in a vacuum. To provide a source of new status symbols, a positive feedback loop is involved which couples social and technoeconomic subsystems. Changes in social mobility, population increase, or status symbol disequilibrium generate a demand for technological innovation to produce new gadgets and produce old gadgets at a lower price to serve as status symbols. New processes and products developed in the technological subsystem lead to unexpected increases in the availability of other symbols. This, in turn, leads to further status system disequilibrium and a demand for additional symbols. Clearly, the positive feedback loop that couples the status grading system to technology in a highly mobile society acts as a powerful engine driving system growth.

At one time, system growth was judged to be beneficial, but now environmentalists, ecologists, and even some economists are calling for an appraisal of the long-term consequences of uncontrolled growth. Some investigators even predict that growth soon will result in system collapse from pollution, resource depletion, and other factors. One way that doom might be prevented or at least forestalled is by the disruption of various positive feedback loops. If the harmful effects of the status-system technology loop are to be lessened and wasteful energy and resource consumption reduced, effort must be directed toward increasing the use of status symbols that are less demanding on advanced production processes and scarce resources than are many now in use. This could be facilitated by artificially increasing the scarcity of certain kinds of material items. The beginnings of this process may be observable in the recent upsurge of interest in art and craft objects, including limited-edition porcelains and junk sculptures. As this trend continues, the positive feedback loop between the social and technological subsystems will assume less importance as a contributor to system disequilibrium and growth. (It should be noted that this model also has clear implications for explaining complex system growth or its absence in preindustrial societies; Schiffer n.d.b.)

When status symbols are replaced by new ones, actual substitution at the level of an individual household may or may not take place. When items in one functional category become devalued and are replaced by items in a different category, the social unit is likely to merely add the new object to its repertoire. For example, when the possession of two or more cars was no longer a status symbol, a color television may have been purchased. But, in many cases, items within the same functional category may replace each other. For example, a car with air conditioning replaces one without it. When this occurs, an opportunity for lateral cycling is created, since the replaced object still may be useful.

Lateral cycling in Tucson, Arizona, was the subject of several undergraduate projects, and the results illuminate some of the processes by which used objects circulate in an urban system. Kassander (1973) found that, as the social distance between the individuals or groups that give and receive laterally cycled goods increases, the greater the likelihood that formal mechanisms with middlemen, such as secondhand stores and thrift shops, will facilitate the activity. Another finding that gives support to the general status-symbol distribution model is that lateral cycling seems to be concerned mostly with items that have relatively long uselives (Young 1973; Brown and Johnson 1973; Kassander 1973; Wood 1973). Of all the lateral cycling mechanisms studied, which include swap meets, thrift shops, and secondhand stores, swap meets—a relatively informal mechanism—seem to represent the greatest diversity of items (Kassander 1973).

The study of swap meets produced some interesting and unexpected results regarding the social dimension of the activity. It seems that there are two major patterns of swap meet use (Brown and Johnson 1973). Some individuals sell items on an irregular or one-time basis. Others are termed "professionals" and repeatedly appear at swap meets, perhaps providing a source of income in that manner. The goods offered for sale by professionals usually are limited in variety compared to those of irregular lateral cyclers. Often, the professional spends other parts of the week in search of goods to sell at the weekend swap meets (Brown and Johnson 1973). Surprisingly, these professionals "maintain social ties with one another even outside the swap-meet functions. Parties and outings often involve friendships started and maintained through the swap-meets [Brown and Johnson 1973:9]."

These preliminary studies now have brought us to the point at which meaningful general questions can be asked about swap meets and other lateral cycling mechanisms. For example, what variables determine when swap meets will emerge as a mechanism of lateral cycling? One might expect that, when population size reaches a certain point in the presence of a critical intensity of social mobility, sufficient material will be available to sustain lateral cycling through swap meets. An important area of investigation is to discover the variables that determine the presence of any mechanism of lateral cycling. One also can examine lateral cycling to determine how materials flow between and among various status groups. Certain mechanisms are likely to arise to facilitate downward flow, others for intrastatus flow, still others for upward flow. One study already has established that, although most secondhand stores are found in the poorer neighborhoods of Tucson, collection points exhibit a slight tendency to occur in the neighborhoods of higher income groups (Brown and Johnson 1973), thus suggesting a downward flow of objects. This also raises questions concerning where lateral cycling mechanisms are situated with respect to givers and receivers. These questions are only a few from among the many raised by these undergraduate studies of lateral cycling.

The importance of the principles of lateral cycling for understanding the archeological record is clear. Less obvious are the implications such studies have for understanding the dynamics of modern systems. At a time when everyone is advocating re-use—both lateral cycling and recycling—as a means of conserving scarce resources, it seems remarkable that so little is known about ongoing cycling processes. It seems to me that before far-reaching re-use policies are implemented by various governments, lateral cycling as it now works should be understood in both its material and social dimensions. Archeologists are eminently qualified to conduct such studies.

In another project, two students attempted to identify the variables determining what materials are likely to be left as de facto refuse when a social unit moves out of a dwelling (Gekas and Phillips 1973). It is likely that many of the variables considered, such as anticipated moving distance, ease of transportation, social status, and available space in the new site, are operative whenever a social unit moves out of its dwelling. This study illustrates that many situations of interest to archeologists, such as de facto refuse production, can be simulated with relative ease in a modern industrial society. Even aspects of Binford's (1973) Nunamiut study can be duplicated in the United States—curate behavior of mobile social units can be studied among modern campers. For archeologists, such as I, who are reluctant to endure the rigors of the arctic cold, even in the name of science, the study of modern material culture offers an appealing and inexpensive alternative for acquiring and testing laws of human behavior. There are, of course, many situations of interest that cannot be simulated under modern conditions; but I suggest that they are less frequent than usually is thought to be the case.

I make no claim that these studies have provided heretofore unknown laws of human behavior that will revolutionize anthropology and the practice of archeology. Instead, I have indicated how modern material culture can be of use to investigators seeking laws of human behavior relevant to both archeological interpretation and the study of the present. One might suspect that, if undergraduates can succeed at discovering regularities in human behavior, professional anthropologists should have somewhat less difficulty. Unfortunately, this is not yet so. Many anthropologists still believe that cultural systems are too complex to yield to general principles. Although many anthropologists are not openly hostile to nomothetic pursuits, benign neglect and indifference have taken a heavy toll on the discipline's output of laws.

If archeologists as anthropologists are to succeed at explaining behavioral variability and change, a major restructuring of anthropological enculturation must occur. Skills in research design, mathematics, statistics, modeling, and logic need to be acquired at the undergraduate level. To discover the laws of human behavior requires training in how to ask general questions and how to devise strategies for answering them. Thus, graduate courses in anthropology should cease being histories of thought. They must concentrate instead on defining the known principles of a subject matter and indicating directions of future inquiry. My experience with undergraduate students unequivocally demonstrates the fruitful results of applying this approach. Only when we set aside ideas about the intractable complexity of culture and seek simple principles to reduce that complexity will we possess the tools to understand human behavior, past or present.

Appendix

Table A.1 Chert Artifact Counts from Several Joint Site Samples[a]

Type numbers	Large roomblock	Small roomblock	Test squares (Phase 1)	Test squares (Phase 2)	Surface
1	1494	204	1123	749	730
2	107	26	142	71	33
3	166	27	250	138	155
4	1703	158	2361	1508	1029
5	386	44	537	215	412
6	24	12	38	11	5
7	665	93	860	528	429
8	275	38	360	116	236
11	42	3	15	6	3
12	44	3	14	3	6
13	34	3	15	11	3
14	88	6	38	16	9
15	11	1	2	3	2
16	5	0	1	0	1
17	2	0	0	0	0
18	16	1	3	3	3
19	20	2	9	7	1
20	1	0	0	0	0
21	120	12	80	25	24
22	265	34	98	47	47
23	365	39	145	69	72
24	567	66	258	107	119
25	57	10	33	23	10
26	55	11	21	15	11
27	43	5	9	14	13
28	120	24	56	48	34
29	7	2	5	0	0
30	56	4	7	10	2
31	118	16	92	60	45
32	273	31	167	96	121
33	930	97	601	313	310

Table A.1 *continued*

Type numbers	Large roomblock	Small roomblock	Test squares (Phase 1)	Test squares (Phase 2)	Surface
34	1080	106	706	381	418
35	96	9	113	76	40
36	149	18	113	86	29
37	314	34	210	162	66
38	509	56	409	301	124
40	1	1	0	0	0
41	199	23	155	63	54
42	425	51	232	104	145
43	1043	106	640	343	343
44	1	0	0	1	0
45	135	17	140	91	46
46	179	27	115	92	39
47	330	37	205	168	70
48	36	6	31	22	12
49	14	0	1	1	0
50	1	0	1	0	0
51	2	0	0	0	0
52	0	0	0	1	0
53	16	1	2	2	1
54	3	0	1	0	0
55	14	0	13	7	3
56	5	2	3	2	2
57	2	0	4	3	0
58	2	0	0	0	2
59	3	0	2	1	1
60	4	0	0	1	1
61	3	1	1	0	1
62	6	0	6	4	0
63	7	2	3	1	4
64	3	2	1	0	1
65	2	0	4	1	0
66	15	1	8	9	5
67	6	1	0	2	0
68	21	1	9	6	7
69	15	3	12	1	5
71	1	0	1	0	1
72	1	0	0	2	1
73	11	1	6	2	2
74	64	7	40	20	47
75	11	4	7	2	2
76	34	1	13	7	7
77	11	0	2	2	0
78	13	0	22	2	10

[a]Large roomblock includes Room 34; small roomblock includes Room 33.

Table A.2 Quartzite Artifact Counts from Several Joint Site Samples[a]

Type numbers	Large roomblock	Small roomblock	Test squares (Phase 1)	Test squares (Phase 2)	Surface
1	97	39	87	43	45
2	4	1	7	1	0
3	21	4	20	12	12
4	166	17	220	104	80
5	11	3	24	5	12
6	1	1	2	0	0
7	154	20	115	110	63
8	23	4	25	9	16
11	16	1	6	2	1
12	25	2	12	4	4
13	17	0	7	0	0
14	40	3	19	6	5
15	4	0	0	1	1
16	4	0	1	2	0
17	1	0	1	0	0
18	5	0	11	2	1
19	1	0	3	0	0
20	0	0	0	0	0
21	8	1	5	3	2
22	40	3	13	8	6
23	50	4	25	9	10
24	78	7	36	17	15
25	4	0	7	7	0
26	16	2	6	6	1
27	8	1	7	2	4
28	25	2	18	14	5
29	7	0	2	1	0
30	59	4	13	6	3
31	2	0	4	1	1
32	20	2	11	9	6
33	69	1	33	25	11
34	80	3	43	32	18
35	5	0	3	4	0
36	12	1	13	4	2
37	44	8	30	17	3
38	59	8	44	25	5
40	0	0	0	0	0
41	17	2	12	5	4
42	65	7	27	15	16
43	117	4	58	32	18
44	0	0	0	0	0
45	9	0	6	12	1
46	26	2	19	10	3
47	51	8	38	19	7

Table A.2 *continued*

Type numbers	Large roomblock	Small roomblock	Test squares (Phase 1)	Test squares (Phase 2)	Surface
48	1	0	0	0	0
49	34	6	10	2	4
50	0	0	0	0	0
51	0	0	0	0	0
52	0	0	0	0	0
53	0	0	0	0	0
54	0	0	0	0	0
55	0	0	0	0	0
56	1	0	1	2	0
57	0	0	0	0	0
58	0	0	0	0	0
59	0	0	0	0	0
60	0	0	0	0	0
61	0	0	0	0	0
62	0	0	1	0	0
63	1	0	0	2	0
64	1	1	0	0	0
65	0	0	0	0	0
66	0	0	0	0	0
67	0	0	0	0	0
68	2	1	0	2	0
69	0	0	0	0	0
71	0	0	0	0	0
72	0	0	0	0	0
73	2	1	0	0	0
74	4	0	0	0	4
75	0	0	0	0	0
76	1	1	2	0	0
77	0	0	0	0	0
78	1	0	0	0	0

[a]Large roomblock includes Room 34; small roomblock includes Room 33.

Table A.3 Chalcedony Artifact Counts from Several Joint Site Samples[a]

Type numbers	Large roomblock	Small roomblock	Test squares (Phase 1)	Test squares (Phase 2)	Surface
1	0	0	0	0	0
2	12	1	3	1	0
3	5	1	3	9	0
4	129	12	107	51	82
5	40	2	34	13	25
6	0	0	0	0	0
7	45	2	34	23	31
8	9	0	11	3	5
11	7	0	0	0	0
12	7	0	0	0	0
13	7	0	0	0	0
14	11	0	0	0	0
15	0	0	0	0	0
16	0	0	0	0	0
17	0	0	0	0	0
18	0	0	0	0	0
19	4	0	0	0	0
20	0	0	0	0	0
21	3	2	6	0	0
22	13	4	4	0	0
23	28	4	7	2	2
24	25	6	12	1	1
25	9	0	5	2	1
26	10	1	3	1	2
27	3	1	2	1	1
28	17	1	9	4	4
29	4	0	1	0	0
30	8	0	0	0	0
31	5	1	6	0	1
32	20	1	9	10	10
33	75	8	26	10	16
34	70	8	30	16	21
35	11	1	8	3	5
36	12	1	4	5	4
37	26	3	18	6	8
38	39	4	27	13	14
40	0	0	0	0	0
41	7	2	7	1	0
42	18	2	8	7	8
43	79	10	27	10	14
44	0	0	0	1	1
45	14	1	12	4	5
46	16	1	7	5	4
47	25	3	17	7	9

Table A.3 *continued*

Type numbers	Large roomblock	Small roomblock	Test squares (Phase 1)	Test squares (Phase 2)	Surface
48	20	4	7	1	5
49	0	0	0	0	0
50	0	0	0	0	2
51	1	0	1	0	0
52	0	0	0	0	1
53	6	0	6	0	2
54	0	0	1	0	0
55	2	0	1	2	2
56	0	0	0	0	0
57	3	0	0	0	2
58	1	0	0	0	0
59	4	0	0	0	0
60	1	0	2	0	0
61	0	0	2	0	0
62	0	0	1	0	0
63	7	0	1	2	4
64	0	0	0	0	0
65	0	0	0	0	0
66	0	0	0	0	0
67	0	0	1	0	0
68	0	0	1	0	0
69	0	0	0	0	1
71	1	0	0	0	0
72	1	0	1	0	1
73	0	0	0	0	0
74	10	1	4	1	2
75	1	0	0	0	1
76	0	0	2	0	0
77	1	0	0	1	0
78	4	0	3	0	0

[a]Large roomblock includes Room 34; small roomblock includes Room 33.

References

Allen, William L. and James B. Richardson III
  1971 The reconstruction of kinship from archaeological data: The concepts, the methods, and the feasibility. *American Antiquity* **36**:41–53.
Ascher, Robert
  1959 A prehistoric population estimate using midden analysis and two population models. *Southwestern Journal of Anthropology* **15**:168–178.
  1961 Experimental archeology. *American Anthropologist* **63**:793–816.
  1968 Time's arrow and the archaeology of a contemporary community. In *Settlement archaeology*, edited by K. C. Chang. Palo Alto: National Press Books. Pp. 43–52.
Baker, Charles M.
  1974 A preliminary archeological field study of the Chicot Watershed, Chicot County, Arkansas. Manuscript on deposit, Arkansas Archeological Survey, Fayetteville.
  n.d. Site abandonment and the archeological record: An empirical case for anticipated return. *Arkansas Academy of Science, Proceedings* (in press).
Bannister, Bryant
  1962 The interpretation of tree-ring dates. *American Antiquity* **27**:508–514.
Bartlett, Katherine
  1933 Pueblo milling stones of the Flagstaff region and their relation to others in the Southwest. *Museum of Northern Arizona, Bulletin* No. 3.
  1936 The utilization of maize among the ancient pueblos. *University of New Mexico, Bulletin* No. 296.
Beaglehole, Ernest
  1937 Notes on Hopi economic life. *Yale University, Publications in Anthropology* No. 15.
Beeson, William J.
  1957 The stages of fill of Room 10 at the Pollock Site. *Plateau* **29**:66–69.

Binford, Lewis R.
1962a   Archaeology as anthropology. *American Antiquity* 28:217–225.
1962b   A new method for calculating dates from kaolin pipe stem samples. *Southeastern Archaeological Conference, Newsletter* 9:19–21.
1964   A consideration of archaeological research design. *American Antiquity* 29:425–441.
1965   Archaeological systematics and the study of culture process. *American Antiquity* 31:203–210.
1968a   Some comments on historical versus processual archaeology. *Southwestern Journal of Anthropology* 24:267–275.
1968b   Archeological perspectives. In *New perspectives in archeology*, edited by Sally R. and L. R. Binford. Chicago: Aldine. Pp. 5–32.
1968c   Methodological considerations of the archeological use of ethnographic data. In *Man the hunter*, edited by Richard B. Lee and Irven DeVore. Chicago: Aldine. Pp. 268–273.
1971   Mortuary practices: Their study and their potential. In Approaches to the social dimensions of mortuary practices, edited and organized by James A. Brown. *Society for American Archaeology, Memoirs* 25: 6–29.
1972a   *An archaeological perspective.* New York: Seminar Press.
1972b   Model building–paradigms, and the current state of Paleolithic research. In *An archaeological perspective*, edited by Lewis R. Binford. New York: Seminar Press. Pp. 252–295.
1973   Interassemblage variability–the Mousterian and the "functional" argument. In *The explanation of culture change: Models in prehistory*, edited by C. Renfrew. London: Duckworth. Pp. 227–253.
Binford, Lewis R. and Sally R. Binford
1966   A preliminary analysis of functional variability in the Mousterian of Levallois facies. In Recent studies in paleoanthropology, edited by J. D. Clark and F. C. Howell. *American Anthropologist* 68(No. 2, Part 2):238–295.
Binford, Lewis R. and George I. Quimby
1963   Indian sites and chipped stone materials in the northern Lake Michigan area. *Fieldiana: Anthropology* 36:277–307.
Binford, Lewis, R., Sally R. Binford, Robert Whallon, and Margaret Ann Hardin
1970   Archaeology at Hatchery West. *Society for American Archaeology, Memoirs* No. 24.
Binford, Sally R. and Lewis R. Binford
1968   Archeological theory and method. In *New perspectives in archeology*, edited by Sally R. and Lewis R. Binford. Chicago: Aldine. Pp. 1–3.
Bonnichsen, Robson
1973   Millie's Camp: An experiment in archaeology. *World Archaeology* 4:277–291.
Bowman, Daniel C.
1975   Preliminary comments on the alluvial chronology of the Hay Hollow Valley, east-central Arizona. In Chapters in the prehistory of eastern Arizona, IV. *Fieldiana: Anthropology* 65:12–16.
Breternitz, David A.
1966   An appraisal of tree-ring dated pottery types in the Southwest. *University of Arizona, Anthropological Papers* No. 10.

Brose, David S.
1970   The Summer Island Site: A study of prehistoric cultural ecology and social organization in the northern Lake Michigan area. *Case Western Reserve University, Studies in Anthropology* No. 1.

Brown, Charles S. and Lane P. Johnson
1973   The secret use-life of a mayonnaise jar . . . or, how I learned to love lateral cycling. Manuscript on deposit, Arizona State Museum Library.

Brown, James A. (editor)
1971   Approaches to the social dimensions of mortuary practices. *Society for American Archaeology, Memoirs* No. 25.

Burling, Robbins
1964   Cognition and componential analysis: God's truth or hocus-pocus? *American Anthropologist* **66**:20–28.

Chang, K. C.
1967   Major aspects of the interrelationship of archaeology and ethnology. *Current Anthropology* **8**:227–234.

Chaplin, R. E.
1971   *The study of animal bones from archaeological sites.* London and New York: Seminar Press.

Claassen, Cheryl
1975   Aleutian Island homogeneity: A Near Island perspective. Unpublished B.A. Honors Thesis, University of Arkansas, Fayetteville.
n.d.   Antiques—objects of lateral cycling? *Arkansas Academy of Science, Proceedings* (in press).

Clark, J. G. D.
1954   *Excavations at Star Carr: An early Mesolithic site at Seamer near Scarborough, Yorkshire, England.* London: Cambridge University Press.
1957   *Archaeology and society: Reconstructing the prehistoric past.* London: Methuen.
1972   Star Carr: A case study in bioarchaeology. *Addison-Wesley Modular Publications in Anthropology* No. 10.

Clarke, David L.
1968   *Analytical archaeology.* London: Methuen.
1972a   (editor) *Models in archaeology.* London: Methuen.
1972b   Models and paradigms in contemporary archaeology. In *Models in archaeology*, edited by D. L. Clarke. London: Methuen. Pp. 1–60.

Coles, John
1973   *Archaeology by experiment.* New York: Scribner.

Collins, Michael B.
1971   The role of lithic analysis in socio-cultural inference. Paper read at the 1971 Meeting of the Society for American Archaeology, Norman, Oklahoma.
1974   A functional analysis of lithic technology among prehistoric hunter-gatherers of southwestern France and western Texas. Ph.D. dissertation, University of Arizona. Ann Arbor: University Microfilms.
1975   Sources of bias in processual data: An appraisal. In *Sampling in archaeology*, edited by James W. Mueller. Tucson: University of Arizona Press. Pp. 26–32.

Collins, Michael B. and Jason M. Fenwick
n.d.   Population growth rate estimates, Grasshopper Pueblo. In Multi-disciplinary research at the Grasshopper Ruin, edited by W. A. Longacre. *University of Arizona, Anthropological Papers* (in press).
Cook, Sherburne F.
1972   Prehistoric demography. *Addison-Wesley Modular Publications in Anthropology* No. 16.
Crabtree, Don E.
1968   Mesoamerican polyhedral cores and prismatic blades. *American Antiquity* **33**:446–478.
1972   An introduction to flintworking. *Idaho State University Museum, Occasional Papers* No. 28.
Daly, Patricia
1969   Approaches to faunal analysis in archaeology. *American Antiquity* **34**:146–153.
Damon, Paul E., Austin Long, and Edward T. Wallick
1972   Dendrochronologic calibration of the carbon-14 time scale. *University of Arizona, Department of Geosciences, Contribution* No. 57.
Darnay, Arsen and William E. Franklin
1972   *Salvage markets for materials in solid wastes.* Washington: U.S. Environmental Protection Agency.
David, Nicholas
1971   The Fulani compound and the archaeologist. *World Archaeology* **3**: 111–131.
1972   On the life span of pottery, type frequencies, and archaeological inference. *American Antiquity* **37**:141–142.
David, Nicholas and Hilke Hennig
1972   The ethnography of pottery: A Fulani case seen in archaeological perspective. *Addison-Wesley Modular Publications in Anthropology* No. 21.
Dean, Jeffrey S.
1969   Chronological analysis of Tsegi Phase sites in northeastern Arizona. *Laboratory of Tree-Ring Research, Papers* No. 3.
1970   Tree-ring dating. Laboratory of Tree-ring Research, University of Arizona (mimeographed).
Deetz, James F.
1965   The dynamics of stylistic change in Arikara ceramics. *University of Illinois, Studies in Anthropology* No. 4.
Dickey, Archie M.
1971   Palynology of the Hay Hollow Valley. M.A. thesis, Northern Arizona University.
Donnan, Christopher B. and C. William Clewlow, Jr. (editors)
1974   Ethnoarchaeology. *University of California at Los Angeles, Institute of Archaeology, Monograph* No. 4.
Drucker, Philip
1972   Stratigraphy in archaeology: An introduction. *Addison-Wesley Modular Publications in Anthropology* No. 30.
Dunnell, Robert C.
1971   *Systematics in prehistory.* New York: Free Press.

Fagan, Brian M.
1972   In the beginning: An introduction to archaeology. Boston: Little, Brown.

Faulkner, Charles H. and C. R. McCollough
1973   Introductory report of the Normandy Reservoir Salvage Project: Environmental setting, typology, and survey. *University of Tennessee, Department of Anthropology, Report of Investigations* No. 11.

Fehon, Jacqueline R. and Sandra C. Scholtz
n.d.   A conceptual framework for the study of artifact loss. Manuscript submitted for publication.

Flenniken, J. Jeffrey
1975   Test excavations of three archeological sites in Des Arc Bayou Watershed, White County, Arkansas. Manuscript on deposit, Arkansas Archeological Survey, Fayetteville.

Ford, James A.
1961   Menard site: The Quapaw village of Osotouy on the Arkansas River. *American Museum of Natural History, Anthropological Papers* No. 48 (Part 2).

Ford, Janet L. and Martha A. Rolingson
1972   Site destruction due to agricultural practices in southeast Arkansas. *Arkansas Archeological Survey, Research Series* 3:1–40.

Foster, George M.
1960   Life-expectancy of utilitarian pottery in Tzintzuntzan, Michoacan, Mexico. *American Antiquity* 25:606–609.

Freeman, Leslie G., Jr.
1968   A theoretical framework for interpreting archeological materials. In *Man the hunter*, edited by Richard B. Lee and Irven DeVore. Chicago: Aldine. Pp. 262–267.

Fritz, John M.
1972   Archaeological systems for indirect observation of the past. In *Contemporary archaeology*, edited by Mark P. Leone. Carbondale: Southern Illinois University Press. Pp. 135–157.

1974   The Hay Hollow site subsistence system, east central Arizona. Ph.D. dissertation, University of Chicago. Ann Arbor: University Microfilms.

Fritz, John M. and Fred T. Plog
1970   The nature of archaeological explanation. *American Antiquity* 35: 405–412.

Garrison, E. G.
n.d.   A qualitative model for inundation studies; for archeological research and resource conservation. *Plains Anthropologist* (in press).

Garson, Adam
1972   Color analysis of lithic material: A cognitive approach to archaeological interpretation. Manuscript on deposit, Field Museum of Natural History and Arizona State Museum Library.

Gekas, Genie and Cathy Phillips
1973   An archaeological study of the variables of moving. Manuscript on deposit, Arizona State Museum Library.

George, Annick and Mary E. Rose
1973   *Carnegiea gigantea:* An application of behavioral chain analysis. Manuscript on deposit, Arizona State Museum Library.

Goodyear, Albert C.
1974   The Brand site: A techno-functional study of a Dalton site in north-east Arkansas. *Arkansas Archeological Survey, Research Series* No. 7.
Gould, Richard A.
1968   Living archaeology: The Ngatatjara of Western Australia. *Southwestern Journal of Anthropology* 24:101−122.
Gregg, Michael L.
1974   Three middle Woodland sites from Henderson County, Illinois: An apparent congruity with middle Woodland subsistence-settlement systems in the lower Illinois Valley. *The Wisconsin Archeologist* 55: 231−245.
Gregory, David A.
1975   Defining variability in prehistoric settlement morphology. In Chapters in the prehistory of eastern Arizona, IV. *Fieldiana: Anthropology* 65:40−46.
Hanson, John A.
1975   Stress response in cultural systems: A prehistoric example from east-central Arizona. In Chapters in the prehistory of eastern Arizona, IV. *Fieldiana: Anthropology* 65:92−102.
Hanson, John A. and Michael B. Schiffer
1975   The Joint Site—A preliminary report. In Chapters in the prehistory of eastern Arizona, IV. *Fieldiana: Anthropology* 65:47−91.
Harris, Marvin
1964   *The nature of cultural things.* New York: Random House.
1968   *The rise of anthropological theory.* New York: Crowell.
Harrison, Gail G., William L. Rathje, and Wilson W. Hughes
1975   Food waste behavior in an urban population. *Journal of Nutrition Education* 7:13−16.
Haury, Emil W.
1934   The Canyon Creek Ruin and the cliff dwellings of the Sierra Ancha. *Medallion Papers* No. 14.
1936   The Mogollon culture of southwestern New Mexico. *Medallion Papers* No. 20.
1950   *The stratigraphy and archaeology of Ventana Cave, Arizona.* Albuquerque: University of New Mexico Press.
Heider, Karl G.
1967   Archaeological assumptions and ethnographical facts: A cautionary tale from New Guinea. *Southwestern Journal of Anthropology* 23: 52−64.
Heizer, Robert F., and Sherburne F. Cook
1956   Some aspects of the quantitative approach in archaeology. *Southwestern Journal of Anthropology* 12:229−248.
Heizer, Robert F. and John A. Graham
1967   *A guide to field methods in archaeology: Approaches to the anthropology of the dead.* Palo Alto: National Press.
Hempel, Carl G.
1965   *Aspects of scientific explanation.* New York: Free Press.
1966   *Philosophy of natural science.* Englewood Cliffs: Prentice-Hall.
Hester, Thomas R. and Robert F. Heizer
1973   Bibliography of archaeology I: Experiments, lithic technology, and

petrography. *Addison-Wesley Modular Publications in Anthropology* No. 29.

Hill, James N.
1966   A prehistoric community in eastern Arizona. *Southwestern Journal of Anthropology* 22:9—30.
1968   Broken K Pueblo: Patterns of form and function. In *New perspectives in archeology,* edited by Sally R. and Lewis R. Binford. Chicago: Aldine. Pp. 103—142.
1970a   Broken K Pueblo: Prehistoric social organization in the American Southwest. *University of Arizona, Anthropological Papers* No. 18.
1970b   Prehistoric social organization in the American Southwest: Theory and method. In *Reconstructing prehistoric pueblo societies,* edited by William A. Longacre. Albuquerque: University of New Mexico Press. Pp. 11—58.

Hill, James N. and Robert K. Evans
1972   A model for classification and typology. In *Models in archaeology,* edited by D. L. Clarke. London: Methuen. Pp. 231—274.

Hole, Frank and Robert F. Heizer
1973   *An introduction to prehistoric archeology.* New York: Holt, Rinehart & Winston.

House, John H.
1975   A functional typology for Cache Project surface collections. In The Cache River Archeological Project: An experiment in contract archeology, assembled by Michael B. Schiffer and John H. House. *Arkansas Archeological Survey, Research Series* No. 8, 55—73.

House, John H. and Michael B. Schiffer
1975   Significance of the archeological resources of the Cache River Basin. In The Cache River Archeological Project: An experiment in contract archeology, assembled by Michael B. Schiffer and John H. House. *Arkansas Archeological Survey, Research Series* No. 8, 163—186.

Howells, W. W.
1960   Estimating population numbers through archaeological and skeletal remains. In The application of quantitative methods in archaeology, edited by R. F. Heizer and S. F. Cook. *Viking Fund Publications in Anthropology* No. 28, 158—180.

Jelinek, Arthur J.
1967   A prehistoric sequence in the middle Pecos Valley, New Mexico. *University of Michigan, Museum of Anthropology, Anthropological Papers* No. 31.
1972   Fundamental problems in the description of lithic industries as exemplified by the et Tabun paleolithic collections. Paper presented at the 1972 Meeting of the Society for American Archaeology, Bal Harbour.

Jelks, Edward
1972   Observations on the concept(s) of association in archeology. Paper read at the 1972 Meeting of the Society for American Archaeology, Bal Harbour.

Kassander, Helen
1973   Second hand rose, or lateral cycling: A study in behavioral archaeology. Manuscript on deposit, Arizona State Museum Library.

Kidder, Alfred V.
1931   *The artifacts of Pecos.* Andover: Phillips Academy.
Kleindienst, Maxine R. and Patty Jo Watson
1956   Action archeology: The archeological inventory of a living community. *Anthropology Tomorrow* 5:75–78.
Krause, Richard A. and Robert M. Thorne
1971   Toward a theory of archaeological things. *Plains Anthropologist* 16: 245–257.
Kuhn, Thomas
1970   *The structure of scientific revolutions.* Chicago: University of Chicago Press.
Lange, Frederick W. and Charles R. Rydberg
1972   Abandonment and post-abandonment behavior at a rural Central American house-site. *American Antiquity* 37:419–432.
LeBlanc, Steven A.
1971   An addition to Naroll's suggested floor area and settlement population relationship. *American Antiquity* 36:210–211.
Leone, Mark P.
1968   Neolithic economic autonomy and social distance. *Science* 162: 1150–1151.
1972   (editor) *Contemporary archaeology.* Carbondale: Southern Illinois University Press.
1973   Archeology as the science of technology: Morman town plans and fences. In *Research and theory in current archeology,* edited by Charles L. Redman. New York: Wiley (Interscience). Pp. 125–150.
Longacre, William A.
1964   Archaeology as anthropology: A case study. *Science* 144:1454–1455.
1967   Artifacts. In Chapters in the prehistory of eastern Arizona, III. *Fieldiana: Anthropology* 57:56–125.
1968   Some aspects of prehistoric society in east-central Arizona. In *New perspectives in archeology,* edited by Sally R. Binford and Lewis R. Binford. Chicago: Aldine. Pp. 89–102.
1970a Archaeology as anthropology: A case study. *University of Arizona, Anthropological Papers* No. 17.
1970b Current thinking in American archeology. In Current directions in anthropology, edited by Ann Fischer. *Bulletins of the American Anthropological Association* 3(No. 3, Part 2):126–138.
1974   Kalinga pottery-making: The evolution of a research design. In *Frontiers in anthropology,* edited by Murray Leaf. New York: Van Nostrand. Pp. 51–67.
n.d.   Population dynamics at the Grasshopper Pueblo. In *Anthropological approaches to demography,* edited by Ezra B. W. Zubrow. Albuquerque: University of New Mexico Press (in press).
Longacre, William A. and James A. Ayres
1968   Archeological lessons from an Apache wickiup. In *New perspectives in archeology,* edited by Sally R. Binford and Lewis R. Binford. Chicago: Aldine. Pp. 151–159.
McCutcheon, Mary and Morgan J. Tamplin
1973   Computer-generated keys for ceramic and lithic typologies. Paper read

at the 1973 Meeting of the Society for American Archaeology, San Francisco.

McDonald, James A., David A. Phillips, Jr., Yvonne Stewart, and Ric Windmiller
1974   *An archaeological survey of the Tucson Gas & Electric El Sol-Vail transmission line.* Tucson: Cultural Resource Management Section, Arizona State Museum, University of Arizona.

McKellar, Judith
1973   Correlations and the explanation of distributions. Manuscript on deposit, Arizona State Museum Library.

Magers, Pamela C.
n.d.   The cotton industry at Antelope House. *The Kiva* (in press).

Martin, Paul S.
1954   Comments. *American Anthropologist* 56:570–572.
1971   The revolution in archaeology. *American Antiquity* 36:1–8.

Martin, Paul S., William A. Longacre, and James N. Hill
1967   Chapters in the prehistory of eastern Arizona, III. *Fieldiana: Anthropology* No. 57.

Martin, Paul S. and Fred Plog
1973   *The archaeology of Arizona.* New York: Natural History Press.

Martin, Paul S., George L. Quimby, and Donald Collier
1947   *Indians before Columbus.* Chicago: University of Chicago Press.

Martin, Paul S., John B. Rinaldo, William A. Longacre, Leslie G. Freeman, Jr., James A. Brown, Richard H. Hevly, and M. E. Cooley
1964   Chapters in the prehistory of eastern Arizona, II. *Fieldiana: Anthropology* No. 55.

Medford, Larry D.
1972   Agricultural destruction of archeological sites in northeast Arkansas. *Arkansas Archeological Survey, Research Series* 3:41–82.

Medlock, Raymond C.
1975   Faunal analysis. In The Cache River Archeological Project: An experiment in contract archeology, assembled by Michael B. Schiffer and John H. House. *Arkansas Archeological Survey, Research Series* No. 8, 223–242.

Morse, Dan F.
1973   Natives and anthropologists in Arkansas. In Anthropology beyond the university, edited by Alden Redfield. *Southern Anthropological Society, Proceedings* 7:26–39.
1975   Paleo-Indian in the land of opportunity: Preliminary report on the excavations at the Sloan site (3GE94). In The Cache River Archeological Project: An experiment in contract archeology, assembled by Michael B. Schiffer and John H. House. *Arkansas Archeological Survey, Research Series* No. 8, 135–143.

Movius, Hallam L.
1953   The Mousterian cave of Teshik-Tash, southeastern Uzbekistan, central Asia. *American School of Prehistoric Research, Bulletin* No. 17.

Muto, Guy R.
1971   A technological analysis of the early stages in the manufacture of lithic artifacts. M.A. thesis, Idaho State University.

Nagel, Ernest
1961   *The structure of science.* New York: Harcourt.

Naroll, Raoul
1962   Floor area and settlement population. *American Antiquity* 27: 587–589.

Nie, Norman, Dale H. Bent, and C. Hadlai Hull
1970   *Statistical package for the social sciences.* New York: McGraw-Hill.

Orton, C. R.
1970   The production of pottery from a Romano-British kiln site: A statistical investigation. *World Archaeology* 1:343–358.

Osborne, Douglas
1965   Chipping remains as an indication of cultural change at Wetherill Mesa. In Contributions of the Wetherill Mesa Archeological Project, assembled by Douglas Osborne. *Society for American Archaeology, Memoirs* 19:30–44.

Oswalt, Wendall H., and J. W. VanStone
1967   The ethnoarcheology of Crow Village, Alaska. *Bureau of American Ethnology, Bulletin* No. 199.

Pastron, Allen G.
1974   Preliminary ethnoarchaeological investigations among the Tarahumara. In Ethnoarchaeology, edited by Christopher B. Donnan and C. William Clewlow, Jr. *University of California at Los Angeles, Institute of Archaeology, Monograph* No. 4, 93–114.

Plog, Fred T.
1973a   Diachronic anthropology. In *Research and theory in current archeology*, edited by Charles L. Redman. New York: Wiley (Interscience). Pp. 181–198.
1973b   Laws, systems of law, and the explanation of observed variation. In *The explanation of culture change: Models in prehistory*, edited by Colin Renfrew. London: Duckworth. Pp. 649–661.
1974   *The study of prehistoric change.* New York: Academic Press.
1975   Demographic studies in southwestern prehistory. In Population studies in archaeology and biological anthropology: A symposium, edited by Alan C. Swedlund. *Society for American Archaeology, Memoirs* 30: 94–103.

Ralph, E. K. and H. N. Michael
1970   MASCA radiocarbon dates for Sequoia and bristlecone-pine samples. In *Radiocarbon variations and absolute chronology*, edited by Ingrid U. Olsson. New York: Wiley. Pp. 619–623.

Rathje, William L.
1973   Models for mobile Maya: A variety of constraints. In *The explanation of culture change: Models in prehistory*, edited by Colin Renfrew. London: Duckworth. Pp. 731–757.
1974   The Garbage Project: A new way of looking at the problems of archaeology. *Archaeology* 27:236–241.

Read, Catherine E.
1971   Animal bones and human behavior. Ph.D. dissertation, UCLA. Ann Arbor: University Microfilms.

Redman, Charles L. (editor)
1973   *Research and theory in current archeology.* New York: Wiley (Interscience).

Redman, Charles L. and Patty Jo Watson
1970   Systematic, intensive surface collection. *American Antiquity* **35**: 279–291.

Reid, J. Jefferson
1973   Growth and response to stress at Grasshopper Pueblo, Arizona. Ph.D. dissertation, University of Arizona. Ann Arbor: University Microfilms.
1974   (editor) Behavioral archaeology at the Grasshopper Ruin. *The Kiva* **40**:1–112.

Reid, J. Jefferson and Michael B. Schiffer
n.d.   Toward a behavioral archaeology. In preparation.

Reid, J. Jefferson and Izumi Shimada
n.d.   Pueblo growth at Grasshopper: Methods and models. In Multi-disciplinary research at the Grasshopper Ruin, edited by William A. Longacre. *University of Arizona, Anthropological Papers* (in press).

Reid, J. Jefferson, William L. Rathje and Michael B. Schiffer
1974   Expanding archaeology. *American Antiquity* **39**:125–126.

Reid, J. Jefferson, Michael B. Schiffer, and Jeffrey M. Neff
1975   Archaeological considerations of intrasite sampling. In *Sampling in archaeology*, edited by James W. Mueller. Tucson: University of Arizona Press. Pp. 209–224.

Reid, J. Jefferson, Michael B. Schiffer, and William L. Rathje
n.d.   Behavioral archaeology: Four strategies. *American Anthropologist* (in press).

Renfrew, Colin
1970   Tree-ring calibration of radiocarbon: An archaeological evaluation. *Proceedings of the Prehistoric Society* **36**:280–311.
1973   (editor) *The explanation of culture change: Models in prehistory.* London: Duckworth.

Reynolds, Paul D.
1971   *A primer in theory construction.* New York: Bobbs-Merrill.

Rick, John W. and Eric Gritzmacher
1970   The spatial-temporal dimensions of lithic raw material in the Hay Hollow Valley. Manuscript on deposit, Field Museum of Natural History and Arizona State Museum Library.

Rinaldo, John B.
1964   Artifacts. In Chapters in the prehistory of eastern Arizona, II. *Fieldiana: Anthropology* **55**:63–109.

Robbins, L. H.
1973   Turkana material culture viewed from an archaeological perspective. *World Archaeology* **5**:209–214.

Robinson, William J. and Richard J. Warren
1971   *Tree-ring dates from New Mexico C-D.* Tucson: Laboratory of Tree-Ring Research, University of Arizona.

Rock, James T.
n.d.   Antelope House methodology. *The Kiva* (in press).

Rouse, Irving
1972   *Introduction to prehistory: A systematic approach.* New York: McGraw-Hill.

Rowe, John H.
1962   Worsaae's Law and the use of grave lots for archaeological dating. *American Antiquity* **28**:129–137.

Salmon, Wesley
1971 *Statistical explanation and statistical relevance.* Pittsburgh: University of Pittsburgh Press.

Salwen, Bert
1973 Archeology in Megalopolis. In *Research and theory in current archeology,* edited by Charles L. Redman. New York: Wiley (Interscience). Pp. 151–163.

Sanders, William T. and Barbara J. Price
1968 *Mesoamerica: The evolution of a civilization.* New York: Random House.

Saraydar, Stephen C. and Izumi Shimada
1973 Experimental archeology: A new outlook. *American Antiquity* **38**: 344–350.

Schiffer, Michael B.
1968 The relationship between economic diversity and population growth: The test of an hypothesis. Manuscript on deposit, Field Museum of Natural History and Arizona State Museum Library.
1972a Cultural laws and the reconstruction of past lifeways. *The Kiva* **37**: 148–157.
1972b Archaeological context and systemic context. *American Antiquity* **37**:156–165.
1973a Cultural formation processes of the archaeological record: Applications at the Joint Site, east-central Arizona. Ph.D. dissertation, University of Arizona. Ann Arbor: University Microfilms.
1973b The chipped-stone assemblage from the Joint Site. Manuscript on deposit, Arizona State Museum Library.
1974 Nomothetic aspects of chipped-stone experiments. *Newsletter of Lithic Technology* 3:46–50.
1975a Behavioral chain analysis: Activities, organization, and the use of space. In Chapters in the prehistory of eastern Arizona, IV. *Fieldiana: Anthropology* 65:103–119.
1975b Factors and "toolkits": Evaluating multivariate analyses in archaeology. *Plains Anthropologist* **20**:61–70.
1975c The effects of occupation span on site content. In The Cache River Archeological Project: An experiment in contract archeology, assembled by Michael B. Schiffer and John H. House. *Arkansas Archeological Survey, Research Series* No. 8, 265–269.
1975d Classifications of chipped-stone tool use. In The Cache River Archeological Project: An experiment in contract archeology, assembled by Michael B. Schiffer and John H. House. *Arkansas Archeological Survey, Research Series* No. 8, 249–251.
n.d.a Archaeology as behavioral science. *American Anthropologist* (in press).
n.d.b In preparation.

Schiffer, Michael B. and John H. House
1975 Indirect impacts of the channelization project on the archeological resources. In The Cache River Archeological Project: An experiment in contract archeology, assembled by Michael B. Schiffer and John H. House. *Arkansas Archeological Survey, Research Series* No. 8, 277–282.

Schiffer, Michael B. and William L. Rathje
1973   Efficient exploitation of the archeological record: Penetrating problems. In *Research and theory in current archeology*, edited by Charles L. Redman. New York: Wiley (Interscience). Pp. 169–179.

Schuyler, Robert L.
1970   Historical and historic sites archaeology as anthropology: Basic definitions and relationships. *Historical Archaeology* 4:83–89.

Semenov, S. A.
1964   *Prehistoric technology* (translated by M. W. Thompson). London: Cory, Adams, and Mackay.

Shafer, Harry J.
1973   Lithic technology at the George C. Davis site, Cherokee County, Texas. Ph.D. dissertation, University of Texas, Austin. Ann Arbor: University Microfilms.

Shawcross, W.
1972   Energy and ecology: Thermodynamic models in archaeology. In *Models in archaeology*, edited by D. L. Clarke. London: Methuen. Pp. 577–622.

Shimada, Izumi
n.d.   Three-fold analysis of human behavior: A case study in experimental archaeology. Manuscript submitted for publication.

Sokal, Robert R. and P. H. A. Sneath
1963   *Principles of numerical taxonomy.* San Francisco: Freeman.

South, Stanley
1972   Evolution and horizon as revealed in ceramic analysis in historical archaeology. *The Conference on Historic Site Archaeology, Papers* 6:71–116.
1974   The function of observation in the archeological process. In Historical archeology papers: Method and theory, edited by Stanley South. *University of South Carolina, Institute of Archeology and Anthropology, Research Manuscript Series* No. 64.

Spaulding, Albert C.
1968   Explanation in archeology. In *New perspectives in archeology*, edited by Sally R. Binford and Lewis R. Binford. Chicago: Aldine. Pp. 33–39.

Stanislawski, Michael B.
1969a   The ethno-archaeology of Hopi pottery making. *Plateau* 42:27–33.
1969b   What good is a broken pot? *Southwestern Lore* 35:11–18.

Stephen, Alexander M.
1936   *Hopi Journal, Part II,* edited by Elsie Clews Parsons. New York: Columbia University Press.

Stickel, E. Gary and Joseph L. Chartkoff
1973   The nature of scientific laws and their relation to law-building in archaeology. In *The explanation of culture change: Models in prehistory*, edited by Colin Renfrew. London: Duckworth. Pp. 663–671.

Stier, Francis
n.d.   The uses of Yucca at Antelope House. *The Kiva* (in press).

Struever, Stuart
1968   Problems, methods and organization: A disparity in the growth of

archeology. In *Anthropological archeology in the Americas,* edited by Betty J. Meggers. Washington: The Anthropological Society of Washington. Pp. 131–151.

Stuiver, Minze and Hans E. Suess
1966   On the relationship between radiocarbon dates and true sample ages. *Radiocarbon* **8**:534–540.

Swan, Lawrence
1972   Testing for status symbol changes in modern material culture. Manuscript on deposit, Arizona State Museum Library.

Tamplin, Morgan
1969   The application of pedology to archaeological research: In *Pedology and Quaternary research,* edited by S. Pawluk. Alberta: Alberta Institute of Pedology. Pp. 153–161.

Thomas, David H.
1970   Archaeology's operational imperative: Great Basin projectile points as a test case. *Annual Report, UCLA Archaeological Survey 1970* **12**:31–60.

1971   On distinguishing natural from cultural bone in archaeological sites. *American Antiquity* **36**:366–371.

1974   *Predicting the past: An introduction to anthropological archaeology.* New York: Holt, Rinehart, and Winston.

Thompson, Raymond H.
1958   Modern Yucatecan Maya pottery making. *Society for American Archaeology, Memoirs* No. 15.

Thompson, Raymond H. and William A. Longacre
1966   The University of Arizona Archaeological Field School at Grasshopper, east-central Arizona. *The Kiva* **31**:255–275.

Titiev, Mischa
1961   *Introduction to cultural anthropology.* New York: Holt, Rinehart, and Winston.

Tracz, Susan M.
1971   The architecture of the Joint Site: A study of building style and its social implications. Manuscript on deposit, Field Museum of Natural History and Arizona State Museum Library.

Trigger, Bruce
1970   Aims in prehistoric archaeology. *Antiquity* **44**:26–37.

Tuggle, H. David
1970   Prehistoric community relationships in east-central Arizona. Ph.D. dissertation, University of Arizona. Ann Arbor: University Microfilms.

Turner, Christy G. II and Laurel Lofgren
1966   Household size of prehistoric Western Pueblo Indians. *Southwestern Journal of Anthropology* **22**:117–132.

Ucko, P. J.
1969   Ethnography and archaeological interpretation of funerary remains. *World Archaeology* **1**:262–280.

Wagner, Philip L.
1960   *The human use of the earth.* Glencoe: The Free Press.

Watson, Patty Jo, Steven A. LeBlanc, and Charles L. Redman
1971   *Explanation in archeology.* New York: Columbia University Press.

Wauchope, Robert
1966 Archaeological survey of northern Georgia with a test of some cultural hypotheses. *Society for American Archaeology, Memoirs* No. 21.

Whallon, Robert, Jr.
1972 A new approach to pottery typology. *American Antiquity* **37**:13–33.
1973 Spatial analysis of occupation floors I: Application of dimensional analysis of variance. *American Antiquity* **38**:266–278.

Wheeler, Mortimer
1956 *Archaeology from the earth.* Baltimore: Pelican.

White, Anta
1963 Analytic description of the chipped-stone industry from Snyders Site, Calhoun, Illinois. In Miscellaneous studies in typology and classification. *University of Michigan, Museum of Anthropology, Anthropological Papers* No. 19, 1–70.

White, J. P. and D. H. Thomas
1972 What mean these stones? Ethno-taxonomic models and archaeological interpretations in the New Guinea Highlands. In *Models in archaeology,* edited by D. L. Clarke. London: Methuen. Pp. 275–308.

Whiting, Alfred F.
1939 Ethnobotany of the Hopi. *Museum of Northern Arizona, Bulletin* No. 15.

Wilcox, David R.
1975 A strategy for perceiving social groups in puebloan sites. In Chapters in the prehistory of eastern Arizona, IV. *Fieldiana: Anthropology* **65**:120–159.
n.d. Sampling pueblos: The implications of room-set additions at Grasshopper Pueblo. In Multi-disciplinary research at the Grasshopper Ruin, edited by William A. Longacre. *University of Arizona, Anthropological Papers* (in press).

Willey, Gordon R. and Charles R. McGimsey III
1954 The Monagrillo culture of Panama. *Papers of the Peabody Museum* No. 49.

Willey, Gordon R. and Jeremy A. Sabloff
1974 *A history of American archaeology.* London: Thames and Hudson.

Wilmsen, Edwin N.
1968 Functional analysis of flaked stone artifacts. *American Antiquity* **33**:156–161.
1970 Lithic analysis and cultural inference: A Paleo-Indian case. *University of Arizona, Anthropological Papers* No. 16.

Winks, Robin W.
1969 Introduction. In *The historian as detective,* edited by Robin W. Winks. New York: Harper and Row. Pp. xiii–xxiv.

Wood, Patrick
1973 Survey of artifact distributions at a swap meet through time. Manuscript on deposit, Arizona State Museum Library.

Woodall, J. Ned
1972 *An introduction to modern archeology.* Cambridge: Schenkman.

Woodbury, Richard B.
1954 Prehistoric stone implements of northeastern Arizona. *Papers of the Peabody Museum* No. 34.

Wright, Gary A.
1974   Archaeology and trade. *Addison-Wesley Modular Publications in Anthropology* No. 49.

Wright, Henry T.
1972   A consideration of interregional exchange in Greater Mesopotamia: 4000–3000 B.C. In Social exchange and interaction, edited by Edwin N. Wilmsen. *University of Michigan, Museum of Anthropology, Anthropological Papers* No. 46, 95–105.

Yellen, John E.
1974   The !Kung settlement pattern: An archaeological perspective. Unpublished Ph.D. dissertation, Harvard University.

Young, Ellen
1973   Lateral cycling of clothing within the nuclear family unit. Manuscript on deposit, Arizona State Museum Library.

Young, Jean and Jim Young
1973   *The garage sale manual: Alternate economics for the people.* New York: Praeger.

Ziegler, Alan C.
1973   Inference from prehistoric faunal remains. *Addison-Wesley Modular Publications in Anthropology* No. 43.

Zubrow, Ezra B. W.
1971   Carrying capacity and dynamic equilibrium in the prehistoric Southwest. *American Antiquity* **36**:127–138.
1975   *Prehistoric carrying capacity: A model.* Menlo Park: Cummings.

Index